IF GOD WAS YOUR FINANCIAL PLANNER

Suresh Sadagopan is the founder of Ladder7 Financial Advisories. A fee-only financial planning and advisory firm, Ladder7 Financial Advisories is one of the most respected firms in the financial planning and advisory space in India. Suresh is registered as an Investment Adviser (RIA) with the Securities and Exchange Board of India (SEBI).

He is an MMS, Certified Financial Planner (CFP^{CM}), Chartered Trust and Estate Planner (CTEP^{TM}) and a Registered Life Planner (RLP).

Suresh is passionate about financial planning and has authored several articles and blogs on the subject. He also speaks at public forums and appears on TV to educate and coach the public about personal finances, achieving financial freedom and creating wealth.

In 2010, Suresh founded The Financial Planners' Guild, India (FPGI). He was its founding President for about four years and is currently the President. He was on the board of directors of Financial Planning Standards Board (FPSB) India—the Certified Financial Planner (CFP) certifying body in India—between 2013 and 2015. He was on the advisory board of the Network FP and FPGI.

A founding member of the Association of Registered Investment Advisers (ARIA), Suresh has also served as the vice chairman in the past, and continues to be on the board.

Suresh was listed in the 101 Top Most Influential BFSI Leaders of the World BFSI Congress in 2020 and 2023.

IF GOD WAS YOUR FINANCIAL PLANNER

SURESH SADAGOPAN

First published in hardback by TV18 Broadcast Ltd in 2020

First published in paperback by Westland Business, an imprint of Westland Books, a division of Nasadiya Technologies Private Limited, in 2023

No. 269/2B, First Floor, 'Irai Arul', Vimalraj Street, Nethaji Nagar, Alapakkam Main Road, Maduravoyal, Chennai 600095

Westland, the Westland logo, Westland Business and the Westland Business logo are the trademarks of Nasadiya Technologies Private Limited, or its affiliates.

ISBN: 9789357767606

10 9 8 7 6 5 4 3 2 1

Typeset by SÜRYA, New Delhi

Printed by Parksons Graphics Pvt. Ltd

CONTENTS

Preface   vii

1. The Lord Paves the Way   1

2. We Are All Birds in Search of a Home   9

3. When One Door Closes, Another Opens   22

4. Real Estate: The Real Story   26

5. The Problem with the Apple of the Eye   36

6. The Need for Speed on Finances   49

7. When Things Seem to Fall in Place,
   Everything Changes   59

8. Everything in Life Happens for a Reason   74

9. Life Has to Move On   80

10. After the Deluge, the Calm   92

11. The Millennial Gets Her Money Lessons   99

12. The Millennial's Lessons Continue   110

13. We Have One Life, We Need to Make It Count   128

14. Arise Arjuna! Your Duty Is to Fight   140

15. The Sceptic Comes Around 147

16. Playing the Role of a Sarathi 168

17. Planning for Retirement 173

18. Getting the Nuts and Bolts of Retirement Right 182

19. The Millennials Return for More Money Lessons 210

20. The Rise of the Scion 226

21. The Calm after the Storm 240

22. Bringing Sundered Hearts Together 258

23. Anshuman and His Family Find Their Mojo 272

Epilogue 295

Acknowledgements 299

PREFACE

Finance is a subject that people often find intimidating and forbidding. People are generally out of their depth when it comes to finance and want to spend as little time thinking about it as they possibly can.

What an irony this is!

You may be wondering why I am saying this. Don't we all work our entire lives to earn money and create wealth so that we can give our families a decent lifestyle and material comforts, and so that we can achieve our goals and hope to retire comfortably?

We dedicate the prime years of our lives to earning money. Don't we need to invest that money properly? Now, for a lot of people, this is the boring part.

If you are like most people, you do not give much thought to the money lying in your bank. It may lie there for weeks, and sometimes even months, till you get a call from the bank's relationship manager or some friendly distributor comes along. The money lying around is then invested in various products according to what is pitched to you, and you heave a sigh of relief when the money has finally been shoved into some product or the other.

Surprising as it may seem, that is how most people handle their hard-earned money.

Finance is not everybody's cup of tea. People run away from this subject all the time. But handling your finances well can build the foundation of a comfortable life, help you achieve your life goals, create wealth and live a worry-free life. Thus, a basic understanding of finance is of use to everyone—especially those who consider it intimidating—and it is to make it accessible and easily readable that I have written this book like a story.

Various characters make an appearance in the book. One of them who appears throughout the book is Lord Krishna himself! Through Lord Krishna and some insightful lessons from the Gita, I have imbued the book with simple philosophies of life and common-sense principles—for they are important to ensure a fulfilling and well-funded life.

I have created different situations, and life scenarios to help illustrate and clarify concepts, offer good financial and life advice, debunk wrong notions and explain financial planning concepts, advisory landscape, etc.

We all need a decent working knowledge of finance—a broad understanding of what needs to be done to meet our life goals and major expenses, an understanding of products, their features and benefits and how they may fit, taxation, strategies to use while creating a financial and investment plan, an understanding of the mistakes people commit with their money, etc.

The objective of the book is to sensitise the reader to various aspects of finance, including broad areas like insurance, investments, taxation, etc. Another objective is to clarify important concepts that investors must know like asset allocation, risk assessment, active versus passive investments, fiduciary, financial planning, life planning and so on.

Many common-sense principles and other information that is important are covered in this book, like choosing a financial planner, remuneration for the services of an adviser, the concept of a fee-only adviser, funding children's education and how one should not overreach for it, etc.

I have also focused on retirement planning and how to fund it, the challenge of accumulating the required corpus and finding meaning in retirement.

Moreover, this book can also be very useful for financial advisers themselves. The various arguments that I have put forth regarding advisory services, engagement with the clients for their success and empathetic client dealings could appeal to practitioners.

I know I have not covered everything there is to personal finances and financial planning. But the important ones are there.

I do hope that whatever is there does make sense. I have strived to make it an interesting read. Hope it is enough to hold your attention and make you finish the book in one sitting.

1

THE LORD PAVES THE WAY

It was pitch dark outside. The clock face informed me that it was forty-five minutes past midnight. Sleep had eluded me so far. A cricket was keeping me company with its intermittent chirping with metronomic regularity. Whether or not the cricket was able to attract its mate I cannot confirm, but its regular chirping gave me that comforting background score to work on a financial plan for one of my clients.

Vishal Bhatnagar and his family had been my clients for four years, and they were not making much progress towards attaining their financial goals. They constantly brought in new elements, which increased their cash burn, and caused their savings rate to go downhill. They had also brought in a couple of new goals, which only added to their pressure.

I had a meeting lined up with the Bhatnagars the following day. I could have worked on this early in the morning, but I preferred to wrap it up before resting. The constant question in my head was: how could we make their plan work?

The Bhatnagars had just told me that they were expecting their third child, but they had not planned for this. As they say in such cases, it was ABC—Absolute Bloody Carelessness! Be that as it may, even before it was born, this new bundle of joy had thrown a huge challenge my way—it was going to test the resources of the Bhatnagars. A roll in the hay had never been more expensive.

I wondered whether Vishal Bhatnagar could work beyond sixty years of age, as it seemed necessary now. Preeti, his wife, would no longer be able to work, with three cherubs about the house. So that option was out. It might have helped had there been a possibility of some ancestral property coming their way— that have eased the pressure a bit. While that was a possibility, it wouldn't be a straightforward affair as Vishal had two siblings and Preeti, too, had one.

As a rule, financial planners do not consider any bequests while planning, as we have seen many siblings fight over hand-me-downs to the extent of sparring over the smallest of items, from the study table down to the paperweight that had been used by their father! And there have been cases where the entire property was donated to a house help or an ashram. Suffice to say, there can be lots of uncertainty surrounding legacies, and it is best not to take them into consideration. I was racking my brain for possible alternatives.

The cricket had stopped its chirping. It looked like it had, after all, managed to entice a mate with its musical renditions and the two of them were now enjoying a romantic munching of leaf stalks together. Time seemed to stand still. My brain had blanked out. And then it happened …

I saw a pale white light emerging from the other bedroom at the far end. My son and wife were supposed to sleep in our regular bedroom today. They knew I would be working late and would sleep in the other bedroom. I was confused. Was my son sleeping in that other bedroom by sheer force of habit? He may be using the iPad then, I thought, and went back to the plan workings of the Bhatnagars.

It was then that I heard a deep hum coming out of the bedroom. For a moment, I ignored it completely. Then I had a thought that made me smile—maybe the crickets had started indulging in a romantic musical celebration of their union and were humming to proclaim that to the world.

And then it hit me. The deep hum sounded like 'Om', the primordial sound sacred to Indic religions.

I got up from my table and started walking towards the bedroom. The bed was empty. I reeled in my tracks. For a moment, it felt like a ton of ice had been dumped on my chest. A nameless fear gripped me, for in front of me was someone who looked like a sanyasi. He was glowing, emitting a pale white light. His body was effulgent.

I heard 'Om' emanating from him, though the sound wasn't coming through his mouth. I could not recognise him. I felt I had become incapable of uttering a word. It was like my tongue had suddenly lost its power to say anything. I was going to ask him who he was and how and why he was here.

But again, my power of speech abandoned me, and all I could do was open and close my mouth like a goldfish. The monk understood my predicament. He gently addressed me: 'Son, you want to know who I am? I thought you knew this, for it was you who had called me …'

At this, my stomach region seemed to have become the nesting area for a million butterflies, and I was delirious. Sensing what was happening, the sanyasi asked me to come and sit on the bed. I obeyed instinctively, as if it was my father telling me to sit next to him.

My power to express was slowly returning. I just blurted that I did not remember calling anyone home. Then, it came to me.

My client Bala, now a friend, was currently undergoing a major crisis. Bala is a bright and affable person who has risen rapidly in the real estate industry and is currently the marketing director of a prominent real estate firm.

The problem was that the real estate industry was undergoing turbulence, and that the cash flows of all companies in the property sector were stretched. He had seen the financials deteriorate in the past few years and had tried his very best to turn the fortunes of his company around. He had once told me that it felt like trying to move ahead against a storm.

His CEO, Kirit, knew that Bala was committed and was flexing his sinews to bring business to the company. But the situation was rapidly turning from bad to worse. The losses were mounting. The Board wanted to do something drastic to stanch the bloodletting. One suggested solution was rationalising the workforce, considering the lower sales and consequent losses. Many in the top management were to be axed. Bala was one of them. The marketing department would be run by just a manager and an executive. All those above the manager position in most departments were getting the heave-ho.

Bala was steeped in despair. He had a family to support and had loans and EMIs to service. His child was still studying. When he came to meet me, his face was ashen. I tried taking him out of his deep melancholia. There were options for him, I tried to point out, but Bala was able to refute every single point. Everything looked like misplaced optimism on my part.

I told him that he could move to some other company in the industry. He replied that most other companies were in a deeper hole than his. I asked Bala why he could not move laterally to another industry. He looked at me sadly. He told me he would have considered that, but he had been in the real estate industry right from the beginning of his career and moving laterally after twenty-five years was just not feasible.

He felt helpless, unable to do anything when everything was crumbling around him. I felt despondent at his situation. It was then that I prayed, 'Oh Lord, why don't you help Bala? Why don't you give a solution to his problem? Why don't you come to rescue someone who is in such a desperate situation?'

When I remembered my prayer, I immediately understood who this sanyasi was. But why had he come in the form of an old ascetic? That part I did not understand. But I let it go. I folded my hands and bowed my head. He nodded.

A wave of compassion and peace caressed my soul. It was an inexplicable feeling. I just kept my eyes closed; I was in bliss. I lost track of myself and the world. All my buzzing thoughts seemed to have come to a grinding halt. When I opened my eyes, He was still there. But lo and behold, he was now my Lord Krishna!

I was overcome with emotion and fell at His feet. Another wave of bliss was washing all over me now. It felt wonderful. There was work to be done, and the Lord had appeared before me out of His infinite kindness to help resolve Bala's situation. There was no time to waste.

With folded hands, I asked the Lord, 'You know what has happened to Bala. What should he do? He is in the midst of a crisis.'

The Lord had a beatific smile on his face. For ten seconds, He did not answer. He said, 'Why should you interpret a job loss as a crisis? A job loss can be the push that can help him move forward to higher planes. Discontinuity and break from the routine, which keeps happening in life, can be good too.'

I got something here, but not all. The Lord was telling me that it was not all bad. Maybe there was a way out for Bala after all. Suddenly, I felt afraid. Could the Lord be talking purely in metaphysical terms and not in worldly parlance at all? Moving on to higher planes seemed to indicate that. Will Bala turn to spiritualism, and will he shun the world we live in? What will happen to his family?

While these thoughts were transiting my mind, the Lord was quiet.

'You people have a worldly problem, and you were exercised by it. There would be solutions if you were to evaluate all options thoroughly. The situation is not as bleak as you people make it out to be ...' I was able to hear all this in my mind, though He was not talking.

I was saying in my mind that I couldn't see any possible solution here.

The Lord continued. 'Since you don't seem to be thinking in that direction at all, let me point out one possible solution. His company is already present abroad. They are doing well there. He can fit in there ...'

Bala had told me about the company's operations in the UK and the Middle East. But there seemed to be no vacancies. Hence, that option was closed, Bala had told me.

The Lord took His time before continuing. 'What Bala had told you was true, but every company would be interested in furthering their business. At this point, they are going through a bad patch in India and have no option but to reduce the headcount. Bala enjoys a lot of goodwill in his company. He could now leverage it and work for the company abroad.'

This did not make sense to me or give any solution to the problem. He continued, 'London is a prime property market. There is a lot of potential. Bala's company also knows that and is keen to tap that market properly. But they don't want to increase their fixed expenses.'

'If Bala is prepared to work for them on a commission basis, they will not have a problem. His company wants to develop the commercial segment, and Bala has experience in that area. His company would be able to procure a work visa and even accommodate him at their guest house in London if Bala is willing,' the Lord concluded.

Whew, this is great! We never even contemplated such a possibility. The Lord had indeed shown the way. I was mighty excited. I wanted to convey this to Bala and see how he would react.

I was lost in my thoughts. When I surfaced and wanted to ask Him my next question, He was no longer there. I thanked Him all the same for His kindness and compassion.

I was atwitter. The excitement of a visitation from the Lord was overwhelming to me. It was inevitable that sleep would elude me for a long time that day. So, the day stretched for me well into the night or, should I say, morning. It was natural that I woke up quite late. My wife, Madhu, had not woken me up. She knew I had worked late but did not know how late I had stayed up.

The first thing I recalled was that the Lord had been with me last night. It felt wonderful and uplifting. Should I tell Madhu? She may ask why I did not wake her up. But there was a higher chance that she may think I'd gone cuckoo.

I was anxious to meet Bala; I did not want to discuss the possibility of him taking an assignment abroad on the phone.

After a cup of coffee, I called Bala. I asked him about his schedule for the day. He told me that we could meet in the afternoon. He had to go to meet his daughter's tutor in the morning. Also, he had some work at the bank.

I asked him to come to my office at 3 p.m. There was a lot of work to do. In the morning, I was supposed to meet the Bhatnagars. This was not going to be easy—not when real estate was involved.

2

WE ARE ALL BIRDS IN SEARCH
OF A HOME

I reached my office and was giving the Bhatnagars' plan a once-over. There was a call from Vishal. I thought he was calling to cancel the appointment. He also must have had the premonition that this meeting would be stormy. He, however, had called to let me know that he would be fifteen minutes late.

I was having a tough time with the Bhatnagars. They had suddenly changed their goalposts. They now wanted an international holiday every three years and a home next year, instead of after five years as originally planned. Moreover, they were going to have their third child, which again would exert considerable strain on their finances.

I was marshalling my thoughts and putting down a few points in my notepad when Vishal and Preeti walked in.

I waved them to their seats, ordered coffee for all of us and got ready for the discussions. I congratulated both on the news of the addition to the family. Vishal sheepishly told me that it had not been planned, which was superfluous information. Preeti was quiet.

I had to initiate the conversation about their financial planning. I approached it gingerly. I told them that I was working on all the things they had wanted me to—international holidays, buying a home next year and also plans for their soon-to-arrive baby. I added that they could see the workings, which would give them some perspective on the discussion that we'd be having that day. I had to explain what I had done. So, I launched forth. I showed them where I had incorporated the goals and expenses and how I had projected the cash flows for the future.

I showed them how their cash flows would look in the future. There was a collective gasp from both of them—there was a sea of numbers in red from the next year itself. Their reaction was good for me as I could not have worked on them had this not got them suitably agitated.

We had earlier discussed the virtue of saving a certain percentage of their income every month. They had accepted that in principle. But they must have been sure that it did not apply to them outside of the principle, because every time they met me, there were new expenses, new goals and now this new co-creation!

I started, 'The last time I had made the plan, I had shared about the virtue of saving. It looks like you mistook that to be the virtue of spending. A rule of thumb is that you need to save about 30 per cent of your income—that way, you will just be as good as other fellow Indians. With all the goals you have now, your savings will be nil. In fact, you will be using your bonus, incentives and the income from your investments just to balance the budget. It's time to get serious, folks.'

I paused for them to understand the gravity of the situation. However, going by past experience, I was being too optimistic.

Nothing seemed to daunt them. After a chastening session, they had returned two months later with elan, piling on more goals and expenses. They must have been liberally cursing me and using the choicest of expletives in their heads. Nothing was verbalised, thankfully. I told them that I want to dwell on the home purchase first. They wanted to buy a new home in Mumbai, which was expected to cost about ₹2.8 crore. Even if they were to sell their home in Bhopal, it would fetch them only ₹60–65 lakh. They had some ₹20 lakh as savings and about ₹12.5 lakh in their Employees' Provident Fund (EPF) accounts. Vishal had told me that he wanted to take out money from the EPF, liquidate the savings and sell the home to have a crore to pay upfront. He wanted to take a loan for ₹1.8 crore. I had pointed out the obvious flaw—he just did not have the money to pay the EMIs for such a huge loan. Vishal said he would save the ₹45,000 monthly rent—which, of course, was true—if he could find a ready-to-move-in property. He, however, would still have to pay a differential of about ₹1.14 lakh every month as the EMI at 8.75 per cent a year for the next twenty years would come up to about ₹1.59 lakh. And unfortunately, Vishal had not been able to save anything significant to date. He was saving about ₹20,000 a month, on average. When I pointed this out, he did not have an answer. He responded philosophically, that he would have to find the money for it and God would help him. Well, that is a wonderful way to escape—but he was digging a hole for himself and his family.

'I'm going to give my opinion on your real estate buy,' I started. 'It is obvious to me that you should not buy a property now. Living in one's own home is highly overrated. Most people stretch themselves to the breaking point while buying a house. And it is not that they are buying a house most suitable to them … but merely end up buying something they can afford. They continue paying their EMIs for years, living in their own ill-suited home.

'For instance, one may be able to buy a one-bedroom house for, say, ₹70 lakh—but that may hardly be suitable. But, because this is what they can afford, they buy it thinking that at least they are living in their own home. Is there another option, you may ask …

'The other option is renting a home, which is what you have done. You are paying ₹45,000 a month. If your requirement is a three-bedroom home, that may come in at ₹60,000 a month. You need not bankrupt yourself by buying a home that will suit your needs. In your case, you may continue to stay in a two-bedroom apartment for a couple of years more.

'When the baby arrives, it will have to be with you all the time. You may require a bigger home two or three years from now. You may say that both your parents may come from time to time to help you. True. But they come often even now to help with the other two kids—you have been able to manage all along. You can very well continue doing the same thing for a couple of years more. We can re-evaluate the buying decision when it becomes feasible.

'Renting is a great decision as the rental yield for the owner is just about 2–3 per cent. When the return on investment is this low, does it not then make sense to rent the property as a tenant? The owner of the property is subsidising your stay and allowing you to reside in a property that, otherwise, you cannot afford.

'You may say that the home would also appreciate in value, and so the owner will anyway gain, which is true. But how much will the gains be? Between 4 and 9 per cent is probably the long-term appreciation potential. At the upper end, it looks somewhat attractive. But when we factor in all the costs—interest, stamp duty, registration, cost of improvements, maintenance, repairs, and taxes to be paid when the property is sold—the return ends up being muted.'

There are many myths surrounding a home, which I wanted to touch upon for their benefit.

Myth 1: Rent paid is money down the drain and EMI is money well spent

'Let us take the case of the three-bedroom home that you want to buy costing ₹2.8 crore,' I continued. 'From your resources, you will be able to brass up ₹1 crore. When you invest in that home, you will lose a potential interest income of about ₹7.5 lakh per annum (assuming an interest rate of 7.5 per cent, pre-tax, from an investment in a fixed income instrument like a fixed deposit).

'When you take a loan of ₹1.8 crore over and above that (assuming you can service that), you would again pay about ₹15.6 lakh as interest in the first year (assuming an interest rate of 8.75 per cent a year on the home loan). That means your combined outgo or notional loss would be about ₹23.1 lakh annually in just the first year.

'As the years go by, the loan exposure would come down, but only glacially at first. So, for the first few years, the interest component would be quite high.

'This interest amount, if added over a twenty-year period, would be ₹2.02 crore. The present value of this money today is ₹1.26 crore (assuming a 7 per cent discount rate). We are talking of big numbers here. You are not paying ₹2.8 crore. The actual cost of the home would be ₹. 2.8 crore + ₹1.26 crore (present value of the future interest amounts), which is ₹4.06 crore!'

'If you had simply rented the place for the entire period (with an 8 per cent increase year-on-year), your ₹1 crore would be intact and will compound over this period. Also, if you invest the same amount as EMI, after deducting the rent along with the original ₹1 crore, it would amount to ₹7.42 crore (assuming a 7 per cent rate of return) after a twenty-year period.'

'This way, you would be completely free of liability, move anywhere your career takes you, your liquidity would be intact, your lifestyle won't be crimped, and you could buy a home at an appropriate time later on, as your savings would have built up by that time.'

Vishal and Preeti were just looking at me without uttering a word. I knew that I was pouring ice-cold water on their dreams, but it had to be done. Vishal, in any case, did not have the wherewithal to pay the EMI of a lakh and a quarter a month.

'I'm trying to clarify your thoughts so that you can see what you need to see. If you were to buy a home, how would you pay the EMI?' I asked. The silence continued. Preeti just said that maybe her uncle could help. I turned to her for further enlightenment, but it was not forthcoming.

I asked, 'If your uncle were to help, how much can he lend you?'

Preeti thought about this for a bit. She informed me that it could probably be between ₹10 lakh and ₹15 lakh. She also immediately realised that the EMI would still be above a lakh. I let it sink in that they just did not have the wherewithal to buy that big flat.

Since we were still on the subject of property, I told them that I would want to exorcise a few more ghosts that may still be in residence in their mind spaces, tormenting them. There are many more myths about property buying, and I requested them to pay attention to what I was going to share, in their best interests.

Myth 2: One should buy property to save taxes

'Firstly, saving taxes is a secondary objective. One cannot invest in a big-ticket item like property, just to save taxes. When one invests in property, one takes on a huge liability for several years, decades even. This kind of leverage does not come cheap; one needs to pay interest, which people breezily ignore.'

'In your example, I have shown that today's value of the interest you'd pay overtime would be ₹1.26 crore. This adds to the cost tremendously.'

'Huge loans can pose a problem if there is a disruption in cash flows in the future. EMIs cannot be stopped. If one is just investing the surplus (after paying rent) on a monthly basis, that investment can be stopped temporarily if there is a cash flow problem.'

'Also, tax savings allowed is just ₹2 lakh per property, as a deduction. Hence, even for those in the 30 per cent tax bracket, the saving is about ₹60,000 per annum. It is a small saving compared with what one needs to invest and the kind of loan one has to take. Tax saving is hence hardly a justification for buying a property, after assuming a huge liability and paying crores of rupees for it.'

In their case, this was not the justification they were giving. But before they could point out tax benefits as one of the possible advantages, I wanted to debunk that premise. I also pointed out to them that the rent one pays, too, can be set off against tax (if you are employed), using a one-in-three formula—lower of House Rent Allowance (HRA), 50 per cent of basic salary for Class A cities (40 per cent for the rest), 10 per cent of rent paid above basic.

In this manner, rent is being subsidised by the government. Hence, buying a home is not the only way to save tax. 'You are saving taxes even now, when you are paying rent,' I told them.

If Vishal and Preeti were getting bored with my soliloquy, they did not show it. They bore my lecture on real estate with the stoicism of Socrates. But they were tough eggs, and I wanted them to get a complete download on real estate so that they would stop talking about it all the time and tear asunder the financial plan that had been painstakingly created for them. So, I took their permission to proceed, and went ahead.

Myth 3: When we rent homes, we will be forced to change homes every eleven months

This is a carefully nurtured propaganda, especially by women who are staunch advocates of owning property. The fact is, a landlord wants a good tenant. Having found one, he is not going to ask the person to move out after just eleven months. It just does not make any sense—the landlord would be an absolute chump to do it.

If he does, then the landlord needs to find another good tenant. This will result in cash flow uncertainties due to vacancy periods after a tenant vacates, brokerage payments, repairs and painting before the next tenant and so on. Therefore, for a good tenant, the house is generally available for several eleven-month periods, blowing this propaganda to smithereens.

The other received wisdom is that it is difficult to stay on rent if one has school-going children. Again, this hardly has any substance. Even if one needs to shift, one can mostly find another home in the same building or society. If not, one can find it in the nearby buildings, the next street or somewhere in the vicinity. One may just have to hire the services of a broker to get the right home. The other nuisance is shifting homes. Movers and packers will be able to help here. While renting, the brokerage and the cost of the movers and packers will have to be paid. But considering all these costs as well, renting homes would still be more economical.

There is still the pain of shifting to consider, even if movers and packers are involved. It takes time to set up the house. Also, one will need to change addresses (this is becoming less of an issue today as communication is mostly electronic, making postal addresses largely redundant) for numerous correspondences. These are certainly the downsides of renting.

But there is an upside to renting, which is not appreciated. If one needs a bigger home, it is far easier to move into one, rather than buy one. And you don't have to attend housing society meetings!

Also, if a better home, with better amenities and ambience, comes up, one can simply move there. A person who has bought a home is going to be stuck with it.

Now I saw boredom writ large on their faces. I had been pontificating on this subject for over forty-five minutes and was hard-selling why they should stay put in a rented apartment instead of buying one, which they desperately wanted. They needed a bit of lift … I ordered a round of juice for them and talked about their children, Shreyan and Ashitaa. That loosened them a bit. They started talking about how naughty they were and how they were driving Preeti round the bend.

Shreyan seemed to display great skill in drawing. They felt he was a precocious child. Most parents feel their child is precocious if they can draw a river, sun and a hut decently! So, I let that go. We imbibed the nourishment, and peace prevailed for a space of five minutes. Vishal had got a call and had excused himself. He came in now. This reprieve was like a tonic for all of us.

Now that I had tackled the toughest topic, I felt I should quickly move on to the other two and wrap up the meeting. I did not want to dwell any longer on real estate—I had made the point and there were going to be other occasions to give them my perspective on real estate.

The international holiday could still be possible, from time to time. But since they were expecting their third child, this trip would not be feasible for at least two years. They agreed as they realised that travelling with such a small child would be difficult.

There would be expenses around the birth of the child. But Vishal's corporate group insurance policy would take care of that. Some expenses may not be covered, but these may not break the piggy bank. I had fobbed them off from their fanciful flights and tried to bring some sanity into their finances.

I threw a challenge at them. I said, 'Let's start a new debt fund in which to put in money for goals like international vacations and other such indulgences. You need to first save and then spend without guilt.' I also insisted on a condition: 'Saving in this debt fund should be after investing a certain sum first for feeding long-term investments, for important goals like retirement and education for the children.'

In a nutshell, they would have to be pragmatic and find money to feed their lifestyle goals. I also suggested they keep a separate fund for buying a house and I wanted them to channel a good proportion of their investments into it. All these proposals were well-received. It was within striking distance of ₹1 lakh a month, and they had not demurred!

Now came the nub. They never objected to anything I had suggested in the past as well. It was their implementation that had been tardy. All their investments needed to be set up and the money needed to get invested just after they got their salaries. Else, they would find a hundred other uses for it.

I suggested that they implement the suggestions completely, without which the plan would not work at all. I told them that the concerned person would call them tomorrow and that they should cooperate fully. They were fine with that.

By this time, unseen rodents were scampering about in my stomach. When I suggested some lunch, they gratefully accepted the offer.

We went to this place which has Gujarati and Rajasthani thalis with an assortment of about twenty different items to savour. Usually, there is a bit of waiting time. But today, this establishment, which calls itself Maharaja Palace, managed to allot us a table in just five minutes.

We settled down comfortably into our seats after which the meal was served. It was a pretty elaborate affair. We had a leisurely meal and after about an hour we had had our fill. The meal was fantastic. Fully satiated and in a mellow mood, we came back to the office.

I had this urge to have a good cup of coffee. I asked Vishal and Preeti if they would join in. Preeti wanted a cuppa, but Vishal declined. I wanted to summarise our discussion and leave them with clear action points that needed to be carried out.

I started, 'We have discussed continuing in the present home for the next two years, at least. In the interest of augmenting your investment corpus, this is the best way forward. We have seen that a new three-bedroom home is not affordable for now, and we need to be pragmatic about this. We can re-evaluate this a few years down the line when you are able to comfortably afford it. For now, the focus should be on investments.

'I have crunched the numbers, and you can up the investments per month to ₹90,000 from the ₹20,000 you are currently at. If you do a bit of belt-tightening, even ₹1 lakh would be possible. But, for now, we can stay with ₹90,000 a month, which is doable after considering all your expenses and short-term goals.

'I'm going to ask our Implementation team to do it for you this time. This is because, in the past, you have not been able to do it yourself. This would ensure that the entire recommendation will get implemented, and that you will not have to be bothered by the nitty-gritty of implementing the suggestions.

Whether it was the stupor induced by the lavish lunch or whether real good sense had finally prevailed, I could not say. Vishal and Preeti enthusiastically agreed to the proposition and assented that this would be the way forward for now. I couldn't have asked for more.

This fortunate turn of our discussion was a huge surprise. I had expected this session to be stormy. Preeti, especially, was expected to be a tough customer to convince when it came to their home—and yet they were both eating out of my hand! The persuasive power of a good meal was on display and it was a revelation for me.

I sent a silent prayer to the proprietors of Maharaja Palace who had the gastronomic delights to dismantle the resistance of the tough eggs I needed to deal with. The place had been full. I wondered whether the establishment specifically catered to the business community who brought in their clients to put them in a mellow mood.

Vishal and Preeti took leave. I told them that someone from the Implementation team would call them that evening and would let them know the way forward. I flopped into the chair, releasing all the pent-up tension of the meeting. There was not much tension, after all, come to think of it. But still, I felt drained.

Another important meeting was coming up and I had to be alert. Bala was expected in another fifteen minutes. I paced the corridors outside my office, collecting my thoughts. A few minutes later, I went inside and wrote down some notes for myself as I waited for Bala to arrive.

3

WHEN ONE DOOR CLOSES, ANOTHER OPENS

Bala came in exactly on time. I was happy to see him. He seemed to be in a good mood. The meeting with the tutor must have gone well, I thought to myself. I was waiting for Bala to start the conversation so that I could get a hint of where his thoughts were. Bala likes coffee, so I ordered some for him.

He ultimately came to the surface. He was quite happy that his daughter, Malvika, was doing well. Her teacher had mentioned that Malvika should be put on specialised training for IIT as she was able to see the potential in her to crack the country's toughest entrance exam. This was like music to Bala's ears. He had then and there resolved that he would look around for a good institute under whose care Malvika could blossom and realise her potential.

But then dark clouds suddenly shrouded his face. He said sadly, 'I don't know where I stand. I need to find some work fast. I do not want to become a stumbling block in Malvika's path.

I let him calm down, and did not utter a word for fifteen seconds. I wanted to broach the topic very carefully. I asked him what he had been doing to find a suitable position. He answered without enthusiasm, and I understood from him that he had pretty much tried everything. He told me he had even looked outside the industry for work. But, as of now, nothing had worked. It had been fifteen days since he had lost his job. He was still on his three-month notice period. But, at the end of it, he needed a job. I was able to see that he was despondent.

I told him, 'For a person with your experience and achievements, many would like to have you. It is another matter that all the companies are down in the dumps and cannot engage you, even if they want to. You have tremendous goodwill in your firm, and your management knows your capabilities. Even the major shareholder knows that you put in unstinted work and, more importantly, always deliver. The answer to your problem may probably be within your firm itself.'

What I said was a bit enigmatic. But I had also touched upon the fact that the solution probably lies inside the portals of the firm rather than elsewhere. Bala just looked at me blankly. He did not understand what I was trying to hint at. I waited for him to react, but he responded with deafening silence!

Some curiosity on the part of Bala would have helped. But, in his current state of mind, that was too much to expect. I had led him to it. Even after that, I was left with no option but to be explicit about what I wanted to convey.

I started, 'You have told me London is a great real estate market, isn't it?' Bala nodded with an utterly puzzled look as to why I was now talking about this.

I continued, 'In a good market like London, it would be great to have competent hands to maximise the impact and harness the potential. You told me that your London office was doing well. You also told me that they were fully staffed. But anyone can use a talented person if they come at no cost, don't you think?'

Bala looked at me as if I had gone insane. In his current pensive mood, he did not say anything.

I soldiered on. 'If a talented person, such as you, were to offer your services on a purely variable basis, would they not lap it up? They have nothing to lose; they pay you only if you get them business.'

I was done. Now I had to wait and see if Bala would latch on to the bait. Bala was quiet for ten seconds. And then, his face lit up.

'Why did I not think of this?' he said. 'You are a genius, Suresh. This is such a simple yet workable idea. I feel like flogging myself for not thinking of this before.'

To push things along, I asked, 'You think this idea will work?'

Bala thought for a bit before answering. 'I think it will,' he said. 'We have to make it work. I have always wanted to work in the London market, and this could be my real chance to have a go at it.' He was smiling now. He seemed to be thinking hard and working something out in his head.

I shared my opinion. 'I have heard that the commercial market in London offers maximum potential. Would you be working in this space?'

Bala was surprised. He looked at me with his eyes peeled open and said, 'Today, you are talking as if you really know our business. Commercial space is the most promising segment and I intend to address that segment if I were to work in London. But how come you got this idea and are suggesting things as if you know all about the London real estate market?'

I answered nonchalantly, 'One of my friends mentioned that London was a great market and had shared a few points with me. I felt that those points may be relevant to your situation. Good to note that I have kindled a thought process that you find useful. Tell me, do you think your London office would offer this commission to you?'

Bala said confidently, 'Of course! They have nothing to lose. Getting an experienced person at no fixed cost would be their dream come true. But it is not going to be as bad as that. I'll ensure that they pay me a base fixed rate and a variable commission. It can be worked out, I'm positive.'

I liked that confident note. 'But how do you know?' I asked.

He said that his management was unhappy to let him go. If he suggested any possible way of continuing to work with them without seriously denting their cash flow, they would be game.

'If I ask for up to 50 per cent of my current salary, they may agree. I propose to ask just 40 per cent of my present income and accept the balance as variable, based on the business I bring.'

Now, it was my time to smile. The ways of the Lord were mysterious. He had used me as a handy tool to give Bala a credible idea and get his confidence back on track. The afternoon coffee came. It tasted like nectar to me. Bala also seemed to savour the coffee today, more than usual.

I had done two good deeds in one day. The time was 5.15 p.m. I wanted to give myself a break. I left the office along with Bala.

4

REAL ESTATE: THE REAL STORY

When I reached home at six that evening, Madhu was surprised. She asked me how come I was back home so early. She quickly ran her hand over my temples and neck to see if I had a fever. She turned and looked at me quizzically. I simply said that I had had completed the tasks for the day and hence had turned in early.

I had an early dinner that night. My thoughts were turned to what had happened during the day, even though I had a book in my hand and was trying to read it.

I could hardly believe that I had been able to prevail upon Vishal and Preeti on a touchy subject like buying a house. The Lord has helped me here too, I thought. I had explained three of the myths of real estate. But there are many, and they are endemic. Almost everyone is in the grip of these myths, which is why people across the country invest heavily in properties.

As some other myths related to buying property came to my mind, I noted them down so that I would be able to relay them to others in the future. Here they are:

Myth 4: We are truly happy in our own house

We all buy a house that we can afford. Many times, the house that we can afford is not always the most suitable one for us to live in. Hence, most people who buy a home somehow adjust and stay in it, even though it is unsuited to their situation.

For others, they can buy a reasonably-sized, comfortable home that will be good to live in. But that home may not be in the neighbourhood they desire.

There is another category of those who can buy the right home in the right locality and are absolutely happy with their purchase. But because they have spent so much, and have taken on massive loans, they have to tighten their finances for years on end. Their lives will be thrown into disarray if there is any disruption in their income. Any new goals or expenses can again cause problems for such people, at least in the initial years. They are often left with no wiggle room.

The last category consists of those who are able to buy the right type of home where they want and have the means to do this comfortably (with some loan, which is easily serviceable). But this is a tiny category.

The number of people who are truly happy in their own homes is quite small indeed.

Myth 5: Buying a home is a way to force saving

It is. But that cannot be the reason to buy a home. It is probably true for an undisciplined person, who will squander money if there are no forced savings, like in the case of home loan EMIs. But everyone is not so undisciplined.

One can set up monthly investments, which can get debited from the main savings account at the beginning of the month, to achieve the same result. Here, one has the flexibility to pause the investment or scale down if an unforeseen event occurs. This option is just not available if one has bought a home on loan. EMIs cannot be paused.

If there is a job loss, one still has to service the home loan. Else, the property will get confiscated by the home loan provider and auctioned. Any default would also impact one's credit score, subsequently affecting one's ability to borrow as and when needed.

Myth 6: Property is the only asset that appreciates constantly and offers good returns

This is the biggest myth of them all. The property market is prone to long up-and-down cycles. Property prices are down or have steadied across the country after about ten years in the dumps. In many places today, one finds it difficult to sell property, even if offered at low prices.

The built-up stocks are high, and the stock under construction is still substantial. When the offtake of property is low, the entire real estate sector gets stressed.

Real estate had given stellar returns between 2003 and 2008. Those returns were a one-off aberration and probably will not be replicated for a long time. The typical return on property (capital appreciation and rent) is between 4 per cent and 9 per cent. That looks like it is very low. That's because we seldom add up the cost of interest we pay on a home loan over time to the cost of the property. In most cases, the interest paid overtime would be as much or higher than the loan amount itself.

Let's take an example. Let us say that one acquires a ₹2 crore property (₹1.8 crore is the cost and ₹20 lakh is for registration, stamp duty and incidentals, which cannot be recovered while selling) with a ₹50 lakh down payment and a loan of ₹1.5 crore.

If the interest rate is 8.75 per cent a year, the interest amount paid over time would be ₹1.68 crore during the loan tenure of twenty years. If the interest rates were 10 per cent, the interest paid on the loan over time would be ₹1.97 crore. This is a substantial cost, which most ignore and calculate returns based on just the quoted cost of the property.

Also, people spend large amounts of money on doing up their homes, which cannot be recovered while selling. Repairs and property maintenance also take up a good sum over time. All these costs need to be factored in.

Even after doing so, there are some properties which give double-digit returns over long periods of time—but they are exceptions.

Property should just be seen as another asset class. People fall in love with it instead. The fact that it has a tactile feel to it and gives a sense of ownership is a deceptive lure that makes people fall for property. As an asset, properties have several negatives—they are illiquid, cannot be partially liquidated if one requires some money and have a huge concentration risk (a huge amount of money gets stuck in just one property; if for some reason that locality is out of favour, then the property price will not increase).

Myth 7: Low-cost home loans allow one to leverage and increase wealth, which no other asset allows

Home loans are indeed low-cost. But the fact is, there is still a cost even if the interest rates are low, the absolute amounts are massive. For a big home loan, the monthly payout would be substantial for a long time. We had shown that for a ₹1.5 crore loan, one would be paying as much as ₹1.97 crore as interest (if the home loan interest rate is 10 per cent a year and the loan tenure is twenty years).

Any disruption in income would cause problems—especially for those with multiple home loans. It is a huge gamble that one is undertaking for a long period of time. If one encounters problems in the future, it may not even be easy to dispose of the property and recover the money. Property is mostly illiquid and takes a long time to sell.

Hence, with such huge leverages, people are taking huge risks. They assume that their income will be stable and rise throughout their life, that there will not be any disruptive events in life in between, that the property invested will appreciate over time and so on.

Life is never linear. It has its ups and downs. Hence, people getting into such a huge gamble invariably get stuck. We have many clients who are in this unenviable situation.

Myth 8: Properties are an excellent way to set up a steady income stream

Properties can be rented out. But there are problems. Property rental yields are very low in India. A residential property costing, say, ₹1 crore can be rented for, say, ₹25,000–30,000 a month. After paying society charges, property tax and income tax, the rental yield comes to just 2 per cent or less. So, if someone wants a good income stream from their investment, their property would not be able to offer that. In this situation, the property they own is like a fixed deposit (FD) that yields only 2 per cent.

In some cases, there are problems with a tenant not vacating on time. It can also get stuck in litigation, which, as we are aware, can be time-consuming and money-draining.

The various problems when a landlord rents out a property have been covered earlier (see Myth 3).

Some people say that commercial property is way better in terms of returns. Commercial property can indeed give better returns when compared to residential property. But even this is not true across the board. Commercial properties bought in the wrong places would be difficult to rent out.

Vacancy periods can be long in commercial property, so one should be extremely careful when choosing them. The loan rates for commercial properties are much higher than for home loans. Unlike residential property, there is no provision for the set-off of the interest portion of the EMI in income tax sections.

The other problem is the black money portion in real estate. While it has come down in recent years, it is still a bane in transactions. The service class struggles with this; they need to convert their tax-paid money into cash as some portion of the transaction is in cash.

A simpler way to set up a regular income would be to invest the money in a financial asset, say a simple FD, and get much more with a lot less hassle.

Other than the many myths that people believe about buying property, there are several mistakes that they commit when it comes to their properties.

Mistake 1: Endowment effect

The property that one owns somehow seems to be much better and worth a lot more than similar properties. The property owner feels that the view from their property is great, is close to the metro station, has more space than most other options and is a 'lucky' home. This is called the 'endowment effect'. Due to this, people abstain from selling their property or keep expecting unrealistically high prices for their property.

There are many cases where sellers get stuck to a price and refuse to budge until that price has been met. Years later, when they sell at 'their price', they lose out on the interest they could have easily earned, which, along with the market price of years earlier, would have been worth much more.

Mistake 2: Buying a holiday home

Holiday homes seem like a wonderful idea. What can be better than your own home in the hills, where you can relax and rejuvenate? It sounds great on paper. But there are lots of negatives to this idea.

For one, one will use this property for maybe twenty to thirty days a year, at the most. For the rest of the time, the property will have to be rented out or would need to be kept under lock and key. Most people keep their property locked, earning nothing. But to keep the property in good shape, a caretaker would be needed throughout the year. This adds to the cost of just holding on to the property.

Coming to the same property every year would get rather boring after three or four visits. Hence, after some time, one would start going to other destinations and end up not using the property at all. The worst thing about holiday homes is that the appreciation is poor and resale is extremely difficult due to the remote locations that they are generally found in.

Mistake 3: Buying a retirement home

It makes sense to buy a retirement home maybe two years before retirement. However, many contemplate buying a retirement home fifteen to twenty years in advance.

The first problem here is that our thinking can change over time. What appears like a great idea today may not appeal to us after fifteen years. The property bought for retirement purposes has to be put on rent, which would yield even lower than 2 per cent, if at all. Retirement homes would be on the outskirts of a city or sometimes so far from the city that they are not exactly sought-after vicinities by those who are still working.

This means that the retirement home may have to be rented out to retirees looking for such options. Since such tenants may be difficult to find, the yield may not be much or even nothing for most of its existence. But one would need to maintain it, pay society charges, property taxes, etc., making it a money-losing proposition. These properties also don't appreciate much.

The home would be old by the time one retires and would require a lot of maintenance and repairs. Also, the property would not be contemporary and may lack many amenities that would by then be available in new developments.

If one wants to sell, the problem is the same as a holiday home. There are few buyers, if any at all. So, if one ends up selling after many years, they may find very little appreciation. All things considered, it would be a loss. It is far better to keep investing in financial assets and buy a home of one's choice at retirement rather than investing decades in advance in a money-losing proposition that may ultimately not be suitable.

Mistake 4: Buying properties to fund important goals like education and marriage

Property markets have long cycles. When one invests in property for essential goals like education, it is crucial that the property be liquidated at the right time, when it is needed. But if the property is in a down cycle (which it can be for several years like 1995–2003 and 2009–2022, out of which 2012 onwards have been severe), one can get stuck and not get a reasonable price. In fact, in such markets, it is difficult to sell at any price—as there are very few buyers.

In such situations, though a person may be asset-rich, they are cash-poor. They end up borrowing for goals like education and marriage, or end up using financial assets that have been earmarked for something else. This happens in lots of cases and is a mistake that should be avoided.

Mistake 5: Prepaying the home loan

A loan is seen as a burden, and rightly so. But a home loan is a special loan with reasonable interest. On top of it, there are tax breaks available that make home loans cheap. For instance, currently, the real cost of a home loan may be just 6–8 per cent. There is just no other loan that can offer money at such low rates; hence prepaying home loans normally does not make any sense. If one has money, it will probably be better to invest elsewhere to earn more rather than prepaying the home loan.

If one is diligently investing whatever surpluses one may have, the loan can be paid off anytime. This way, one would also have liquidity throughout, and the amount being accumulated (in lieu of paying off the loan) would take care of any interim needs and act as a liquidity or contingency buffer.

There is one instance when prepaying a home loan would make sense. If initially the home loan taken is huge and the EMI being paid is over 40 per cent of one's monthly take-home pay, then it may make sense to bring down the loan to manageable levels, where the EMI is up to 40 per cent or lesser than the take-home pay. This would be a prudent practice as any disruption in income would otherwise have a ruinous effect on one's finances.

Mistake 6: Property is an asset

While property is an asset, it is a liability too. There are regular payments to be made for properties, like maintenance charges and property taxes. Property repairs and maintenance regularly require money to be put in, which we do not consider while calculating returns. The property must be occupied, or else it starts atrophying. Once the property is unoccupied for long periods, it requires a huge amount of capital to make it liveable. Also, even if it is given on rent, there will be vacancy periods—sometimes extending to several months.

There are other liabilities too, in the case of a property. Property titles are unclear in many cases, and property development itself comes to a grinding halt for years, bringing with it uncertainty, leaving the owner in despair, confused whether one would ever get possession of the property. In some cases, there could be litigation too.

Dealing with builders and sundry others is often a tiresome affair as well. Sometimes, there are also escalations in prices and charges that had not been disclosed at the beginning; these further jack up the price of the property for the buyer. However, the Real Estate (Regulation and Development) Act, 2016 (RERA) has tried to address this and provide relief to property buyers.

Also, properties often don't get the occupancy certificate, and the owners are left in a limbo, even after fully paying for it. All these risks and liabilities of investing in a property are not fully factored in, and we erroneously call property an asset.

5

THE PROBLEM WITH
THE APPLE OF THE EYE

The next morning found me well-rested and ready to take on the world. Since I woke up early, I reached the office early too.

Half an hour into work, I got a call from Vishal, who wanted to discuss his children's education. He said he wanted to talk about it during the previous day's meeting, but in all the other points we discussed, this got left out.

I told him that we could have this conversation in the evening around four over the phone, which he was fine with. I wanted to finish up a few things before having this conversation, which could take a while.

Now is the best time to be a child. Parents fawn over their children and do their every bidding. So there is nothing that children will not be able to make their doting parents do for them. Much more than ever before, parents are concerned about their children's education. Nothing wrong there, but this is becoming an obsession. A good education has lots of connotations these days.

Well-rounded personality: Parents want their children to start life with an advantage. They want them to have the best education as well as other life skills. They are prepared to pull out all the stops and spare no expense in giving their wards that push to keep them ahead of the crowd.

Parents want their children to have a well-rounded personality and look for schools that provide that opportunity as a part of the curriculum. There are schools which have horse riding, swimming, football, archery, etc., as part of the routine. What were once extracurricular activities have gone centre stage now.

These things have become very valuable—so valuable that parents are ready to spend a small fortune for the benefits a certain education may confer on their wards. 'International' schools hold the promise of activity-based learning, rather than rote learning and have various extracurricular activities as well.

Many schools also do not want to judge and exert undue pressure on their students and hence only give grades. Parents want to shield their children from the adverse effects of hyper-competition. All these are seen as positive aspects by parents.

But Bill Gates had some penetrating insight on this. He had said that only in school will everyone pass, and there are no winners and losers. In life, however, competition is endemic, and one needs to strive hard to win. No. 1 and No. 2 are clear when it comes to life, as it is in sports. There are clear winners, and there are also-rans.

Children studying in 'international' schools in International Baccalaureate or other similar curriculums would not be able to easily integrate into the Indian college education stream.

Admitting children to such schools virtually ensures that the children have to be sent abroad for education. Hence, children's education becomes a massive expense, where school education itself is costly, and college education is a king's ransom. Even those earning very well would find it extremely difficult to fund their children's education in such situations.

These schools charge between ₹4 lakh and ₹12 lakh yearly (sometimes more) for the spit and polish job. High fees are hardly a deterrent these days. In fact, for parents today, high fees are often a heuristic to determine whether the school is really good or not.

Unintended consequences: Other unintended consequences exist when parents admit their children to fancy schools. Children from such schools usually come from upper-middle-class or wealthy households. In such a situation, even children from fairly well-off families tend to feel poor, as many of their peers are from wealthier households. Some of these children tend to develop an inferiority complex, after comparing themselves with other kids in their class or school.

Children get upset that their parents don't take them on foreign jaunts every summer. And the fact that their parents own only an 'ordinary' car, as opposed to the Jaguar, BMW or Mercedes Benz of their friends' parents, rankles them. The list goes on. They are unhappy with their shoes, birthday parties, bags, etc. They are poor by comparison! There are also instances where children have started seeing their parents as 'failures', just because their parents are not CEOs, executive directors or business owners like the parents of their classmates. This is very unfortunate, given the fact that parents put their wards in these fancy schools in order to help them put their best foot forward.

Values, ethics and morals: Parents don't have time due to their hyper-busy careers. In many households, both parents are working. They now want their children to learn moral values from their schools. Previously, parents (and grandparents) used to don the mantle of educating children and inculcating strong values in them. Now, this vital job is getting outsourced. Parents have little time, and they want moral education to be imparted at school as well as regular subjects.

Tired parents find cricket matches and soap operas more comforting. Tutoring children on the nuances of ethical conduct and being morally right, conveying and anchoring those through stories which pass on such precious wisdom, takes time and patience. These days, parents just don't have the time or patience to answer questions raised by children. Schools of various persuasions 'mould' children and teach 'moral values and ethics' according to what they want to propagate. Schools are producing deracinated zombies who believe that the West is somehow superior in everything and there is nothing worthwhile that has ever come out of India. Such schools are well-funded by Western missions and influence groups and are meant to mentally colonise our children. One such school did not even want the Indian national anthem to be sung and wanted a foreign anthem to be sung by students!

Yet, schools which dangle the promise of teaching values, ethics and morals are in huge demand, and parents are voting for these schools with their money, without realising the perils of outsourcing this vital function and polluting impressionable minds.

Ambitious parents: Parents want their children to become 'superman meets Leonardo da Vinci'. Many parents put their wards in a variety of after-school classes which are not part of the curriculum. Children are hence packed off to karate, spelling bee, abacus, skating and dance classes, to further aid their 'holistic' development. Children are often tired of these routines and are mostly not interested in any of them.

Parents want to produce the next Jack Ma, but most children end up as Jacks of all trades. The generous amounts that parents lavish on these activities generally end up as money down the drain. Giving a positive spin, one can say that these parents create a considerable amount of employment, and there are lakhs of beneficiaries who would be thankful to them for being able to put three meals on their family tables.

Vicarious achievement: Some parents live their dreams vicariously through their children, and the children end up being held hostage to the dreams and wishes of their parents. Many parents want their wards to pursue a particular vocation—say, medicine, as they had always wanted to be doctors. To pursue their dreams, parents display a single-minded focus, pressurising their children to choose the streams they wanted to, shovel money into tuitions, coaching classes, and so on. But even if the child becomes a doctor, the child may not have an aptitude for medicine and may be an average doctor. The child could have fared far better in their own field of interest.

Don't know the pulse: Many parents are not aware of what's happening in the economy, the new directions in various industries, and the new sectors and options that are emerging. Parents still want their children to pursue engineering even though there is a surfeit of engineers. These days those who have completed their engineering degrees are not able to land jobs. There are survey statistics to show that out of three million or so engineers who complete their engineering courses every year in India, less than 20 per cent are employable. That is a damning statistic and one that parents should know about, and thus refrain from pushing their wards over the cliff.

But even today, a vast majority of students pursue engineering only to find themselves left standing in the cold, as they cannot find any job. Such students end up pursuing some other courses to increase their 'marketability'. Many of them end up doing jobs that have no connection with what they have majored in.

So, a simple subject like the education of children becomes very complicated indeed—complicated by their own parents. Children themselves have added complexity to their lives. They are very much affected by their peer group. That skews their choice of school, classes, hobbies, the stream they would want to pursue and so on. This unnecessarily adds complexity to the education pursuit as there are multiple requirements from both parents and children.

The latest fad: To add to it, studying abroad has now become a trend. These days even those with comparatively modest means plan to send their children abroad—at least at the postgraduate level. Again, parents want to give their children that advantage— nothing wrong with that. The only problem with it is that education abroad is frightfully expensive. On average, education in the US or UK at the graduate or postgraduate level would cost about ₹50 lakh per year, maybe more. Hence, education abroad is a very costly affair. In their enthusiasm to send their children abroad, parents end up emptying their coffers. Money which has been kept aside for goals like retirement gets diverted to education, which leaves many parents exposed in the future. With average life expectancy increasing, the retirement period has only become longer—between twenty-five to thirty years—and so retirement funding needs to be taken even more seriously. If there is a shortfall, parents will have to depend on their children for sustenance, which is hardly the best option.

There is, however, a way to manage foreign education expenses. Apart from parental funding, three other options need to be explored.

The first is to explore the possibility of a scholarship for the chosen stream. The second is to take an education loan to fund the goal partly. And the third is to find work abroad and partially defray expenses when there.

If all the above options are considered, education abroad would be a lot less taxing for the parent. Also, one needs to be realistic about the possibility of securing employment after completing the course abroad.

There are many instances where students have not been able to get employment and have had to return to India. One needs a plan B if their child has to come back.

I was thinking of all these matters, which were essential for Vishal to know. Every time Vishal comes to meet me, it is with trepidation that I look forward to the meeting. Vishal called around 3 p.m. and informed me that he was in the vicinity of my office and would prefer to meet me personally. He postponed our meeting to 5 p.m.

He walked in at the appointed hour. His face was inscrutable. I ordered tea, and we settled in for our discussion. Vishal started. 'We did not discuss the education for Shreyan. We have to admit him to a regular school in kindergarten this year. Ashitaa needs to be admitted to playschool next year.'

'There is a good school near our home called Pristine International School. Admissions are open now. They are asking for a non-refundable deposit of ₹1 lakh. The school fee currently is ₹2.85 lakh a year for kindergarten. From the first standard onwards, the fee will go up to ₹3.75 lakh. They have also given a guidance of about 5 per cent escalation in school fees, year on year.'

He paused, half expecting me to interrupt and say something. I kept quiet. He continued. 'We are both interested in putting Shreyan into this school. As I mentioned, this is a very good school with an international curriculum. The quality of education, I have heard, is very good. They have various activities for children beyond regular education like swimming, singing, drawing, etc. Also, they teach children morals and ethics, which are very important in their formative years. The only problem is that we must pay the deposit and yearly fees, which we need to arrange.' It looked like he had come to the end of his monologue. I paused to find out if there was more coming. But there wasn't.

When Vishal wanted to meet me, I knew he would let off an explosive device under my feet—I was not mistaken. With Vishal, one did not get surprised. I was staring at a long argument against the move he was suggesting. I had to prepare him for what was coming.

'What is the amount currently in the bank, Vishal?' I asked.

'₹4 lakh, approximately,' said Vishal.

'You would need ₹2.5 lakh at least for liquidity, which leaves ₹1.5 lakh free. The advance will be taken care of. But, tell me, does the school fee have to be paid fully in advance?' I enquired.

'There are two options. One, where I can pay ₹2.85 lakh in advance, or I could pay ₹75,000 per quarter in four equal instalments. I thought paying up in advance is a good idea as we would be saving about ₹15,000 in the process,' he said.

'But for that you need to dip into your savings, which is not something that I would advocate. The savings you have now are only at ₹20 lakh, and eroding that further would not be prudent.'

Vishal considered this. I cashed in on the opportunity to do some probing.

'Have you considered all the options for schooling in your vicinity? Are you sure there are no other schools that offer good education at far more reasonable rates?'

Vishal saw this coming. 'We have looked at all schools within a five-kilometre radius, and this is indeed the best school. We did some fact-finding on other international schools, and their fee structure is much more expensive. So, this school is indeed the best bet,' Vishal said.

'Your expenses will go up, the monthly savings will come down by ₹25,000. This will have an impact on other goals. I hope you remember what I showed you the other day,' I said.

Vishal nodded. I had shown him the effect of various expenses and how he may have to work till about sixty-five years, at least, to make things work. I was surprised as to how he could be so adamant about this. It was Shreyan now; Ashitaa would come next. The new baby would come after that. It will be a very expensive proposition for Vishal, I thought.

I excused myself and did some quick calculations, considering the education of all three children till the twelfth standard, starting at their respective points. I then included graduation and postgraduation abroad for all three. It just did not work.

I turned the laptop around, showed Vishal what I had done and quickly explained to him the problem with such funding. I explained all the points I had pondered over, regarding the parents overextending themselves, before he had come. He listened patiently.

Vishal asked, 'What would you do in my position?'

'I would put them in regular schools, considering there are three kids to educate. It is practically not possible to give such an education with the current income stream you have. But expecting a much higher income stream is also not pragmatic. Frankly, 'international school' education is overhyped and does not necessarily mean better education.

'Their method is somewhat different and ostensibly produces better outcomes. But there is no real empirical evidence to prove that. Also, there are enough and more success stories of children from modest backgrounds, studying in municipal schools who have risen to occupy positions of power.

'The former President of India Dr Abdul Kalam and the eminent scientist and former director of the Council of Scientific & Industrial Research (CSIR), Dr R.A. Mashelkar studied in municipal schools and were able to reach the pinnacle of their chosen fields.

'I know that I'm relying on anecdotal evidence here, and admittedly they are the outliers. But there are many who have had humble early lives, who have gone on to become achievers in the fields of their choosing.

'Education is important. It does light the spirit of enquiry and widens vistas. But thinking that only one kind of education or curriculum could confer your children with the winning advantage is incorrect, especially when there is no evidence of this education system producing excellent performers or super successes.

'A regular school has other advantages. Such schools have students from middle-class backgrounds and your children will not face peer pressures that have monetary implications for you. Students in 'international schools', who generally come from more affluent backgrounds, end up giving an inferiority complex to others from relatively modest backgrounds.

'And children's expectations rise—be it in terms of holidays, cars, the neighbourhood they live in, entertainment, partying and so on. That can exert significant pressure on you, especially when all your three children start going to such a school.

'Also, as we have seen, it will not be feasible for you to service fees and other incidentals when all your children start studying in such schools. You just don't have the cash flow. You may be forced to shift them to regular schools at some point in the future, which even your children may not agree to then. Both of you need to think through this properly before taking any decision.

'This is a very important decision. Why don't you bring Preeti along tomorrow so that we can meet and get this out of the way?' I suggested.

'Sure,' said Vishal, and I sensed relief in how he said it. He was very clearly dreading the possibility of conveying my thoughts to Preeti and getting shredded in the bargain. He did not want to be the messenger who carried bad news.

The next day when I met Preeti, it appeared that her guard was up. I brought her up to speed on my thoughts regarding their children's education, and I should say that she patiently heard me out. After that, she asked me a difficult question.

'Would you, knowingly, send your children to a lesser school when better options are available?' was how she started her campaign. It was a loaded question, and my integrity was on the line.

I ventured forth, 'We need to define quality education and what we mean by a good institution. The quality of teachers, the infrastructure, the values and morals they inculcate, the understanding and grounding the students get from the subjects they study, overall personality development, the success of their students in the real world, etc., are some of the measures to gauge the worth of an institution and the education they are able to provide. By that token, my children are going to good schools. I'm suggesting the same to you.

'A seemingly wonderful institution, with international affiliations, may not necessarily offer the best education. Even if it does, there can be other institutions that may also be as good and offer quality education at reasonable fees.

'They may not confer you with bragging rights like those international schools. But there are several advantages to such a choice. The children who study in 'normal' schools are from typical middle-class backgrounds. Hence, your children may not feel the weight of expectations that they may feel in a snooty institution.'

'The focus in a normal school is education, and there are not too many diversions—which is, after all, good. Plus, you will be meeting other regular parents in the meetings organised by the school—not some snooty fat cats to whom you cannot relate. Lastly, it's perceptibly light on the pocket and offers space to plan for other important goals too.'

Preeti was combative. 'That's your opinion. But the international school we want to put Shreyan in is really good, and has produced several excellent students who have been able to secure admission in some of the best colleges. Their fees are high, I agree. But they are very good.'

I said nothing. I just pulled up the calculation that I had shown Vishal the previous day and explained to her that, in their case, they would have to educate three kids and the school fees alone would be over ₹10 lakh a year. I also showed her that it would not work, given their current level of income and expenditure. The other goals they have would also be impacted.

'We have to be pragmatic. We need to deploy the available resources in the best possible manner so that they can produce good outcomes for you overall. That's all from my side. You need to decide what you want to do,' I signed off. There was silence for ten seconds. I had no intention of ending this uncomfortable silence.

'Let's take a day to decide. We will think about this and then come to a decision,' said Vishal.

With that, the meeting was over, and they departed. This was one of those meetings which I loathed to do but was necessary to keep my client away from a self-destructive path.

After the meeting, I could not conclude what they might decide. It could be a fifty-fifty chance, either way, I reckoned.

6

THE NEED FOR SPEED
ON FINANCES

That evening, I was mulling over the meeting. Madhu noticed it and asked if something was troubling me. There was nothing, I told her. But the conversation we had had earlier in the day was going over and over in my head.

There was this suspense as to what Vishal and Preeti would decide regarding the school. It puzzled me as to why I got so involved in it. Would they not know what is best for them? Still, this one decision regarding their children's education was crucial for their overall plan, and I have to admit that it was troubling me more than it should have.

As a financial adviser, I should have been far more dispassionate. But I was getting involved—which was not how it should be.

To change track, I picked up a book and was going through it for some time. The phone rang, and it was Vishal. My heart skipped a beat.

'Hi, Vishal, what's up?' I said. It was Preeti. I stiffened. What is it now? Why was she calling?

'Yes, Preeti. Go ahead,' I said with as much nonchalance as I could muster at a moment's notice.

'Sorry for calling you so late. I hope I have not disturbed you,' Preeti said.

'No, no, not at all. Go ahead,' I said, almost dreading what she might say.

'I was talking about you to my sister, Sunaina. You have met didi once, when you came to our place, you remember?' she asked. I did not get the drift. Where was this leading? Was she going to draft her sister into convincing me about the importance of admitting Shreyan into that international school?

'Didi and Raj need your help. I have asked them to call you and fix an appointment with you. They want to meet you tomorrow itself. Is that possible?' Preeti queried.

I heaved a sigh of relief. Thank God, it was not about the school.

'Certainly. Would half past ten in the morning suit them? If it does, they can come right over,' I said.

She talked to her sister immediately and confirmed. She said that she would come along with her sister tomorrow.

This was a new turn of events. But it was much better than what I had anticipated. This calmed me down a bit. After dinner, I was browsing through a book. It did not grip me. But at least I was no longer apprehensive about what Vishal and Preeti might decide. While talking to Preeti, she appeared relaxed, which had a calming effect on me.

I heard the squawk of parakeets. The sky was lit, and I knew I had slept well the previous night. The clock informed me that it was quarter past six. I jumped out of bed and, in five minutes, was ready to do my yoga and pranayama. This should be done every day, but I do it whenever I can.

A shave and a shower later, I was ready. Madhu had prepared breakfast, sensing that today was one of those rare days when I may leave early for the office. I reached the office at half past eight. It was a wonderful feeling to be there before everyone else.

The silence of the office was soothing like a balm and proved conducive for work. I marshalled my thoughts on what I needed to do for the day, made some notes, called for tea and sipped it contentedly.

The phone rang. It was Preeti. She was enquiring if they could come a bit early at 10 a.m. I agreed. The clock's face proclaimed that there were twenty minutes to the tête-à-tête with Preeti's elder sister.

When they arrived I let Preeti and company in. I was introduced formally to Sunaina (Naina to the family and didi to Preeti) and Prithiviraj Mathur (Raj to family and friends). Preeti was doing the talking initially, and then she wanted them to take over. She said she would now have to step out for some other work. That left the three of us in the room.

I smiled at them and asked them what they wanted to accomplish. Naina was the one who was quick on the uptake. She quickly gave a brief about their situation.

Raj and Naina were both working—Raj in a packaged food manufacturing company as a production manager and Naina at a private firm. They have a daughter Ritika, who was eleven years old and studying in the sixth grade.

What I was able to gather was that they had built a house in Bhopal but were staying on rent near the factory in Himachal

Pradesh, where Raj worked. They had saved some money, but not as much as one would have expected. When asked about it, they said they had to invest a lot of money into the Bhopal home and had also given money to Raj's parents and his brother, who is a businessman.

Raj was forty-five years old, and Naina was forty-two. They wanted to know whether they were on course to achieving their goals and whether their investments were right. Naina especially wanted advice on their investments. She was insistent that that was all the help they needed. I had faced these kinds of clients before—those who insisted that we just look at their investments. I had to explain to them why we had to take a holistic look at their life and their goals to see what needed to be done about their investments. In short, I had to explain to them the concept of financial planning.

What is financial planning?

Financial planning is a process where the client's goals are kept in focus, and a blueprint is created after considering their current financial situation and various factors impacting them so that the salient goals can be achieved in the timeframes needed. This calls for an analysis of the client's situation, evaluation of alternatives, strategies to achieve desired outcomes and, finally, coming up with appropriate recommendations to implement the plan.

In the financial planning process, products come at the end as investment recommendations—as a by-product of all the planning and deliberations. Along with it, there will also be recommendations on what to do about loans, properties, liquidity and contingency to be maintained, risk mitigation through appropriate insurance suggestions for investments in various assets based on the client's risk tolerance.

The focus here will be on efficient management of resources at the client's disposal and optimising them based on their specific needs. That means choosing the right vehicles for the right purposes, ensuring tax-efficient investments and meshing the investments with the overall requirements on risk-return, tenure and so on.

Financial planning is an ongoing engagement that starts with a plan that continues to engage clients and offer appropriate advice going forward.

Now with that out of the way, most people still think that they are not rich enough to hire the services of a financial planner.

Who is a financial planner or adviser?

Customers have a problem in understanding who a financial planner or adviser is. Most people just sell products and call themselves planners and advisers, which confuses customers.

There is a huge confusion in their minds as to who is an adviser and what to expect from them. The Securities and Exchange Board of India (SEBI), which is the capital markets regulator and oversees the area of financial advice, had come out with the Investment Adviser (IA) Regulation, 2013. And those who have chosen to come under this regulation are called Registered Investment Advisers (RIA). As per this regulation, an RIA should advise clients on a fee-only basis and should not receive any remuneration by way of commissions or brokerage. IA Regulation enforces a higher standard, compliance, education and certification norms, and an avoidance of conflict of interest. Any residual conflicts of interest are to be disclosed to the client completely.

Many RIAs also have commission income as they continue with the legacy investments of their clients or continue to solicit new business too. In such cases, RIAs who have a distribution practice along with their advisery practice must segregate the two practices clearly and maintain a distance between the two so that the client's interests are not compromised. If there is a conflict of interest, it must be clearly disclosed to the client. The latest iteration of the regulation suggests client-level segregation for advisery and distribution services for corporate entities.

Also, the SEBI regulation wants the RIA to be a fiduciary. Fiduciaries are those who put the client's interests above everything, including their own. That should be comforting for a client to know as they would now have someone, apart from their close family, who is thinking in terms of their best interests.

Why should one deal with an adviser who is a fiduciary?

Fiduciary responsibility is the guarantee that the adviser is acting truly in the client's best interests. To act in the client's best interest all the time, the adviser needs to be independent and should receive the remuneration only from the client by way of a fee.

This way, the adviser's interest can be aligned to the client's. Conflict of interest gets minimised when they just represent a client, unlike a product seller who represents his principal.

Also, since the remuneration is by way of fees from the client for a fee-only adviser, he would need to demonstrate his value and usefulness on an ongoing basis to justify the fee he is charging. That ensures that the adviser has a clear incentive to stay updated and offer high-quality services to justify their remuneration.

This is in sharp contradistinction to product sellers who would be paid a fixed percentage on product sales, which is in no way linked to their knowledge levels or the service received by the client. The client has no control over what they are indirectly paying—they can do nothing even if the service quality is bad.

Is financial planning the preserve of the rich?

A lot of people tend to think that they do not make enough money to hire the services of a financial planner. People have this impression that financial planning is for the rich and well-endowed. The other opinion that is widely prevalent is that financial planners are wildly expensive and hence not affordable.

Everyone requires financial planning. It is needed more by those who are moderately endowed compared to those who are rich—for the margin of error in the former is much smaller. Hence, financial planning is needed more by those on a tight leash than by those who are rolling in money.

A good adviser would be able to help the client manage their money efficiently, bring in tax efficiencies in their investments, suggest the right investments in line with their goals and risk profile and ensure that mistakes are avoided—all of which will save money for the client.

Hence, the fee would be more than offset by the savings. Most importantly, there will be a blueprint to follow, which could lead to clarity and peace of mind.

Is it necessary to always go to a financial planner or adviser?

If one has the necessary knowledge, interest, skills and time to understand one's requirements and evaluate options, an adviser may not be necessary. There are people who can do it themselves. But they are a miniscule minority.

For most people, it would be advisable to seek professional advice from a financial planner. This is just like going to a lawyer, doctor or an architect to get appropriate advice in their area of specialisation. However, when choosing an adviser, one must exercise caution. Verify whether the adviser or planner is an RIA with SEBI, their credentials, experience and so on. Half the battle is won if you choose the right adviser. With someone falsely posing as one, you are sunk.

The myth that investing in products for goals is financial planning

Many people claim to do financial planning—insurance agents, distributors, banks and just about everyone! They tend to portray that by buying some of their products, consumers will be able to do their own financial planning. So, consumers at large seem to think that financial planning is accumulating one product after another for various goals.

Insurance companies do this all the time. Other financial product manufacturers, too, use the term 'financial planning' rather liberally and loosely. Mutual fund companies have come up with pension products and other goal-achievement products like children's education funding products which they dub as financial planning.

Most times, there is another problem. Any product can be twisted enough to make it appear suitable for a goal. For instance, a multitude of endowment plans maturing every year in retirement are touted as retirement planning solutions. Many insurance agents offer this as a retirement solution.

This is the problem with agents and distributors. They will coax and twist their product to suit any and every goal one may have. At times, making these investments can assist in the achievement of certain goals. But ad hoc investments to achieve goals seldom results in a cogent plan. In fact, it is the other way round.

In financial planning, one needs to understand their clients' multiple goals and requirements, look at what they have done in terms of investment and insurance, find out what is an appropriate asset allocation in line with their risk profile, and then finally suggest products that meet with their requirements over time and achieve financial freedom.

A financial plan is hence a blueprint for achieving the client's goals holistically. The suggestions in a financial plan or advisory exercise would be far more well-deliberated and thought out than just a mere matching of products with a goal. The financial plan would consider the various life events and client requirements and provide the necessary money as needed.

After I had given them a full download, Raj and Naina seemed convinced about financial planning and about how different it was from just focusing on product investment. I offered to repeat it if they had not understood some portion of it. Raj hastened to affirm that they had heard and understood me correctly (lest I launch into another soliloquy).

It emerged that they had been making random investments. There was absolutely no pattern. For instance, they had invested in shares when one of their friends had suggested it. They got into mutual funds when the relationship manager of their bank pestered them about it and got them to start a few systematic investment plans (SIPs) to channelise their monthly surpluses productively.

They bought their second property when Raj's brother bought one for himself and suggested that they, too, buy with him. Raj and Naina were not from Bhopal nor did they intend to ever settle there. They just bought it so that their money could be channelled into an asset instead of spending it. So, that is where they were—they had a patchwork of investments that did not have any underlying logic.

They had the usual goals like their children's education, retirement planning, cars, vacations, etc. They also had to support Raj's mother. Naina's parents required some support occasionally, but mostly, they were financially independent. They had their daughter's education and wedding to plan for in the future along with a retirement home. And Naina wanted to retire early as well.

I was doubtful if all their goals could be met, considering that their investment corpus was limited and the free cash flow, though reasonably good, were not very big. Raj had a good income, but it was not flamboyant. I suggested that it would be good if they filled out the required data in our information sheet and sent it to me before the next meeting. They nodded. The meeting was over.

7

WHEN THINGS SEEM TO FALL IN PLACE, EVERYTHING CHANGES

I was in the office when I got a call from Vishal. Whenever Vishal calls, my heart is aflutter. My mind begins to race and thinks of all the new ingenious ways he would have thought of to spend money—and come up with some fait accompli! Oh no, not again, I thought.

'Yes, Vishal,' I said with as much equanimity as I could muster.

'Hi, Suresh. We wanted to meet you. Got some time for us in the first half?' he queried.

'You want to meet today? It is 10.30 now. Can you come by noon?' I asked.

'That's just fine. Both of us will be there. Thanks,' he ended the call.

I had a bit of work to complete before they came. I was immersed in work when they arrived precisely at the stroke of 12. Pretty nifty, I thought.

I smiled at them and looked at them expectantly. I looked at them with an expression that said: You have me by the beard, go ahead, tug it!

'Last time we met, we had discussed about the school in which our children would study. We had further discussions after we left. After deliberating on this for quite a while, we came to the same conclusion as you,' Vishal paused.

I couldn't believe my ears! That was quite a turnaround, I thought to myself. Was there a buy-in from Preeti? Had Vishal somehow bulldozed this decision and made her accept it? These were the thoughts flashing in my head.

'We were both not happy to let go of this opportunity to put Shreyan in that international school,' Vishal continued. 'But what clinched the argument was that if we cannot educate all three children in the same manner, we should not venture into it at all.

'Educating only one or two children in an international school and putting the third child in a regular school would be a huge problem for us later. Also, we understand the costs involved and the fact that we need to meet our various other goals.

'Your working sheet, that you showed the other day, was helpful. It showed in a crystal-clear manner that the indulgence we wanted with regards to the children's education would be disastrous in the long term.

'Also, the profile of the parents who put their wards in the school was something we had to confront; we would probably not have the money to spend like them, and that could give an inferiority complex to our children.

'We also thought that this was an entirely avoidable turmoil for our children. And so, putting them in a regular school seemed like the right thing to do,' Vishal concluded and looked at Preeti.

Preeti nodded. 'Initially, I was disappointed and crushed. I have always wanted my children to study in such high-class schools. I could not accept the fact that we were unable to do this for them. But it was clear that this would have been ruinous for us.

'Your calculations showed that it was the elephant in the room. We had to be sensible about it. With our third child on the way, we understand more than ever that we need to be careful with our money.

'We have overcome our reticence to putting our children in a regular school. We have found a good CBSE school in our vicinity. Our enquiries show that the quality of teaching in the school is fine and the school produces good students who go on to do well in life.

'The best news for us now is this school's overall outgo. Everything, including a school bus, books, uniform, etc., comes to under ₹90,000 a year. That certainly helps in our situation. And that is why we bit the bullet,' she concluded and smiled.

'Wonderful' I exclaimed, extremely relieved. I was beaming, and I knew it. Since they had reconciled to the new situation, they would not have taken it offensively. They beamed back at me.

'So, that's it then,' I said meaninglessly. Then I added, 'We need to have something special to celebrate a satisfactory resolution to a pesky problem. What would you like?'

'I don't mind something cold, if that can be organised,' said Preeti.

'Of course,' I said and asked my assistant to get the menu card of the friendly neighbourhood joint.

Preeti settled for an anjir milkshake while Vishal and I wanted our caffeine fixes.

In a cordial and uplifted frame of mind, we continued our

banter. Vishal was saying that there was an office picnic coming up that was to be a two-day trip. But he was not very enthusiastic about it.

Preeti interjected, 'I've been telling him to go on this picnic. It is just a couple of days. I can take care of the kids. He is not agreeing. He thinks I cannot take care of the kids alone now since I'm carrying ...'

Vishal was giving me a blank look. As inscrutable as ever, I thought. I did not say anything at all and looked at Vishal for enlightenment. It was not coming.

By that time the anjir milkshake and our coffees had arrived. We contentedly sipped our coffees and Preeti her milkshake.

'Where is the office picnic?' I asked Vishal.

'Dandeli,' he said.

'That's a great place. The Kaali River winding through the forests is a treat to watch. The river will be in full flow now. Then you could go into the forests in the morning on a safari. It could be good fun,' I said.

'How can I go? I cannot possibly leave Preeti alone now, can I?' he asked rhetorically.

Preeti pitched in. 'Didi can be with me for two days. It's not a big deal. All of Vishal's friends from the office are looking forward to him joining them on the picnic. A couple of them even called up and offered to send their spouses to keep me company.

'It looks like Vishal is the soul of the party. Only that, at home, he is silent as a tomb and usually expressionless.' Preeti teased him, smiling.

Silent as a tomb and expressionless—that fits Vishal like a glove, I thought as they left.

Out of the blue, I had got a call from someone called Ajay Sharma. He wanted to come over and meet me, along with his wife, Arundhati. He told me that he had been following my blogs, articles and media quotes for years.

I had asked him then and there as to why he had not come to me earlier. He said he was waiting for the right time to come to me! What a repartee!

Anyway, they were expected in half an hour, and I decided to devote some quality time to savour the sandwich I had ordered for lunch and be suitably nourished before I faced the young couple.

Ajay had briefly told me about him and Arundhati. They were pulling in north of ₹3.4 lakh a month—very credible considering their age. There were many decisions they needed to take now, and that's why they were seeking my assistance.

They came through the portals and were ushered into my cabin. These guys were tall. Ajay must probably be a strapping six feet two inches of alpha male. Arundhati was a tall lady herself—probably five feet seven. They seemed to fill the room. I waved them into their chairs, ordered their beverages and settled down for a conversation with them.

'Really appreciate you guys coming over on a weekday. Would you want something to munch on? I can order something,' I ventured to ask.

'Nothing needed, really. We just had our lunch,' Ajay said.

'Go right ahead and tell me—what is it that brings you here? Tell me a bit about yourselves, your situation and what you want to accomplish,' I gave them the lead.

Arundhati was the one who took the initiative. 'We have been married for two years and have been in Mumbai. I work in a global e-commerce firm as an HR manager. I have been with this firm for three-and-a-half years. The job is interesting, and the remuneration is decent.

'The job front is running along smoothly. Ajay is a techie and works in an IT firm. Together, our earnings are good. We have a good surplus every month, but only some of it is getting invested.

'A lot of money is accumulating in the bank account, and I fully realise that it is a poor way to manage money. We have bought some plots as per my father's advice since we did not have a clue about what to do.

'We have also bought some insurance plans recently. Apart from that, we are investing in bank FDs. Recently, the bank advised us to start some SIPs, which we started for about ₹20,000 a month. In a nutshell, our finances are not properly managed, and we need help,' she concluded.

I thanked her for these inputs and looked at Ajay. Ajay seemed to be collecting his thoughts. He came to the surface now.

'Aru has nicely summed up our situation. We need you to look into the investments we have made and suggest what we need to do. We need to, of course, tell you what we want to plan for in the future. We would like to buy a house in the next two years.

'We are planning to start a family next year. While there is no real decision on it, we may have two children—that's at least the tentative plan. Both of our parents are not dependent on us financially. We intend to travel the world, though we have not yet started on this. We have a car and would like to buy one more in the next six months. Those are some of the goals. In the long term, we need to plan for our children's education and future as well as our own retirement.'

'Thanks, Ajay. You have listed most of the goals. You both

have also shared some details about your finances. I will send you an information sheet that you need to fill out so that we can have complete and comprehensive information before we analyse and offer advice.

'I would like to briefly explain the financial planning process. In this process, the investment recommendations come at the end of the financial plan. Most people expect an adviser to just look at what amount needs to be invested and suggest schemes. That is not planning.

'While planning, we need to consider all the aspects that impact a person, from goals to financials like incomes, expenses, investments, insurances, assets, liabilities, specific family situations and many other such factors that need consideration. We need to explore and establish overall feasibility, assess risk, consider the risk profile of the person and come up with an appropriate allocation of assets, which would ultimately result in a detailed recommendation of what one needs to do.

'This is a multi-stage process where we would collaboratively build the plan to meet your needs completely,' I said.

'All fine till now … any questions?' I asked. They had none.

'Let me ask you now … What is really important in your life right now? What is it that you are truly excited about, the something that adds meaning to your life? What would energise you to look forward to each day with anticipation? What is sapping your energy? Paint a life that would be truly elevating, meaningful, empowering and wholesome for you individually and as a family. Both of you may dwell on this for a few minutes and then tell me,' I said.

They got immersed in thought. I let them be. I put forward the same questions on paper and gave them a notepad each. I told them that they could ponder this for a bit and then put down what they individually felt was important to have or to achieve in their lives.

This was new to them, and they were struggling. I offered to order them something to drink. Ajay said he would have coffee, and Arundhati settled for orange juice.

I excused myself and went out of the cabin so that they would be under less pressure to come up with the answers to my questions. When I came in after five minutes, Ajay had written about three points and Arundhati had one.

'How does life ahead look?' I asked. They looked at me bewildered. I asked them if anything was wrong, and they just said that they had never gotten around to thinking about what was really, truly important to them. Life was going on; they had no complaints and took that to be the life for them.

'That happens quite a lot. You need time to think it through. You may take this home and complete it at leisure,' I pacified them.

'Why did you ask us this question? We came to you for our finances. Your questions were … um … different … something we hardly expected. What is all of this about?' Ajay managed to blurt out.

It was time for me to explain.

'We all work to earn money. We work hard and keep going on with life as it is. For many of us, life is fine, and we ease into a routine. There are all kinds of things that are important that we want to achieve. We call them goals. These goals just pile up—we don't even have to think. A home, a car, holidays, funding for children's education—the works. We unquestioningly accept this. But just think for a moment—are these the real goals or the only goals?

'We take loans to buy a home, car, etc., thinking these are our goals. But are they? Why are many of us unhappy, even when these goals are achieved?

'That's because these are not the things we really want in life. These are incidental …' I trailed off to see whether they were with me or dozing off with their eyes open.

'Makes sense till now?' I asked. They nodded.

'We need to find out what really excites and inspires us and what makes this life worth living. We need to find out what will energise us, and make us look forward to every new day with gleeful anticipation. There are things that charge us, bring vigour and vitality and empower us.

'We all would like to live an authentic life where we can live in consonance with our highest ideals and achieve our true potential. That is what will make life truly satisfying.

'We need to find those things and make them part of our life—NOW,' I stopped.

'Wow,' said Arundhati. 'But how do we find what it is that will truly excite us? I'm not sure if there is anything like that for me. I could not come up with anything credible when you asked me a while ago. What if I don't find anything? What if I'm satisfied with life as it is?' asked Arundhati.

'Excellent questions there,' I said. 'One should be attempting to find out what will make life truly exciting, meaningful and wholesome. If the current life you are living is that life, then you are truly blessed. Then, you don't need to do this part. This part which we are now discussing is called life planning.

'This is a precursor to financial planning, where we find out how to achieve the goals we have. In life planning, we find out what it is that we really want to do in our lives and in light of that, what is it that we need to do. Is it not logical to understand what we want to do with our life before working on a plan to achieve something? If we have the wrong goals, we will be moving in the wrong direction, away from the real fulfilment we crave. Would that not be ironic?' I paused.

They were now nodding. The expressions on their faces told me that I had caught their attention.

'How would you want us to go about this?' Ajay asked. 'Is there a way you can help us kick-start this process?'

'Actually, there is. There are three methods of life planning. One of the well-known methods is the one propounded by George Kinder. That is the method I follow. To help you with narrowing down on what is truly important, and for me to understand and assist you, there are some worksheets and questions you need to complete.

'Once you do that, we will be on our way. I can send the material over email and you can fill that out and send it over to me before you come next. I would also need some financial information from you. There is another worksheet for that, which I can send out', I said.

'Okay. We can fill those out. This sounds exciting! Do all your clients do this?' Ajay asked. 'And by the way, what do you charge for all of this?'

'All my clients do not do life planning. The life planning portion is done by me as I'm certified for this. I charge for this separately. The financial planning process, which starts after you have identified what you want to do, is done by three planners. I'll be the principal planner guiding them. The plan itself will be created by our associate planner and checked by our lead planner, after which I will give my input. So, you get the wisdom of three financial planners.

'Our plan will be created in three steps; there may be more if required. The first step is to establish the feasibility of what you want to achieve. In the second and third levels, we will go deeper, assess risks and suggest remedies, check your risk tolerance and come to a suitable asset allocation, and then go on to make the recommendations. At every stage, we will have a plan walk-through so that you know what we are doing,' I stopped.

Ajay was looking at me intently. I was fully aware of the fact that I had not come to his point of the fee. He was going to have that now.

'We spend about 60–70 hours in all. We would be charging about ₹1 lakh for this. It can be more. I can tell you the exact amount only after I see the data.'

Ajay looked surprised. He clearly had not expected me to quote what he seemed to consider an astronomical figure.

I waited for about ten seconds before reacting. I asked whether they had come by car. They nodded. I then asked them if they had a driver. They said they had.

'I am assuming you are paying your driver ₹15,000 or more per month. That makes it ₹1.8 lakh a year. You may also be paying him a Diwali bonus and some overtime as well. That should make his remuneration well over ₹2 lakh per annum. I suppose you will also retain the driver in the future,' I asked. They nodded.

'Assuming that your driver is with you for thirty years and his salary increases by 5 per cent every year, you will be paying him over ₹1.3 crore in all that time. A driver is useful, of course. But what he does is help you reach from one point to another with comfort. The job he does is useful, even vital. But it is transactional.

'The job we advisers do will be transformational. The direction of your life can change. The complexion of your financial future can transform completely. Would you not want to pay for a transformational service and let your life blossom?' I queried.

Ajay said, 'Wow!' He was shocked by the revelation that he would be paying his driver over ₹1.3 crore, over a span of thirty years.

I told him to calculate that for the maid for fifty years. Arundhati told me she pays all her maids a total of ₹12,000 a month, which would come to ₹1.7 lakh a year after bonuses and everything else she gives is accounted for.

I told her that she would be paying the help just under ₹2 crore, in fifty years' time, even assuming a very modest 3 per cent increase per year. I told them that between just these two, they would be paying north of ₹3.2 crore. I could hear a collective gasp. I smiled at them. They smiled back sheepishly.

I told them not to worry too much about the fees and confidently told them that it would be worth every paisa. Firstly, we would help them clearly see for themselves the life they truly want and get a blueprint to achieve that. This by itself would be invaluable.

I then went on to inform them that the entire fee and more could come back to them because of the efficiencies that we would be bringing through money management strategies, the right asset mix based on their specific situation, tax efficiency, avoidance of mistakes and other measures.

I told them that I would send them more information about this by email for them to go through.

I informed them that I could confirm the fee after they sent me all the information from their side.

'Is there anything else you would like to know?' I asked.

'We are good for now,' said Ajay, getting up from the chair. We shook hands and they left.

My day ended with some routine work and phone calls.

The next day was a hectic day at work. I had meetings with our advisers about clients' plans, their portfolios, some calls and so on. I was also working on a new service that we wanted to roll out in the next three months. It was exciting conjuring up all those service details, how the service would be delivered, what it will be priced at, etc. I was immersed in it till it was almost time to go home.

My phone started to ring; it was Preeti. She sounded worried. There had been some mishap at the picnic that Vishal had gone to. She had got a call from the wife of one of Vishal's colleagues. She had heard that the dinghy had capsized during white water rafting. She was not sure who all had been on the dinghy.

She had called to ask me if I had any information about this. I had about four clients, including Vishal, from his company. I had not heard from anyone and said so. She was disappointed and said she would call if she got more information.

Now, it was my time to worry. This did not sound good. I called Alex, another client of mine who worked in the same company as Vishal, but he did not answer. I called his home. His wife, Alice, picked up. She had heard about the mishap from Alex, who had not gone on the ride. She informed me that there were eight of them on that dinghy and that it had capsized at one of the bends in the river.

The Kaali River would have been in full flow at this time of the year. White water rafting on it could be dangerous, especially for people who didn't know how to swim. Even for those who knew how to swim, the current would be intense and difficult to manage. Hence, the forebodings were grave. I was hoping that the guide had taken the necessary safety precautions and equipment to ensure people's safety.

I tried to reach Krishna, another client from the same firm. He picked up immediately. He confirmed that Vishal had been on the dinghy. He informed me that four people had already been rescued and were fine. Vishal was not one of them.

The search was on for the others, he said. They were hopeful that the others would be found in due course, like the four they had already found. Krishna mentioned that the search would resume in full force the next day, at daybreak.

This did not sound good at all. I felt a churn in my stomach. I must have looked forlorn, for Madhu asked me at least three times that night if something was wrong. I did not tell her at first, but since she persisted with her enquiry, I told her eventually.

'I'm worried. Vishal and three others have not yet been found. Do you remember the time we went to Dandeli? The river swells and is in full flow at this time of the year. I don't even know if Vishal knows how to swim … not that it would help in the Kaali River. Let's see …' I trailed off and cupped my face in my hands. Madhu came around and comforted me.

'Don't you worry. They have managed to save four. Come tomorrow we will hear the good news. Be patient for now,' she pacified me.

I nodded. That was the hope, of course. I was trying in vain to read the paper and some magazines. It is going to be difficult to sleep tonight, I thought.

I woke up with a start, and the clock informed me that it was 12.30 a.m. What woke me up, I could not tell. But there I was, fully awake, bathed in sweat. The AC was on. I wondered if I had had a heart attack.

I was not feeling uneasy or experiencing any symptoms that presage heart problems. The sweating could have been due to a nightmare, I presumed. I was not able to remember any of it, though.

I had a strange premonition that I had woken up for a reason. Then, I heard a sound.

8

EVERYTHING IN LIFE HAPPENS FOR A REASON

It was the deep hum of the primordial Om. I had heard it once before. My hair stood on end. Was it what I thought it was?

I got up and entered the living room. There was nothing there. I checked the kitchen, the other bedroom, even the washrooms … no one was there. But I was still hearing the distinct, low-frequency intonation of Om. I was transfixed. Then I realised that it was coming from outside the door. When I opened the door, there was no one. I closed the door and came back inside.

Suddenly, I could smell fragrances that one would encounter in a temple—sandalwood paste, camphor, tulsi and agarbatti. I peeped into the living room to see where these were emanating from. My heart leapt out and was in my mouth. There he was, the same old sanyasi sitting on the far end of the sofa. I recognised him immediately. He was my Lord.

He seemed to be looking out of the window and into the horizon. I inched my way towards him. I bent my head slightly and brought my hands together in pranam. He was still peering out. He slowly turned his head and looked at me.

I felt a wave of bliss and compassion wash over me, and it felt like I was floating in the air, like a feather. It was an other-worldly feeling, and I completely lost consciousness.

Time stood still.

He was indicating that I should sit on the other sofa. I complied. There was a mild glow around him like I had seen last time. He was just looking at me and just that look was infinitely comforting. It was as if time was standing still.

Then a sudden chill entered my heart. Why has he come now when Vishal has had this accident? Is something wrong? On the other hand, I thought that this was a God-given opportunity (literally) to inquire about Vishal's well-being.

I mustered the courage to speak. 'Is Vishal fine?' I asked.

'What's the problem with Vishal?' he asked.

I was elated. This signalled that Vishal was fine. I must have been beaming.

'Please understand that what you call life is but a fleeting period when the atma resides in your temporary body. You experience life through the senses that the limited body affords and you feel that that is life. The life that an atma experiences in a body is like a day, in an eighty-year human lifetime.

'Is every day not a new day, a new start with twenty-four hours stretching ahead, beckoning with infinite possibilities? Every new body that a person is born with is a new opportunity for the atma to rise to higher planes from their baser selves.

'The body that we get is like a garment. It is worn for a time, after which we need to change it, just like we change a garment when it gets soiled. Do we feel sad when we change into a new garment? We do not.

'The previous garment has done its job. The new garment has a job to do now. It's as simple as that. Sometimes we achieve what we need to achieve in that life much sooner than anticipated. When a mission is achieved, what do we do? We go back to where we came from, don't we? That is what happens to the atma too.

'In our ignorance about the permanence of the atma and in our attachment to the evanescent body, we grieve when the body perishes. The body perishes only when the mission in that life is accomplished. Is that a reason to celebrate or feel sad? We do not know what happens to the atma after death. It is that ignorance that causes sadness,' he finished.

This monologue was driving me to the edge of despair. I understood without an iota of doubt what he was hinting at. I knew now that Vishal was no longer with us. God, what will happen to his wife and kids? She was carrying their third child. How would she be able to bear such a huge shock?

It is easy to philosophise and say that he had cast away his body like a garment. But it would unleash a tsunami in the lives of his family members. Their whole life would now come crashing down.

'The Lord of the universe knows precisely what each one is capable of. He never would allow someone to take what they cannot fulfil.

'Hence, what a person has chosen is something that will make them a better person. Every person on Earth is an atma in transition.

'The purpose of every atma is to get better with every birth, evolve from their base selves, get more refined and inexorably move to higher planes over lifetimes. The atma decides the extent of progress it wants to make in a lifetime and chooses the kind of life that will facilitate that progress.

'So, a lot of times, it is a choice that is made by the atma who is born in the world as a human being. It is not for us to despair about what is happening in someone's life. We do this without understanding the context.

'The Lord is always happy to see spiritual progress and supports such intentions. The Lord lends strength and resolve to meet lofty targets an atma sets for itself. Difficulties encountered on the way then become the runway to spiritual ascendancy.

'Even in the world we live in, struggles and difficulties are not always bad. In fact, they are pivotal to success in many cases.

'A coach makes a champion out of a merely talented individual. The coach pushes his ward to the limits. He knows how to develop his ward and what his pupil can endure. A champion does not get built just like that.

'A goldsmith melts the gold in the furnace to purify the metal. The resultant gold, that has gone through trial by fire, emerges pure. Would we be unhappy that the goldsmith put the gold through this process? No. We fully understand that this is done to ensure purity and refinement.

'The gold in each one of you needs to go through the furnace of life and needs to get refined. In the process, one may face trials and tribulations and what looks like an extremely rough patch. But they are necessary rough paths that act as catalysts for toughening up the person, elevate the soul and aid in the soul purification process. Let us not grieve unnecessarily.

'You know not what Vishal's atma desires, nor the purpose for which it was born as Vishal. You also would not know why his wife came into his life and what her purpose is in this life. Preeti also wants to refine herself.

'There was a reason she was married to Vishal. And she is destined to move ahead and fulfil her mission in this life, in the overall long march of an atma over millennia. When we see and understand so little, is it not a little silly to grieve for something transient?' the Lord concluded.

So, it was sealed. I was dumbfounded. I did understand completely the philosophical underpinnings of what the Lord had shared. It was all there in Hindu theology. But all the well-construed philosophical arguments were just not good enough to convince me to accept Vishal's passing away with equanimity.

I felt the loss. I was unable to view it dispassionately like the Lord was urging me to. Nor did I think Preeti would. For her, it was going to be a body blow. Raising three children single-handedly would be enormously challenging, to put it mildly. I just could not think of how I would face Preeti.

While I was immersed in my thoughts, I forgot that the Lord was still there, seated on my sofa, his effulgence blinding me now, with the Om pranava mantra resounding and the enchanting smells casting a spell on me. I did not know what to do or what to ask.

'O Lord Krishna, please have mercy on Vishal. What will happen to his family now? Their situation will be like a small boat caught in a stormy sea, where mighty waves will toss the flimsy boat like a matchstick. How can they survive this massive tragedy?' I asked.

'You do not understand my child. Like I said before, each person born in the world comes with a purpose and once it is achieved would want to move on to the next, in the onward journey of refinement and purification.

'It is the atma that wills and events unfold to help it to move on. The others who are with them also have come together in a pact to achieve something together and individually. When their achievement together is accomplished, they part ways, and their individual journeys continue.

'You people tend to attach too much importance to worldly events and don't look at the angle of self-improvement that the atma is trying to accomplish.

'Allow things to happen as they do. Don't get perturbed. Whatever is happening is happening for good. Whatever has happened is also actually good. The future events are also going to be for good. There is no reason to grieve for something that was already chosen by those souls.

'Learn to watch life as it goes by, like a bystander watching the traffic below from his balcony. Learn to be in this world and yet be detached from it. Why worry about something over which you have no control? Also, why underestimate those who have chosen the difficult path? They know what they have chosen. They have the fortitude and capacity to see it through,' he concluded.

That was a wonderful exposition. It was like a private Gita upadesh session for me. I folded my hand and bent my head in prayer. I clearly got what he had so lucidly put forward. But then, I still did not have the maturity to watch things as they unfolded, like a bystander, as he wanted me to.

When I straightened, he was nowhere to be seen. The smell of a temple was the only reminder of his visit.

9

LIFE HAS TO MOVE ON

The next day, I contacted my other clients for news about Vishal. I did not have any hope. But I still wanted to know definitively before I contacted Preeti. It was already afternoon, and there had been no news about three of the four people who were still missing from the previous night, though one of them had been fished out.

This was depressing and indicated ominous portends. I finally called Preeti at about 2.30 in the afternoon. She came on the line with the first ring. Maybe she was expecting my call; maybe she was expecting some good news which was marked by its absence.

'Hi, Preeti. Just thought of calling you. Don't worry. Everything will eventually be fine,' I said.

There was silence for two seconds. 'Do you have any news of Vishal?' she asked. She was expecting some specific information. I did not want to tell her about the recovery of one body down the river course, if she already had not heard about it. I just said that I did not have any further update. She was deflated.

She said, 'I'm getting a very bad feeling about Vishal. Hope God helps us in this crisis. I want my Vishal back.' It was a plaintive expression of her inner turbulence. It was sad to hear. But I could do nothing to assuage it. I could not even offer her any hope about Vishal, for that would give her a false sense of assurance.

'God is always there to help. He has his mysterious ways while dealing with the world. He is the one who nourishes us and takes care of us. He gives us challenges to test us, makes us resilient and strong and helps us become that person who we have the potential to become.

'We have all come into this world with a purpose and we need to accept our responsibilities with equanimity and discharge them. Happiness and sadness will cycle in life. We need to be able to accept them, transcend them and evolve,' I said.

'Where are you now?' Preeti asked. I did not expect this. I told her that I was in the office. She said she wanted to meet me immediately. I was perplexed. What did she want to talk to me about now? I told her that she could, of course, come over, but I offered to go and see her, as that could save her the trouble. But she insisted on coming over.

Preeti came in some time. She seemed composed. I had kept a glass of water for her. She came in and without any further ado came straight to the point.

'Suresh, please tell me what you know about Vishal. Tell me straight. I have a very strong feeling that you know something but are not telling me,' Preeti said.

I was taken aback. How did she know? Did I inadvertently blurt out something? I quickly went over our conversation a few minutes back and nothing seemed to indicate such laxity on my part. I played innocent and asked her what made her think so.

'The way you spoke seemed to indicate that you knew something that I did not,' she said with tears in her eyes.

I really did not know how to console her. I told her that I'm in touch with people from Vishal's office and till about half an hour back, they did not have any specific news about Vishal.

I was debating internally if I should put her out of the depressing uncertainty and agony. Her next comment left no room for any further debate and I had to tell her.

'You know Vishal is dead, right?' she said, looking directly into my eyes. It was a gaze looking for the truth. It had sadness, tiredness and, at the same time, a grim determination to learn the truth. My eyes automatically averted. Tears had started streaming down her cheeks. I felt extremely sorry for her.

I had to tell her now. 'It is true that I have not heard anything about Vishal from his colleagues. But there is something else which is a source of insight. But you may find it bizarre and hard to believe and hence I did not want to tell you anything about it. But now you have forced my hand …' I trailed off.

Preeti's eyes widened. There was surprise and hurt in equal measure. 'If you know something about Vishal, don't you think I need to know it?' she asked, half-angrily and half with incredulity.

'Let me tell you all that I have encountered. Then you are free to make your own conclusions,' I said and told her the entire episode of the Lord's visitation and what he had indicated. She was stunned.

There was absolutely nothing to indicate that she did not believe me. In fact, she seemed to completely buy it. Tears were rolling down her cheeks in profusion. I went out and ordered coffee for both of us, without asking if she wanted. I felt that she needed one.

'I'm so sorry to be the bearer of bad news. I wanted you to know through the normal channels … but you sensed it and kind of made me confess what I knew. I'm extremely sorry about this,' I remarked sincerely. I had tears in my eyes too.

She just waved it off, to indicate that all that was okay. She was still unable to talk. I was silent. For about two minutes, there was stony silence. The coffee came.

I took my mug and put one before her. She instinctively took a sip. She took another long sip before she started talking again.

'I have to bring up three children single-handedly. It's daunting to even think about it. But is there an option?' she signed off rhetorically.

All I could do was nod sadly. 'Like the Lord had said, He only gives situations that one can handle. Time is the healer and time will show that you are more than up to the task. I'm here to help in whatever way I can. We will now have to wait for a confirmation,' I diplomatically quipped.

She just nodded. She was again deep with her thoughts and tears had started streaming down once more. This time, she was sobbing. I did not console her, for I did not want to disturb her while she was grieving and slowly coming to terms with her new reality. Tears are a safety valve in such situations, and they should be allowed to run their course.

After about ten minutes, she was herself again. She tried to get up, but she collapsed back into the chair. I was worried. When I looked at her, it appeared that she had aged about ten years since she had stepped into the office.

She tried getting up again. I gave her a hand and helped her hoist herself up. She was due in three months and the baby inside her must be bigger now and weighing her down. What was really weighing her down was not the baby inside but the weight of responsibility that was now placed upon her. I did understand how she must be feeling.

I volunteered to drop her home. She did not say anything. At this point, she needed all the help she could get. I dropped her and came back to the office.

The office phone rang after ten minutes of my return. It was one of Vishal's colleagues. He was talking with bated breath. He informed me that a body had been fished out 10 kilometres downstream. It appeared like it may be Vishal. But the body was partially decomposed and possibly eaten by marine creatures, which made the identification difficult. He was wondering if I could convey this to Preeti and ask her to come over to Dandeli for identification.

I was transfixed with the phone to my ear. Here I was hearing the bad news, finally. Though they were calling for identification, it appeared to me that the confirmation had come. I told him that I would first convey this to Preeti and then let him know as to when she could come.

I first thought of calling up and telling her. Then I thought that going around and telling her in person would be a lot better. I reached there in fifteen minutes. Preeti was surprised to see me again within the same hour. She instantly knew something was up.

'I got a call from Ramki about Vishal. They've found a body about 10 kilometres down the river. They are not able to determine whether it is Vishal or someone else. So, they want you to come over there,' I managed to blurt out.

Tears welled up in her eyes once more. She started staggering but fortunately she found the sofa just in time. Shreyan came running from inside. He saw tears in Preeti's eyes and asked why she was crying. She managed to fob him off by saying that she was having a little pain in her stomach, which the little kid bought completely and went running back inside.

A minute later, he came running in with an ointment tube, asking his mother to apply it to alleviate the pain. This brought even more tears to Preeti's eyes and she gathered Shreyan in an embrace and gave him a couple of loving kisses.

It was my turn to despair, seeing the innocent act of a child. How will they even understand that their father is no more? How will they reconcile to that fact? How will Preeti inform them that, from now on, she was going to be their father and mother? It was truly a difficult task which, I was sure, Preeti dreaded.

Preeti asked me, 'Can I talk to Ramki?'

I immediately dialled the number and gave the phone to her. She asked him various details about the body recovered, the clothes that were there on the person, an identification mark on the chest and more. The call went on for about fifteen minutes with them checking and giving information to her. At one point, she fainted.

I took the phone and asked Ramki what had happened. He said as per the identifications given, it seemed like the body recovered was Vishal's. I told them I had to disconnect the call as Preeti had fainted.

I sprinkled some water on her face. She stirred but did not open her eyes. I sprinkled even more water. She regained consciousness with a start. She started sobbing loudly. Again, I was a helpless bystander. I did not want to interrupt her grieving.

I fetched a glass of water for her. She was going through bouts of intense emotions and kept crying and sobbing for about fifteen minutes. She must have realised that I was sitting there all along. She got up, went to the bathroom, washed her face, tied up her hair and sat before me on the sofa.

'It's him alright,' she said and started sobbing again. 'He's gone, he's gone,' she kept saying and went on crying. I waited for her to calm down.

She said, 'Tell Ramki to get the body to Mumbai.'

I was quiet for a while. I asked her in low tones if she was sure that it was Vishal. I suggested that we go to Dandeli for an identification. She said she was sure, and did not want to go to Dandeli. She did not want to see the river, the setting—nothing. I understood why.

Vishal had a couple of birthmarks that Preeti had asked Ramki to check on the body recovered and he had found them. There was a big butterfly-shaped mole on the chest and an oblong one on the right arm just above the elbow. She was able to clearly identify the T-shirt he was wearing. So, she was sure it was him.

I called Ramki and conveyed what Preeti had said. Ramki was reluctant, but I told him that Preeti did not want to come, as it would be traumatic for her. He relented and said he would talk to the people concerned and make arrangements to bring the body to Mumbai.

I told Preeti what had been arranged. She did not show any sign of having heard it. Her sister, Naina, was to be here with her when Vishal was at the picnic. But she was nowhere to be seen; I surmised she must have gone to her workplace. I felt that I needed to inform her about this and wanted her to come over immediately.

I stepped out into the foyer and dialled Raj's number. He picked up immediately. I came straight to the point. I briefly told him all that had happened and asked him whether he and Naina would come over immediately. He told me that they would be there in thirty minutes.

Sure enough, they were there in half an hour. Naina ran into the living room and hugged Preeti. Seeing Naina, Preeti began crying loudly. It was painful to see this. But I was relieved that someone from the family was there to comfort her. Raj and I were talking outside in the foyer. We were discussing the twists and turns life takes and how unpredictable life is.

In this context, Raj mentioned that planning was such a futile exercise, for we didn't know what would happen in the next moment. I said I agreed with the second part about life being uncertain but, due to that very reason, we needed to plan, keeping in mind potential problems and unfortunate events.

In Vishal's case, last year, I had suggested a life insurance plan of ₹1.5 crore. I had no information if he had done that. He, however, did have a ₹1 crore term insurance plan. I told Raj that if he had this level of life insurance, the family would get ₹2.5 crore just from the insurance claims alone.

Apart from this, they would also get Employees' Provident Fund (EPF) dues, gratuity, leave encashment and other benefits. His company also had life insurance for all their employees. That alone would probably amount to ₹1.5 crore. What I was trying to convey was that planning helped in all situations, especially in worst-case scenarios.

One of the most important things we do while planning is protect our clients by putting up appropriate security nets. Appropriate insurance will cushion the fall and ensure that the family will still be able to comfortably achieve their goals and be able to maintain their standard of living without any problem.

I told him that we would discuss this in detail when we move ahead with their planning process. We peeped in to see what was happening. No one was there in the living room. I suggested that Raj go inside to see what was happening. He came back to tell me that Preeti was lying in bed and was still crying with her sister trying to comfort her.

I did not know what to do there. I told Raj that I would like to head home, as it was already 7 p.m. I told him that I would inform them about what they intended to do from the Dandeli end.

Before leaving, I spoke to Ramki. He understood the situation and told me that he would make arrangements so that the body could be sent to Mumbai by the next evening.

The next day, I was in the office but was unable to concentrate on my work. I called Naina from time to time to find out how Preeti was doing. I called Preeti once during the day. She sounded low but thanked me for all that I was doing for them.

I told her that I would come by in the evening. I was in touch with Ramki. True to his word, he had made arrangements to send the body. But he said that it had ultimately been done only by 7 a.m. It would reach Mumbai by 5–6 p.m., he had said.

I left the office at 5 p.m. and was at Preeti's home soon thereafter. A few people had come over to be with the family. Preeti's father was also there. She was nowhere to be seen. Her children, Ashitaa and Shreyan, were running about playing.

It must have been exciting for the children to have so many people fawning over them. They were blissfully unaware of the tragedy that had befallen them. It was tragic to witness this. Oh God, what is this mess that has descended upon them? How are they ever going to recover from this catastrophe?

It was 6 p.m., and I decided to call Ramki to get details on where the vehicle carrying Vishal's body was. He confirmed that it was already in Mumbai and should reach in about half an hour.

Raj came around to my side and we had a bit of general chit-chat. Neither of us was in the mood for a real conversation. The vehicle arrived. It was an ambulance. Two white uniformed personnel came out of the vehicle and dragged the gurney out of the ambulance. We saw that the whole body was shrouded in a white sheet, as was usually the case.

We asked for it to be taken into the house. The hospital personnel started talking to us and wanted to find out who the next of kin was. Raj stepped in and introduced himself. He was told that the identification needed to be completed, and some paperwork had to be done.

Before showing the body to Preeti, we wanted to see the face and check if it was really Vishal. When they removed the shroud, we saw that the body was heavily bandaged. They explained to us that since the body had been in water and had also been partially eaten, it was disfigured in many places. The face was partly visible. I was able to make out that it was Vishal, even though the face was somewhat swollen and disfigured. Raj and Preeti's father confirmed the same.

We now had to call Preeti as she also had to make the identification, after which she would need to sign the required documents. Preeti came in ten minutes later. She was being supported on either side by her relatives. When she came into the living room, she started wailing. She was trembling and probably losing consciousness as her legs seemed to give way. She seemed delirious.

She asked for the shroud to be removed. When she saw the face, she let out a wail. It was obvious that she was able to identify it as Vishal. She was made to sit on the nearby sofa, and someone offered her water. After about five minutes, she was somewhat normal and we could talk to her. Her father was calming her down by gently stroking her head.

Raj asked her whether she was able to identify the body as Vishal. She nodded emphatically. Raj took charge. He quickly explained to her the identifications and paperwork that needed to be done and got the whole thing out of the way in just five minutes with supreme efficiency.

We then sat in a corner and read the documents and filled in all the necessary details. We handed over the papers to the hospital staff. I thought it was necessary to take a full set of copies before we handed it over to them. I volunteered to do the job as I knew there was a photocopy shop in the next street. I was back in ten minutes and handed over all the original forms.

The hospital staff was patient and understanding. They never made us hurry up at any point and patiently waited for us to go through the motions and hand over the papers. We apologised for making them wait.

They said that this was the fastest they had ever got the entire thing done. In this case, the whole process had been completed in under an hour. They were now thanking us for the extremely quick turnaround.

Arrangements were being made for the cremation, right then and there, for the hospital staff had suggested that the body could not be kept for long. Most of the relatives were to arrive before 10 p.m. Hence, a pundit was engaged, and the arrangements for Vishal's final journey were now well underway.

The last rites commenced just after 10.30 p.m. and the body was taken for cremation close to midnight. We were all there at the cremation ground and returned well after 1 a.m. It was all over now with a depressing finality.

Vishal was gone. But his family was now like a small piece of wood that was being tossed by mighty waves. They needed to go through the tumult of life alone—without Vishal. It was going to be tough for Preeti. But then and there I prayed to the Lord to give her strength, courage and fortitude to go through the trials and tribulations she was to face in life and emerge victorious.

10

AFTER THE DELUGE, THE CALM

I went to bed after 2 a.m. that day. I couldn't sleep. The question haunting me was: what would happen to Preeti now?

The calamity was so huge that even I, an outsider, was feeling overwhelmed. I was worried about Preeti. Would she take it in her stride, pick up the threads and move on? That seems to be the logical thing to do, but extremely difficult to put into action in real life.

I was not too worried about the money aspect. That could be managed, I thought, as huge amounts of claims and final settlements would soon pour in. Judiciously invested, she could sail through without much trouble. But I was worried about whether she would hold up, considering the crushing burden of responsibility on her. These thoughts kept churning in my head and driving me insane.

Finally, I consoled myself with the thought that she would walk the path ahead in one piece for the sake of her children, if for no other reason. This gave me some solace. And some sleep.

When I stirred, the clock showed 8.35 a.m. I had overslept as I must have gone off to sleep only around 4 a.m. or so. I got ready as soon as I could and went to work. There were a few matters that needed my attention. I was immersed in them.

The phone rang; it was 1.25 p.m. Raj was on the line. He was asking whether Vishal's family had medical insurance. This was an unexpected question. I said they had and wanted to know what had happened and why he was asking about their medical insurance all of a sudden.

He then told me that Preeti had cried almost the entire night and was in a bad shape. She was running a high fever and seemed to be in a delirious state. A doctor in her building had examined her and had suggested that they take her to the hospital. They had taken her to the nearest hospital and doctors were attending to her. She was stable now. The doctors were asking whether she had medical insurance and that's why he had called.

I asked him a few quick questions, sent the policy and other details to him, talked to the medical insurance company, logged a hospital admittance case and asked them to process the case cashless. There was some further process involved for which I sent across someone to the third-party administrator (TPA) stationed in the hospital.

I asked Raj if I could come and see Preeti. He asked me not to come now as doctors were not allowing anyone to go into her room. She was not in the ICU, but in a ward. Even so, they did not want anyone to disturb her for now. She was sleeping and the doctors had said that this was essential for her recovery.

Raj told me that the doctors opined that it was trauma and dehydration and nothing more. They said that she could be discharged the next day. That sounded reassuring. I wound up work early that day and was in the hospital by 6 p.m. Raj was there. He said that Preeti was fine now and I could go and meet her.

When I entered the room, I saw Preeti on the bed with a thick blanket till her chest. She smiled weakly on seeing me. I returned the smile. Frankly, I did not know what to say. It just did not occur to me to utter inane pleasantries. So, I just stood there.

Naina, who was there in the room, took charge. She welcomed me, gave me a brief summary about the happenings since last night and finished by telling me that Preeti was much better now than she was in the morning, when she got admitted.

I was absorbing the information absent-mindedly. I knew most of it anyway. But I was now worried about Preeti all over again.

I despaired. What was she going to do? She seemed to be taking the news rather badly.

I hung around for another half an hour and then took leave. I told them that they could call me anytime, if they needed.

After dinner, I was ruminating over the events of the past forty-eight hours. These thoughts were running incessantly, as if on a Möbius strip. I could not help thinking and getting angry with the way their family was being tossed around like a twig in the ocean. How were they dealt such a bad hand? What was their crime? I was thinking all this despite what the Lord told me.

Thinking thus, I was fiddling around with a Rubik's Cube. I was aimlessly turning the faces. I don't know for how long this continued. At one point, I stopped. I was deep in thought and intently looking at the Rubik's Cube in my hand. It did not have any answers for me and continued being just that.

There was a sharp sound and I straightened with a start. The steel tumbler which was on my bedside table had fallen. My hand must have touched it while I had slumped and fallen asleep unwittingly. My mobile informed me that the time was 2.40 a.m.

It was logical to go back to sleep as there were still about four hours to sunrise. I pulled over the blanket to get some rest.

The river was flowing serenely and the water was making soothing, gurgling sounds. There was a gentle breeze. It was very early in the morning and quite dark.

The stars were only faintly visible as there was almost a full moon. The river looked beautiful by the moonlight. It looked like liquid silver was cutting across the dense forest.

There was a gentle breeze. Time stood still and it seemed like the universe was in suspended animation. It was a sublime feeling. There were no thoughts. I was able to experience that calm oneness with the entire creation.

Dawn was near. There was a bit more light now. Who was that walking in the distance?

I was able to make out a silhouette. It looked like Vishal.

It really was him! There was an indescribable joy I felt upon seeing him again. I ran to him and embraced him. Vishal was beaming. He reciprocated my warm embrace and patted me on my back with genuine friendliness. I felt ecstatic.

Where did you go, Vishal? We all were paralysed thinking you were dead, I was saying in my mind. Vishal was on the same frequency, and he was answering.

Vishal was now communicating with me through his mind.

'I just finished the portion I was assigned in this edition,' he began. 'Life is like a play. You act in some scenes, and then you are not needed for the rest of it. You know from the beginning that you are there only in some scenes. Every actor knows that.

'Then why should we despair when an actor whose scenes are over does not make any more appearances?

'Actors come together with this clear understanding and play the drama called life. Every actor chooses a role to further their progress in the long march of life. They choose a role in order to pursue some objectives.

'They may despair in their current scene, as even this is part of their act. But make no mistake—they are acting their part to the last detail. There is nothing to despair when you understand that all these are merely acts, to get better and rise higher.

'The ultimate purpose for all of us is to merge with the Supreme and be relieved of this endless cycle of life and death, which is tiresome to say the least.

'But for that, we need to evolve and ultimately come to the state where we are able to treat pain and pleasure, the highs and lows, fame and ignominy, riches and poverty and other such extremes, with equanimity.

'We should neither be carried away by riches or fame, nor be plunged in sorrow over our monetary misfortunes or other troubles. We will need to evolve to a state where we have the maturity to accept bouquets and brickbats with the same grace and composure. Such people are called Sthithapragyan.

'That state would be that of a yogi. Such a person can be in this world and experience all the ups and downs of life like everyone else and yet be unaffected. This is easy to say and very difficult to achieve. But this is what helps in rising higher in the quest to finally merge with the Lord of the universe.

'Preeti and our children are willing actors in this drama. They have their parts to play. They have chosen those parts, including the tough ones. There is no need to feel sorry. It is part of their uphill climb in their evolutionary journey. Why despair then?

'Even you are an actor in this drama, and you are playing a specific role, some of which impacts the family that I was a part of. Let us understand this fact and move on. There is no need to feel bad at all. Remember, these are the paths they have chosen. Let us move on without blaming anyone about the unfairness of life.

'We are all manifestations of the divine. Only that we don't understand that. We create unwanted divisions and unnecessarily spar over perceived differences. We don't see that we are all connected and are in fact one, though we exist in many forms.

'Seen this way, it will be silly to harm someone as we would be harming ourselves. When we realise this, we are truly one with God, for we won't be able to see anything apart from Him.

'In this life, I have chosen to cast my body away the way it has happened. I could have chosen differently, but did not. There are reasons for that. We need not go into them now. Hope you have got the answers to the questions that were tormenting you,' he concluded.

There was silence now. I waited for some time. But nothing more was coming.

It was profound. I was stunned that this had come from Vishal. Never had I thought of Vishal as someone who understood life's philosophy. But here he was, explaining it like the Lord himself! I was awestruck and kept looking at him with open-eyed wonder.

One moment he was Vishal who was smiling at me. The next moment he was Lord Krishna himself with his beatific smile, in all his divine glory.

I knew what the Lord had done. He had created this entire rendezvous to make me understand and let me see the happenings in the right perspective. As an aside, I also got the benefit of an exposition into the ultimate purpose of life and the futility of our petty crabbiness.

'Thank you, O Lord,' I bowed in sincere deference. The Lord was magnetic in his appeal, with his captivating smile and his ethereal countenance. I was bathed in a wave of bliss and again had a moment of oneness with the entire creation, a moment of complete revelation and supreme understanding.

Then I blinked. What happened, I asked myself. Where am I now? I realised that I was at home. It dawned on me that the meeting with Vishal and the Lord was a dream.

It was so real, and I still remembered every word of what Vishal had said. It was like the Gita upadesh. It gave me so much clarity. I would now be able to move beyond anger about how unfair life was, to acceptance, reconciliation and transcendence.

I was now able to understand that it was about the choices we made. There was no one else to blame. We, therefore, needed to accept life as it came.

Now I understood what Lord Krishna had told Arjuna: Whatever has happened and is happening is all for the best. I felt light and was now at peace. I wished this same epiphany for Preeti as well.

I must have dozed off again after this.

11

THE MILLENNIAL GETS HER MONEY LESSONS

It was Bala who wanted to meet me that day. He had briefly gone to London to hustle the team there into hiring him. I had heard from him earlier, over the phone, that he had been very successful at it.

Their London office had made a fabulous offer, which Bala could only have dreamed of. He was offered almost 60 per cent of the remuneration as salary and the rest in commissions. The terms of the commission were quite generous, he had informed me.

He had started working and was enjoying every bit of it. He had done two small deals in the first month itself. The deals had not been worth a lot to the company, but they were pleased that he had gotten cracking and was able to show something in the very first month. He had told me that he was working on about eight deals, out of which two were very big.

He expected at least a couple of them to fructify, in less than thirty days. He told me that he had cracked one of those deals, sometime before coming to India. It was a medium-size deal, but the London office had been thrilled about it. They had thrown an impromptu party and Bala had become a star overnight. While it was a medium-sized deal, it was very profitable and was expected to yield revenues for the next ten years.

Bala sauntered into the office around 2.30 in the afternoon. He seemed to be in a great mood. I waved him to the seat and asked him to tell me about his London experience. What I wanted to hear was how the dealmaking was going and what kind of money he would be earning.

Bala's eyes lit up. This obviously was his favourite subject and needed no persuasion. He started talking animatedly about the deals he was pursuing.

'There are as many as thirteen deals in different stages. The one I closed was an office rental deal for a 2,50,000 sq. ft office space for a ten-year tenure. That was in Chelsea. Most of the other deals are in even more prime localities in premium properties.

'The prized deal I'm pursuing is a premium office block under 5 million sq. ft in Kensington. This deal, if struck, will be valued in hundreds of millions of pounds and will catapult our company to become one of the top property firms in the UK. There is a lot of competition for this deal, which is natural. You don't get a deal like this every day. But we do have some aces up our sleeve, which can help swing the deal our way.

'This deal should fructify in six to eight months. Let's see if I can swing this one. About eight of us are working on it as a team. If the deal comes through in our favour, all of us can retire with that money, if we want to.

'Only that, after such a deal, no one would want to retire. It's not the money alone. It's the excitement of the pursuit itself, the people you meet, the strategies you devise to convince the party and ace the competition, the dealmaking itself!

'I should have gone to London a long time ago. It is probably the most exciting market in the whole world. London is not just English. The whole world is investing there. You will deal with Russians, Germans, many from countries in the Eurozone, Chinese, Indians, those from the Middle East, etc. That's quite an eclectic mix of people, you would agree. Knowledge of foreign languages places you at a significant advantage.

'I know French. But so do many others in this field. Hence, my advantage is blunted. But I'm learning Russian and Chinese. I only know a few words for now. But I'm determined to learn it to a level where I can hold some basic conversation.

'Things are great in my office. I'm already well-regarded in just the two months I have been there, and I don't mind confiding in you that I'm tickled pink. Things are looking very bright after all. Like you had mentioned once, the bad situation here did me a lot of good. I would have never explored this opportunity, but for the push I got from my company in India. And, thanks a lot to you for suggesting this idea. I would not have thought of this in a million years.'

I was able to see a lot of typical British slangs in the way he spoke. He still did not end sentences with 'What' though and the tongue-in-cheek English humour had still not caught up with him. But I was sure it would be there the next time. He seemed to love the place and had taken to it, like a fish to water.

We continued talking about his projects for a while. He was saying that he had about £10,000 surplus now and wanted to know how to invest them. I weighed it and told him to invest it in some liquid funds, as a safety margin. Some of this would help to fund Malvika's education as well, I told him. I did not want to start investing anything before he found his feet.

The topic now shifted to Malvika. Bala was telling me that Malvika had applied to some universities in the US and some in the Netherlands, Germany and England as well. He said that he was encouraging her to pursue English universities, especially London or its suburbs, as he was now there and reckoned he could put her up with him and bring down the boarding expenses. Also, they need not have to worry about her well-being if she was going to stay with her father. Malvika had also warmed up to the idea, he said.

She has zeroed in on the London School of Economics and was now hoping to get in. Bala wanted me to meet Malvika and talk to her about investments.

I was curious. She was going to study now. She would only start earning a few years later. 'Do you still want me to give her the lowdown now itself?' I queried.

Bala wanted me to do it right away. For one, he said, he wanted her to get a hang of her personal finances. He was not sure she knew even the basics. He also said that she would have opportunities to work and earn a bit, during the time she would be studying there. Hence, there may be some money she could invest. I agreed. He wanted to bring Malvika in three days later, which was fine with me.

Bala had his favourite cold coffee before he left.

He had given me some food for thought. His unexpected success in London was music to my ears. I thanked the Lord for his guidance. That Malvika would probably be going to London sounded good too.

How could everything change so dramatically in just a few moons, I thought. It had brought about a sea of change in Bala's case in a positive way while it had completely shattered Preeti's household in a trice.

It was three days since I met Bala. As my thoughts went back to his dream success in London, I received a call from him, asking if he could come at 3 p.m.

In time trooped in Bala and Malvika. I had seen Malvika three years back. She was now a young woman who had become several inches taller since then. She had delicate features and came across as a pleasant girl.

Bala introduced her to me. Quite unnecessary, if you ask me, for we knew each other. Bala again started off with some other tidbits from his London sojourn. Bala was a raconteur par excellence, and he had our attention for thirty minutes.

I asked Malvika what she'd prefer to have. She was in for a coffee. So, I ordered two coffees, knowing that Bala would have his usual, and then we turned to the work at hand.

Bala indicated through his demeanour that it was my time to take over the proceedings.

I asked Malvika about what she intended to do. Malvika informed me that she had got an offer from a university in Canada and another from Iowa in the US. She was happy with both. But she was now waiting for a call from a university in the UK, specifically the London School of Economics. She told me that she had another month in which time she was confident that something from the UK would come up. She had applied to four universities there.

I asked her about the fees, and she gave me ranges for various foreign universities. She told me that the UK colleges were costly and living expenses were high as well. But in her case since she would be staying with her father, it would bring down the expenses.

She also told me that she intended to work wherever she finally went for college. 'So, I will be getting some money, at least to take care of my incidental expenses. Appa will have to pay the college fees, for that would be difficult for me to manage with the income that I expect to make.'

Bala chimed in that he would gladly do that. He now wanted me to weigh in and give her a bit of personal finance 101.

Malvika realised that it was time for her to hear a long-winding soliloquy on personal finance. She, diplomatically and deferentially, told me that she would be glad to get some knowledge on personal finances, as she confessed that she knew next to nothing about the subject.

The coffees came and we were suitably primed for the job at hand—I for what looked like the makings of a long lecture and Malvika for the upcoming ordeal.

Frankly, I did not know where to start. Have you gone to a bank, I asked Malvika. She said that she had. I learnt that she knew about savings accounts, FDs, recurring deposits (RDs), etc. She was also aware that one does get an interest when one invests money in a bank FD or RD.

I explained to her why it is always a good idea to keep the money invested instead of keeping it as cash. 'The value of money keeps eroding over time. This is known as inflation. Hence, you need to earn a certain return just so that you at least preserve the value of what you have. If you can earn a bit over that, only then would you earn a real return on your investment. Real return is the return one earns above inflation. All good so far?' I asked her. She nodded. She seemed to know all the basic stuff.

I then took a detour and went into the kinds of investment options that are available.

Fixed income instruments

I told Malavika about some instruments, similar to FDs, that would give a fixed return on the investment. These instruments are called debt instruments or fixed income instruments, as one loans the amount to another party and one needs to get an interest on the amount loaned, which the other party pays for the privilege of using that money.

There are many kinds of fixed income instruments. But there are differences in terms of risk, tenure, liquidity, periodicity of returns, etc. Also, there are differences in terms of the risk inherent in the instruments.

What kind of instrument one chooses will depend on various parameters, some of which have been listed earlier. For instance, one would choose a bank FD, if one wants a safe, low-risk product that can offer monthly or quarterly returns. This kind of product, however, will offer low returns.

Risk and returns

The question would arise as to why a product with low risk cannot give high returns. While that is a situation that most would love to have, risk and returns go hand in hand. Whenever the risk is high, the lender, who is probably a high-risk borrower, would want a higher return to compensate for the higher risks their money is exposed to. They would want a higher payoff. That is why riskier products have to offer higher returns to compensate for the risk and in this way attract lenders.

How does one know which entities are risky and which ones are less risky, Malvika wanted to know. That was a good question.

As a rule, the investment options from the government are the least risky. Hence, government bonds can even be called risk-free. Government papers, like bonds, are said to carry a sovereign guarantee.

In the worst-case scenario, governments can print money and give it back to those who gave them loans. Or they can raise more loans, just to pay off previous loans. Raising money to pay off the old debt using money raised in a new scheme is a dangerous proposition. This means that the old scheme is not good enough to generate enough returns to pay the interest. Also, probably, the principal is stuck someplace or even spent. This is a loan spiral which will work for some time and will collapse at some point. These are termed as Ponzi schemes.

The only difference is that the government can keep running Ponzi schemes for a very long time as they make the laws of the land and control the mints that print currency. However, such profligacy is not without its own problems.

Such irresponsible acts from the government have their own backlash—higher inflation due to increased money supply (a surfeit of money chasing products resulting in higher prices), crowding out others raising money due to the government's privileged position to raise money at lower rates (than others) and higher deficits that affect the country's international ratings, devalues the nation's currency against other international currencies and affects the country's ability to raise money at decent rates.

The private operators will crumble much faster if they are operating Ponzi schemes, for they do not have the benefit of a currency printing press or legislative powers.

The general public would be hard-pressed to understand which entities are genuine and have good creditworthiness, and which ones are in poor fiscal health. That is precisely why they need someone to ascertain the creditworthiness of the various entities that are issuing papers.

Credit ratings

There are credit rating agencies who do the job of going through the information about the entities, their activities and their finances, and come out with a rating to indicate their credibility. For the public, this is a yardstick to measure the ability of the company to meet the interest obligations in a timely manner as well as its ability to return the principal amount when due. This works well most times. But there have been notable failures by credit rating agencies worldwide.

During the years preceding the 2008 financial crisis in the US, which triggered a global shakeout, credit rating agencies had been giving high ratings to junk instruments which were packaged as high-quality instruments. In India, too, we have had many instances of credit rating agencies getting their calls all wrong.

It is not just incompetence. Part of the problem is the way they are remunerated. The credit rating agency is remunerated by the party for whom they are doing the credit rating. This is clearly a conflicted model where the one engaging the service of a credit rating agency can 'influence' them and get better ratings than what they deserve.

Credit rating agencies claim to maintain their independence, but that is truly suspect. Better models need to be evolved. But for now, the general public has no other system to understand the creditworthiness of the entities. This has to do for now.

'Does this make sense till now?' I asked Malvika, after going over the details of the various instruments and explaining the risk-vs-return trade-off to her. I was not sure whether she was even listening to the harangue that I had inadvertently waded into.

Malvika was delighted. She told me then and there that this was the best explanation she has ever got about risk–return, credit ratings, sovereign guarantees, Ponzi schemes, etc. She said none of her economics professors had explained these concepts so simply and in such a short time. The praise was genuine, I was able to see that. I thanked her and asked her if this was good for the day or if I should continue.

She asked me to continue and the day wore on.

I said I would now explain the concept of equity to her. I suspected she already knew about it and asked her if I should. She said that she wanted to hear it from me.

Debt and equity instruments

In the case of debt instruments, one loans an entity a certain sum of money for a certain period. For the privilege of using that money, the borrowing entity pays the lender an interest.

There is no ownership interest created in this transaction. Whether the entity does well or otherwise, the borrower has an obligation to return the principal and interest as per the agreed terms.

Equity is completely different. Here, one buys into the enterprise and participates in its performance. The equity one owns hence confers a certain level of ownership of the enterprise, which is in proportion to the shares one holds in the enterprise.

Hence, when one buys a company's equity shares, one becomes the owner of a fraction of that company. The equity holder will participate in the performance of the firm and be able to enjoy the fruits of profitable operations of the enterprise. However, if the entity makes losses, the equity holder would participate in that too.

Hence, when we are equity holders in the company, there is no way to predict what returns one may get and whether the returns will be positive or negative. It is for this uncertainty that those investing in equity want risk compensation. They look for outsize payoffs as the risks involved are high.

Equity and fixed income (also called debt) vehicles are hence different kinds of assets. They behave differently at different points. They are mostly uncorrelated and, therefore, good to have in the portfolio.

There are other assets that we invest in as well. Gold and precious metals are one, real estate is another. There are many other asset classes, such as commodities, currency (including cyber currency), art and collectibles, fine wines, etc., which are now gaining acceptance.

It is important to put together one's portfolio wisely, based on the specific needs of the individual and the family. We call this asset allocation. There are broad principles which we follow here.

As I went about explaining all this to Malavika, Bala was getting restless. He told Malvika that she could continue the discussions, but he wanted to go now. Malvika, though entirely involved in the discussions, stood up immediately, saying that she, too, would leave with him.

She said she wanted more time with me and also wanted to bring two of her friends along the next time, whom she thought would like the lecture too. I said that should be okay and gave an appointment for Friday evening.

12

THE MILLENNIAL'S LESSONS CONTINUE

The next three days went by and then came Friday. In the evening, Malvika landed up in my office with her friends Urvi and Priya.

I offered them seats, ordered some juice and we were ready to start.

Malvika quickly summarised what I had covered three days earlier. She did it so impeccably that it came as a surprise to me. She then said that I would be covering asset allocation today, among other topics.

'Wow, Malvika! What an amazing grasp and what a pithy summarisation you have done.' I couldn't help appreciating her, before I continued with the financial literacy lecture.

'There are many assets like equity, debt, gold, real estate, currency, commodities, etc., which have different characteristics, and would help in portfolio diversification as well as offering the right mix of benefits at various points.

'Some assets, like fixed income instruments, are less volatile and are liquid, and hence are ideal as assets if one has goals in the near future. Other assets, like equity, are volatile and cyclical. The returns can swing from abject haemorrhage in sub-zero territory to soaring like a rocket in stratospheric zones. Volatility in the equity market can be enormous and can unnerve even the most intrepid.

'However, that is no reason to abandon equity as an asset class. Equity has proved that it can offer excellent real returns, if one has time on their side. This is an asset which works in the long term. Liquidity is good in many stocks. However, some stocks can become illiquid, especially the smaller ones where the free float of that company's equity shares itself is low.'

I then went on to talk about real estate.

'Real estate is again another asset class that is very popular worldwide. It is an asset class that involves huge sums of money, in most cases.

'Loans for purchasing residential property are available at attractive rates. This is so, as the government wants to encourage its citizens to buy homes for their use. However, liquidity is a big problem as real estate cannot be easily sold. Also, price discovery is poor, unlike in the case of equity or gold, where the prices are quoted on an exchange every day.

'Many buy multiple real estate assets and think it is a great investment. They believe that real estate will never lose value and will give regular rental returns. But rental return, at least in residential properties, is poor, especially after factoring in the society charges, income tax and so on.'

I then gave them the lowdown on all the myths and mistakes pertaining to real estate, which I had mentioned earlier to Vishal and Preeti.

After a lecture of about thirty minutes, I took a breather. Urvi was the one who commented this time. 'We never knew there are so many things to look into while considering real estate. It was a good eye-opener for us,' she said.

I had a sip of water and ordered some more juice and coffee. I wanted to give them some information on the other asset class that is a big draw with Indians—gold.

'Gold is a traditional asset that has been popular for millennia. Gold is a unique metal, in the sense that it is very malleable and ductile and lends itself to making intricate jewellery. Across the world, ornaments have been made from gold throughout human existence,' I began.

'Gold is seen as a storehouse of wealth and as an asset which would always have a certain intrinsic value. Gold has been used as a currency for a very long time.

'Gold is a rare metal. It is available in a limited quantity and its supply cannot be increased at will. Hence, this ensures that the price of gold stays at a certain level.

'This comes even more in focus as governments today are printing currency to infuse liquidity as well as fund deficits. This stokes inflation which ends up eroding the value of the currency. In these kinds of situations, gold will continue to hold its value and thereby act as a hedge.

'Gold as an asset has a negative correlation with equity and currency for the most part, which brings down the risk in any portfolio when gold is included.

'The point we need to understand is in what form should one make investments in gold. Gold investments in the form of ornaments are not an investment at all.

'For one, ornaments are a personal possession and would have a lot of emotions attached to them. Hence, one may not sell gold ornaments unless one is truly in dire straits. Ornaments are consumption items. This can be likened to a residential home which cannot be treated as part of one's wealth as it cannot be liquidated.

'Added to this, gold ornaments have many charges which cannot be recovered while selling, making it a poor investment choice even otherwise.

'One may want to buy gold bullion, that is, in the form of pure gold coins, bars, etc. Even in this situation, there is a differential of 8–12 per cent between the market price of gold and the price at which one would buy bullion. Also, there would be storage and insurance costs in case of physical gold, which depresses the returns.

'A better option would be to invest in gold through financial instruments which track the prices of gold.

'Gold exchange-traded funds (ETFs) invest in gold. It is a financial instrument traded on the stock exchange and one can buy or sell these anytime. The one running the ETF will buy gold in bulk and handle storage, insurance, purity checks, etc. The cost differential between the market price and the price at which they buy will be negligible.

'The gold index fund, which again tracks the price of gold, is another financial instrument worth considering. These typically will invest through a gold ETF. The cost to the investor might be slightly higher here. But gold index funds have guaranteed liquidity from the mutual fund house, which will buy the seller's units.

'The best option for investing in gold comes from the Government of India in the form of Sovereign Gold Bonds (SGB). This instrument comes with a tenure of eight years and it will track the price of gold. Also, this bond will offer a return of 2.5 per cent a year. This clearly makes it superior to all other gold investment options since this 2.5 per cent is an extra return. Also, there is no capital gains tax if it is held to maturity. However, unlike other options, this is not available for purchase throughout the year. But one can buy it from secondary market sources, as per the availability.'

Now that this was done, the next topic that I wanted to get into was asset allocation. I asked them if they wanted a quick summary or a detailed expounding on the subject. They voted for the detailed exposition.

Asset allocation

'Asset allocation is at the heart of portfolio planning and management,' I started. 'Each of the assets like equity, debt, gold, etc., that we have discussed have different characteristics. We need to have the right amounts of these in our portfolio based on a number of factors.

'The risk tolerance of an individual is important to assess. It indicates the level of risk a person is comfortable taking in their quest for returns. This is important to know as asset allocation done without this can go horribly wrong.

'Apart from this, one will have to consider various other parameters, like when the goals are coming up and how critical they are, liquidity, volatility, taxation, regular income needs, years to retirement and so on. Based on this, the right mix of assets needs to be chosen.

'First, we need to allocate for the short-term goals of up to three years. This must be allocated in short-term instruments where the capital is preserved and the amount available for the goals. This can be done in a mix of low to short duration debt funds and arbitrage funds.

'What is invested for short-term goals of up to three years will need to be excluded from the corpus where we do long-term asset allocation. This is because we are forced to invest in debt funds for all short-term goals and nothing by way of true asset allocation can be done there. For the assets that are truly long-term, we will look at allocation across asset classes.

'Let us understand why I have suggested arbitrage funds for short-term goals, coming up in the next three years, and not FDs, which is a favourite among the public. It is because of the tax treatment.'

Tax treatment of investments

'There are two kinds of tax treatments,' I continued. The returns from the investments are either treated as income or capital gains. If the returns are treated as income, it will be added to whatever other incomes one may have and taxed as such.

'For most people, this will put them in the higher tax slabs, and they will end up paying taxes at the rate of 30 per cent plus applicable surcharges and cess. Hence, the real return from an FD post-tax will come down by about one-third, making it not such a great investment vehicle.

'Also, FDs usually have a tenure. If they are broken before the stipulated time, penalties are levied. But one may need to access FDs based on when the goals are coming. That further depresses the returns.

'The question that may arise is when the goals are known, why will there be uncertainty about timing. For instance, in the case of a goal like education and the fee that needs to be paid towards it, the timing may be clearly known and can be planned for accordingly.

'However, there can be uncertainties about the timing of some goals. Goals like car purchase or vacations can get delayed or come earlier than anticipated, and the timing cannot be estimated exactly at the beginning. For these goals, we need more flexible vehicles that can be liquidated without any penalties.

'One such vehicle is a debt mutual fund (MF) scheme. We can choose a shorter duration fund that largely matches the durations at which the goals may come up. That way, they will be the most appropriate vehicle in a situation wherein the exact point the goal will come up is not known.'

Capital gains

'Another thing to understand is capital gains,' I continued. 'The returns from debt mutual funds are treated as capital gains. Till thirty-six months from the initial investment, they are treated as short-term capital gains (STCG). After thirty-six months, they will be long-term capital gains (LTCG).

'STCG is the difference between the purchase and sale price of units that are cashed out. STCG tax is as per one's applicable tax slabs.

'However, STCG can be less than the typical income tax one may pay on an FD, especially if we are taking out the equivalent of the interest from a debt fund. I'm not going to go into that now, for that would call for explanations and calculations, and it will be a big detour.

'LTCG is calculated differently. The units to be cashed out are adjusted for inflation. The difference between the sale price of the units and the indexed cost price is the LTCG amount. On that, 20 per cent tax is applied. The effective tax works out to below 10 per cent in most cases.

'Since the short-term goals are mostly going to be within three years (according to the plan), LTCG may not become applicable in these cases. However, we have found that some goals coming in the next three years may get postponed. In such cases, LTCG will apply.

But this kind of tax treatment for debt MFs has changed from April 2023. Now, the returns from debt MFs are treated as Short term Capital gains (STCG) irrespective of the holding period. This has taken away the favourable LTCG tax treatment that debt MFs used to enjoy earlier. 'Equity investments are also subject to STCG and LTCG. In equity, STCG applies after twelve months of holding the investment and the tax applicable is 15 per cent plus surcharge and cess.

'For periods beyond twelve months, LTCG will apply. LTCG tax rates are 10 per cent without indexation if the amount goes beyond ₹1 lakh in a year. If it is within the ₹1 lakh limit, no taxes need to be paid. Hence, even in the beyond twelve-month situation, a person may not have to pay any tax at all, if the gains are under ₹1 lakh.' I said.

Debt and arbitrage funds

'I must also tell you a bit about debt and arbitrage funds to take care of short-term goals,' I continued. 'Let us look at the payoffs in debt mutual funds. In debt funds, there are two kinds of payoffs. One is the coupon (that is, inherent interest rate offered) that the underlying instrument would offer.

'The second is the capital appreciation that accrues when the interest rates in the banking system go down, due to action by the

Reserve Bank of India (RBI). It can be capital depreciation, too, if the interest rates start going up. Hence, it is always a good idea to match the portfolio duration with the approximate duration after which the goal may come up.

'This ensures that the fund under question would be able to roughly deliver the portfolio yield one sees while investing, even if there is some interest rate volatility in the interim.

'Though the favourable LTCG tax treatment is not available any longer for debt MFs, they continue to be a good choice to park money for important goals. Debt MFs have low volatility, high liquidity, excellent price discovery and professional oversight.

'Arbitrage funds are what we recommend for short-term investments as the first choice. They are equity products where the fund manager cashes in on the difference between the current and future prices of securities. The fund manager typically does this by buying the stock now and selling the same in the futures/options market, and pocketing the difference. The return potential is low here. However, there is a clear tax advantage that arbitrage funds enjoy, as they are treated as equity investments.

'Hence, arbitrage funds should do well when it comes to parking the money till the time it is needed for the goals. But there is a caveat. Arbitrage funds tend to do well in volatile markets and are a good place to park one's funds in such a market. These are hybrid funds with a certain allocation to debt instruments at every point in time. In a range-bound market, these funds may not do well.

'So, we have now dealt with what investments we need to make to take care of short-term goals of up to three years. As mentioned earlier, we will not consider this in the overall asset allocation, as these are pass-through vehicles and will not be there at the end of three years.'

Strategic and tactical asset allocation

'Now, let us come to the real asset allocation for meeting goals over the entire lifecycle. This is also termed as strategic asset allocation. The term denotes that for an individual or family unit, this asset allocation constitutes what an optimum asset mix would be, considering various parameters like risk, tenure, return expectations, taxation and diversification.

'There is another concept called tactical asset allocation, which some advisors believe in and use. Here, based on the advisor's estimation of where the market is going, they would vary how much they may allocate to equity, debt, gold, etc. This looks like a great idea.

'There are two problems here. This presupposes that the adviser would be able to predict the direction of the market. This in itself is dangerous. It's extremely difficult to predict the direction of the market, especially in the short term. Hence, tactical asset allocation can go wrong as many times as it can go right.

'The second and even bigger problem is that the portfolio will be changed from time to time, based on just the return potential in the future and nothing else. A portfolio that has been carefully put together, based on multiple parameters, gets undone for nothing more than a potential for better returns.

'If tactical allocation is used to just tweak the asset allocation mildly, it should be fine. For instance, a 5–10 per cent change should still be okay. But wholesale changes in the portfolio would be detrimental, and we do not advocate such a strategy. In fact, we do not subscribe much to the tactical allocation theory. We would prefer to stay with the well-thought-out strategic asset allocation for our clients.

'Asset allocation is an art and a science. The broad allocation can be arrived at based on various parameters. To that, the advisors need to apply the touchstone of their experience and wisdom and arrive at what may be most suited to the individual or family. The adviser would need to factor in softer aspects like the client's emotions and biases, their preferences and choices, their fears and inhibitions. Accounting for these and then arriving at the asset allocation makes it an art and a science.

'The quantifiable parameters to first look at are risk tolerance of the person and the number of years to retirement. These two will determine how much of growth assets (like equity) one can have in the portfolio. Equity assets, along with real estate, are considered to be growth assets, which have the potential to offer returns that are substantially over the inflation rate. This is needed for the wealth to grow in real terms.

'If one does not have too much time before retirement, then equity allocation will have to be low in the portfolio. How low it will be is a factor of one's risk tolerance.

'If one has a good number of years to retirement, then allocation to equity and real estate assets can be higher. Again, how much we allocate to these is a factor of one's risk tolerance.

'All portfolios will have a certain level of debt or fixed income instruments as a part of strategic asset allocation. Debt gives stability to a portfolio and, therefore, is much needed.'

How to choose the right instruments

'The exact choice of instruments within equity and debt depends on factors like liquidity, tenure, income needs, taxation and credit quality.

'Now, within equity, an adviser will need to decide what kinds of equity mutual funds they would want to offer. There are large-cap-oriented mutual fund schemes, midcap-oriented mutual fund schemes, multi-cap funds, hybrid funds, international funds and so on. An adviser will have to decide which sub-categories to choose for which kind of client.

'Generally, one would offer large-cap and hybrid funds as part of equity allocation for those who have a low-risk appetite or those who have only a few years left to retirement. The more the investor's risk tolerance, the higher one can go on the risk meter of equity categories.

'For instance, a small-cap fund is riskier than a large-cap or a hybrid equity fund. Hence, a small-cap fund can be considered for someone who has both high-risk tolerance and a long working life.

'Some may want to directly invest in equity, that is, stocks. There is nothing wrong with that, as long as the investor understands equity, does her own research to identify companies with potential, monitors the company, sector, economy, etc., and reviews the portfolio from time to time.

'The problem is that most investors don't do this. Most investors in equity just rely on tips from brokers or others. They also invest based on what they read in the media, what the talking heads on TV are recommending and according to which stocks are in the limelight and gaining momentum.

'Invested this way, there are more chances of losing money than making money. The other misconception is that a stock that has offered good returns in the recent past will continue to give good returns in the future as well. Hence, a majority of investors get it all wrong.

'That is why mutual funds are a great way to invest in equity, where a fund manager and the analysts' team would take the investor's money, pool it and invest as per stated objectives. There are portfolio management services, too, which may be a bit more customisable and specific, and are suited for more mature as well as more monied investors.

'Let's talk about asset allocation at various stages in life. Let us consider someone who is thirty-two years of age, earning well, will work till they are sixty years old. If such a person has a high-risk tolerance level, the equity allocation can be between 70 per cent and 75 per cent. Allocations to equity can be in midcap and even small-cap funds, considering these factors.

'Now, someone who is forty-five years old, has a moderate risk appetite, is expected to retire at fifty-eight and has good surplus every month can probably invest 50–55 per cent in equity assets. The equity investments we may suggest for this person may be lower since the risk profile is moderate and the number of years to retirement is only thirteen years.

'Take yet another case of a person who is fifty-five and is slated to retire at sixty years. This person has a moderate risk appetite and has good surpluses every month. The allocation in equity assets for this person can probably be about 40–45 per cent.

'For a person nearing retirement, we typically bring down the equity allocation close to 40 per cent. For retired people, we will allocate anything from 10–40 per cent in equity, based on their risk tolerance levels, risk capacity, income needs and hence how much of the corpus needs to be locked in for that, their upcoming goals in terms of travel, gifting and so on.

'There is a rule of thumb which says that the equity allocation should be 100 minus one's age. That is a broad approximation. This should be relied on for broad guidance about how much equity one may have in the portfolio. But the actual allocation to equity or other assets in one's portfolio is dependent on various factors we talked about earlier.'

Asset allocation over the life cycle

'Asset allocation will need to change over the years. The risk profile itself slowly comes down over the years. One of the contributing factors is that capital preservation becomes much more important in the later years as compared to the earlier years of life. The other reason is that a person's risk tolerance itself slides over the years.

'Hence, one needs to lower the allocations to equity assets over the years and bring it near about 40 per cent or less, around one's retirement. This is something I, as an advisor, would be comfortable with and advocate. Other advisors may have different levels of growth asset allocations, which they advocate at various stages of life, including at retirement.

Managing finances for millennials

'Millennials and their needs are different from other categories. They would have joined the workforce recently, and their incomes usually would be fairly low. However, millennials would have a lot to spend on, like buying gadgets, bikes, travel, gifting, entertainment, etc.

'These are important for them at this stage of life, and hence a proper mechanism for this needs to be found. There is no point in saying that they need to save a big portion of their income as they don't have many commitments. These days, some of them have education loans they need to pay back.

'Their interests and indulgences are many. These need to be carefully sequenced for ensuring that these would be financially possible.

'The first thing we do is build a liquidity fund from which they can tap money for their various needs. For this, we need to direct a good portion of their surplus, say 75 per cent, to such a fund. The liquidity fund would be a debt fund from which one would be able to withdraw at any point.

'If this is not done and they end up spending their income, they will start taking loans and using credit cards for many of their needs. This can plunge them into a debt trap. It is always advisable to first build the corpus, and then spend from that.

'The other suggestion for millennials is to allocate a small portion of their income towards investments. Even if it is a small amount, it is fine. But the investment should be started right from the first salary itself. A regular monthly investment in a mutual fund scheme may be a good place to start.

'Millennials, though young, should get medical insurance, even if their employer is offering one. This is because they tend to change jobs frequently, and some employers may not have medical insurance for their employees. Hence, it is always a good idea to have a personal medical insurance policy.

'Life insurance will be needed if they have taken a loan or if they have dependants like a spouse, parents and so on.'

Risk capacity

'There is another aspect to consider called risk capacity of a person. The risk capacity is the person's potential to take risks. Let us take a few examples to illustrate this.

'A person who is thirty years of age is said to have a very good risk capacity since he is almost thirty years away from retirement. This measure is different from the risk tolerance measure, which suggests the inherent risk-bearing ability of a person. A person with a low-risk tolerance level can have high-risk capacity. When risk capacity is high, one can push till the upper limits of the risk tolerance scale.

'Another thing that affects the risk capacity of a person is the quantum of wealth. A very wealthy person even at the age of sixty-five may have a high-risk capacity. Such a person may be able to take risks due to the wealth they have, which affords a good cushion to any adverse effects of such risks. Many times, very wealthy people do take high levels of risk even at advanced ages, and this is due to their risk capacity. Wealth managers give risky investments to such people, as their risk capacity may be quite high even though their risk tolerance may not be that high.

'There could be other reasons for risk capacity being high. Suppose a senior citizen has a good pension coming to him every month, and that pension amount will keep getting revised to adjust for inflation, the risk capacity of such a person would be very good. That is again because there is income certainty in the future as well and this allows that person to take risks on the existing corpus.

'The other reason could be that the spouse is working and is also pulling in decent money. This could increase risk capacity too.

'Risk capacity will be high when risk does not affect a person as adversely as compared to most people, due to specific reasons. When there is high-risk capacity, it allows one to push the envelope of what is possible within one's risk tolerance levels. It is good to largely operate within the tolerance zones.

Risk required

'There is a third terminology called risk required. This is in the context of one's goals. To achieve certain goals, one may have to take on some amount of risk. When the risk required for achieving a certain goal is very high, the right approach would be to find out whether the goal can be postponed. If that cannot be done, one needs to see if the goal needs to be scaled down or more funds need to be allocated to this goal, while channelling funds from other goals to this. When the risk required is very high, it may be good to truly reconsider if the goal is worth pursuing.

'Risk required will need to be subservient to risk tolerance and risk capacity.'

I paused. I asked them if they had followed all that I had covered till now. They nodded vigorously. They had been taking notes all along, which impressed me no end.

Priya said that this was a wonderful session and came to know so much about putting together a portfolio and the various parameters that need to be considered before the assets are allocated to a portfolio. I thanked her. I asked them if we should continue or break here.

They chorused that I should go on. It was very encouraging to be around such minds that were thirsty for knowledge, I thought. We had a short break, after which I started again.

'When we construct a portfolio, the percentage allocations do not stay the same over time. That is because different components of the portfolio will be offering different returns. That will change the allocations in the portfolio over time. If we need to maintain certain weights in the portfolio for various assets, we need to do portfolio rebalancing from time to time. Another reason to do this is the changing requirements of the person over time, which would necessitate a rebalancing.

'When goals come near, we need to have the money in a form that can be liquidated anytime and would not fluctuate much in value. Only then would one be able to meet the goals with ease and without a hitch. Hence, we usually suggest moving the required money into debt funds, FDs or arbitrage funds well before it is required. We generally recommend that the money should be ready before one to two years, especially before any major goals like children's education or wedding.'

This completed the discussions about this topic. I told them that we should meet another day to discuss the various instruments that are available for investments. I also told them that I would cover how a young adult should go about investing.

This somewhat deflated them. After the break, when I started again, they must have expected another forty-five-minute session at least. I wrapped up in just five minutes, and the disappointment showed. I tried to mollify it.

'I have covered asset allocation and all the related topics in detail today. You have also taken notes on this. You should go through all this, read up a bit and then come prepared four days from now. Please call me that morning and we can fix a time,' I told them.

Reluctantly, they got up, thanked me and left. I was sorry that I had to ask them to leave. I remembered that I needed to work on one of my client cases and had to get everything ready before he came the next day by 2 p.m. I wanted to wrap that up before leaving for the day. I consoled myself by saying that they needed to learn to cope with small disappointments in life.

13

WE HAVE ONE LIFE, WE NEED TO MAKE IT COUNT

I had been thinking of Preeti off and on over the past few days, after Vishal had passed away. It had now been twenty days. I had talked to Preeti once over the phone and had been to her place on the thirteenth day. On that day, Preeti seemed composed. But I could not fathom what her mental state was like.

That is why I was looking forward to meeting Naina, her sister. They had sent across their information and goals. Like I had estimated after hearing them out the first time, the picture was not very pretty. We would need to sort out the dross in their portfolio and refocus it in a manner that would be helpful in achieving their goals.

They wanted to meet me. I thought I could use this meeting to get some insight into their goals and what they wanted to achieve.

More than anything though, I wanted to learn a bit about Preeti. At about 11.30 a.m., they trooped in.

After the pleasantries, I asked Naina about Preeti.

Naina said that Preeti seemed fine on the surface but the wound caused by Vishal's untimely demise would probably take a long time to heal. She seemed calm and composed externally, but was completely unsettled inside. She was still in shock and was extremely worried about the future. She was worried about how she would now bring up three children single-handedly.

I knew that Vishal's company had credited the leave encashments, EPF, gratuity as well as other arrears. All that had come to about ₹1.15 crore. They were also processing the life insurance that Vishal was entitled to; that amount was ₹1.5 crore.

As far as his personal insurance was concerned, I got to know that he had not taken the ₹1.5 crore insurance that I had recommended and instead took just a ₹50 lakh cover. He already had a ₹1 crore insurance plan. I had asked the concerned insurance agents about the claim settlement. That process was underway, and they had assured me that the claim would get settled in about fifteen days or so.

So, overall, the insurance amount due to them would be about ₹3 crore. That was a tidy sum and could help the family greatly. The total corpus which they now had at their disposal would be ₹4.15 crore. Vishal's company had very graciously offered a job to Preeti, in line with her qualifications, if she was interested. Preeti had told the HR department that it would be rather difficult for her to take it up, with three children in tow.

I made a mental note to contact her so that we could discuss the way ahead and deploy the funds.

I now came back to Raj and Naina. I told them that I had seen their information and had some questions. Despite good incomes in their case, their savings were low. When I pointed this out, they said that this was in fact a problem area which they wanted to address. I told them that though their expense pattern did not indicate very high spends, it did not reflect in their savings.

They admitted that they were not really on top of their spending. There was a lot of leakage and they struggled with money management, despite their good incomes.

I wanted to know what the solution to this could be. They looked at each other. Raj said that they had come to me thinking that I would be able to come up with a solution. I explained to them that we needed to budget all expenses carefully and stay within the budget. This was something that they needed to do and I told them that I would give them an expense tracker.

One needs to track expenses for at least three months to understand their expense pattern.

The next thing I wanted to know was about their daughter, Ritika, and what we needed to factor for her educational needs. I wanted to understand whether they had given any thought to this subject at all.

They again looked at each other for inspiration. Nothing apparently presented itself and they looked at me blankly.

Raj mentioned that since Ritika was still in the sixth standard, they still had no idea about which stream she may pursue. That was a fair point. I asked them whether they had ever considered college education costs and whether the education would be in India or abroad. This seemed to take them deeper into the swamps.

They were tongue-tied. I told them that education was an expensive affair these days and that it needed to be planned properly. While the stream Ritika may pursue may get decided later, we would need to set up some corpus for it. It is true that the stream one would pursue would decide how much would be spent on the course. However, it was important that we got to a reasonably realistic number for the purpose of planning for her education.

Raj again looked blank. He just said that I may have more experience on this and could probably guide them. I told them that the cost of college education would be dependent on the stream one may choose. Also, it would depend on whether it was a public college or a private one. It would also depend on whether the education was in India or abroad.

'The latest trend is to send children abroad. Parents are spending a king's ransom on this. The reason for this is the perception that when one is educated abroad, prospects brighten. While there are many high-quality educational institutions abroad, one will have to be cognizant of the costs involved. A proper cost–benefit analysis does not always establish a foreign education as a financially better option.

'But then, both parents and their children are not looking at education abroad merely in monetary terms. They are looking at this as a chance to settle abroad. There are problems which some face even with that and return to India. Those who return to work in India find that the extra premium they can command is not all that much, especially when seen against the money they have spent for their education abroad.

'The approximate fees and living expenses per annum when one does an undergraduate programme in the US or UK is about ₹50 lakh a year. One rarely gets scholarships in undergraduate programmes. Hence, one will have to be prepared to spend a lot of money for sending children abroad. The only other way by which the cost can be defrayed is by taking an education loan. Even that will take care of only a fraction of the costs.

'Postgraduation can again be as expensive. But the chances of scholarships for a PG course are higher.

'The other way of taking care of expenses, apart from education loan and scholarships, is for the student to work while they study there. This can get them some money to take care of most of their living expenses while there.

'But whichever way one looks at it, foreign education is a costly affair, costing crores of rupees. A sane way would be to educate them in India till graduation, allow them to work for a little while so that they get some experience and money and then go abroad for studies. This should be an option for the child to pursue instead of the parents trying to fund the entire education binge.

'A ballpark amount can be planned for education, since we do not know what she may pursue. We could plan for an amount of about ₹30 lakh for her. If more funds are required, we can evaluate our options closer to the time when we have more information. Based on the information you have shared with me, this is the option we should consider.'

I then had a query for them. 'You have mentioned early retirement for Naina. Can you please give me some more inputs on that?' I asked.

Naina suddenly came to life now from being an unblinking statue. She thanked me for providing clarity regarding the education bit. Apparently, even she was toying with the idea of sending Ritika abroad for education.

'I'm working with a private firm that is into infrastructure projects. I'm into bidding for projects and need to come up with quotes for the project after considering the manpower, material and time involved in them. It is very interesting and challenging. Sometimes the deadlines are a bit stretched, but overall the work is fine.'

'But having done this for about eight years, I'm getting bored. I do not want to keep doing this for the rest of my life. I'm starting to feel the drag now. Hence my urge to quit as soon as I can,' she said.

There was a pause. She said that she may quit when Ritika goes to the eleventh standard. That would be about four years at least.

'Let us say you have quit after four years. What is it that you intend to do?' I queried.

There was a long pause. I waited. She replied that what she would be doing was not clear, but she would probably be doing some work with an NGO, teaching children. I asked her if she had ever worked as a teacher in the past. She answered in the negative. I was intrigued.

'Why would you want to teach? How do you know that you would like that or if you would even be able to do it? What is it that you are trying to achieve?' I asked.

She was not sure herself. She felt that teaching was a noble thing and wanted to do that. I let that lie there.

I asked her if it was okay for her to continue with her work even though she was getting bored for more than four years. The look on her face said it all. I was able to see the boredom and tiredness written all over it.

'We all know what happened to Vishal. If your current job is sapping your energy and is boring, would you want to do that for four more years, before pursuing what you heart truly desires?' I asked.

Hearing this, Naina was struggling with her emotions. There was a lot going on under the surface, I could see that.

She finally blurted out, 'What can I do? The job may be boring, but they are still paying me north of a lakh a month.

'We need that money and I don't know which teaching job can give me that. Hence, I'm here doing it irrespective of whether I like it or not. Also, I do not know if I can quit after four years. The dilemma will be the same then as well. You have seen that we have not done anything significant with our finances till date. We need to fix that immediately. That, I guess, is the reason why we are here.'

I was able to feel the crushing burden she was experiencing and the consequent caged-in feeling. I felt her deep, searing pain. It was heartrending.

I was not going to talk about this. But I felt it was the right time to bring in the topic of life planning.

I sought their permission to go into this subject. I told them that this may be quite meaningful to them. I also told them that it may take some time and hence they could tell me if that was okay by them.

They were okay with it. Raj said that if I felt it was worth knowing about, they were open to listening. That gave me the freedom to expound on the subject.

I had already given them an understanding of financial planning in the previous meeting.

'Financial planning starts with understanding the needs and aspirations of the family and their financial situation. Then the planner analyses and checks the feasibility of achievement, comes up with alternative scenarios and evolves a strategy that would work best for the client.

'Many times, our goals may not be the ones that bring true satisfaction, a sense of achievement or happiness.

'When we pursue goals that don't really matter and spend time and energy achieving them, we feel tired, burnt out and exhausted. And once we achieve them, there is no satisfaction or delight because these were meaningless goals to start with. These goals take us away from the real goals that would liberate us, inject vitality, a sense of achievement of one's potential and the exhilarating feeling of looking forward to life itself.

'There is no set formula on how a life needs to be lived. The life we have is the only life there is (not counting rebirth, for now) and we have the option to make it meaningful, blissful and in accordance with our highest ideals.

'But, for that, we need to understand what our true values and motivations are. This will help us get a life that is truly meaningful for us and elevate our everyday to something cherished and sublime.

'Life planning precisely addresses this. This is a new area where the focus is to find out what is truly important for us in life—our values and motivations. Once we understand that, we determine what our goals and objectives are, around which our future life needs to develop.

'Based on these, we would then envision a life that would deliver freedom from the bondage of a humdrum existence, live our life's true purpose, live an authentic life, achieve our highest potential, find meaning in our lives and achieve our cherished goals and objectives that truly resonate with us.

'Life is always about choices. It is up to us to create the life we want. We are the ones to decide what our life should look like. We all have one life; we should make it count. We need to bring meaning back into our lives.

'But most of us have not even begun to visualise what such a life could be. We just conform, blend in and live our lives in a templated manner. We are all running around like headless chickens, filling the time in our lives with meaningless activities.

'We are not talking about some esoteric philosophy that is difficult to grasp. Life planning is all about understanding what we truly want in life and doing those things by which one's life is meaningful and truly enjoyable and fulfilling. Life planning is all about intentionally crafting a life we long for.

'So, you may ask, is having monetary goals like children's education, a home and vacations part of life planning?

'The answer is yes. All those things that are important to you should be there in the life vision canvas. Many of the goals like children's education, buying a home, going on vacations, etc., that are important will be a part of your overall life plan. What one wants to achieve in life is the locus around which all the important financial requirements should revolve, not the other way round.

'So, you need to envision the life you want first. When you do this and see life the way you would like it to be, you experience tremendous excitement about life itself, and it transforms into a canvas on which to paint with iridescent hues. Such a vision would lend vigour and infuse emotional energy to realise that compelling vision.

'Once the life vision is clear, we draw up a plan to lend financial architecture to support that life plan.

'How does one find out what is meaningful? To facilitate this, there are exercises that will help the client focus on a meaningful life they always wanted to live. There are some fundamental questions one needs to ask themselves, which will help them narrow down what they really want to do in life.

'Once they discover their true, heartfelt goals and see the vision of that wholesome life they can create for themselves, they get hugely excited. The life planner acts as a guide and mentor and paints that ideal life for the clients to see. This helps the client realise what an amazingly fulfilling life they can live, and they get to experience the entire repertoire of emotions that would arise out of such a life.

'This may call for a reworking of the client's life as it exists today. Some of the goals that one had in the past may not retain their appeal anymore. New goals would take their place, there could be adjustments in income and expenses too, depending on what one may want to do.

'One may feel an anticipatory thrill as well as trepidation that comes from a leap into the unknown. Obstacles may present themselves, which the client would need to resolve, drawing strength and support from the life planner. The next step would be to consider all these goals and create a financial plan and implement it so that life ahead is smooth.'

The role of the life planner

'Let me tell you a bit about the role of the life planner. The initial portion of life planning is extremely important. This is where the client and the life planner jointly explore what may make the client's life truly well lived. Once the client understands what would make their life meaningful, they get veritably excited.

'The new life envisaged may have problems that need to be surmounted and the planner plays a huge role here in ensuring that the client does not get disillusioned and slides back into their erstwhile existence.

'The life planner holds and keeps the torch of their dreams burning till the client can reconcile with the adjustments needed and gets the strength and fortitude to make it happen. Then a financial plan which accommodates the new life is drawn, and the recommendations implemented. From time to time, the life planner would be in touch with the client to find out if they are on track and offer any guidance that may be required.

'We all deserve a life where we experience the freedom to achieve our true potential and live a life that is meaningful, garnished with vigour and vitality in good measure and look forward to each day with anticipation. Life planning can make this possible.

'When life planning is made a part of financial planning, it becomes a tremendous force multiplier for the client. As George Kinder, the father of the life planning movement, says, 'Life planning is financial planning done right.'

'That's about life planning.' I wanted to know if they had any questions.

Raj had a question. 'I heard you about life planning. You made a good case for life planning with financial planning. It seems logical to me. Is there anyone at all who would want to only do financial planning?'

This brought a smile to my lips.

I explained. 'Most people don't seem to care too much for life planning. They do hear me out politely enough and then tell me that they would prefer doing the financial plan.

'Only some want to do life planning and financial planning together. It's an irony, as it makes sense to do the life planning bit first. As I see it, many people don't get that this is an opportunity for exploration that they should welcome with open arms.

'Most have never thought about their lives seriously, about where they are headed, what they really want to do and how one can reconfigure their lives to make them infinitely more satisfying and interesting. We end up like driftwood on a river, going where it takes us, with nary a concern for whether it makes sense or where we will land up.'

'Many don't even realise that they can envision and come up with a more fulfilling life than what they are currently living. They have accepted life as it is now and have resigned to that existence.'

Raj heard this out. He was genuinely intrigued by the fact that people may not want to imbue their lives with meaning. He clearly told me that this was what he wanted to do. He looked at Naina. She also nodded in acquiescence.

Raj asked me if the goals he had articulated earlier still made sense to me. I smiled and told him that these were their goals personally and as a family. They needed to agree on them and let me know. This deflated him a bit.

I again reiterated that my job was that of a facilitator. It is they who needed to envision the life they would like to have in the future. The goals would be a consequence of that vision.

I assured him that by following the life planning process they would be able to figure out the life that they truly wanted.

'There is work to be done and you folks need to contemplate and complete the exercises and worksheets I will be sharing with you,' I told them.

Raj wanted to know how to get started. I quickly explained the process of engagement and told him the fees. He did not say anything upfront. But I did sense that they were taken aback by the quantum I had quoted.

I took permission to go into this a bit at first. I then saw the time and realised that I had other things lined up that day. Hence, I told them that I would first send them some information to go through, after which we could meet again and handle any questions they may have.

14

ARISE ARJUNA!
YOUR DUTY IS TO FIGHT

It had been twenty-six days since Vishal had passed away. Time flew by. The image of the burning funeral pyre was etched in my memory. It seemed like yesterday, and yet, it was going to be a month.

I had had brief conversations with Preeti during this time. The last one had been about three days ago. The money that was lying in the bank needed to be taken care of. It had been there for about ten days now. We needed to have discussions about picking up the threads and getting on with life. For that, I had suggested that I could come over to her home when convenient.

But she had said that she would call and let me know. I understood that she needed some time to think through the next steps. She had to take charge and take care of her two children and the yet-to-be-born child. She would now be their father and mother. The thought scared her, she had told me in one of the previous conversations. It was daunting, no doubt.

When the call came, she asked me if I was free that afternoon. I said I was. She said she may be able to make it anytime between 2 p.m. and 4 p.m.

When she arrived, she looked calm enough, externally. Her face had aged perceptibly. She seemed preoccupied as she sat across the table in an absent-minded sort of way. She was looking down and it looked like she was crying.

When she looked up, there were no tears. She must have simply been collecting her thoughts, I figured. I waited.

'How do we go ahead?' she finally asked.

That was too broad a question. I wanted to understand what was on her mind. I asked her what she wanted to do going forward.

She looked intently at me without answering. I was taken aback for a moment. Did I ask something inappropriate, I wondered. But then, on replaying, it appeared to be an innocuous enough question.

'What choices do I have now? The life ahead involves taking care of three children. Is there anything else at all?' she asked.

This is an extremely difficult stage for her, I thought, and made a mental note to be a lot more circumspect and mindful when I spoke to her.

I changed course. I enquired about Shreyan and Ashitaa. This immediately brought tears to her eyes. She had told me earlier that she was worried sick about them. She had told them that Vishal was on a spiritual journey to meet God and he may not be around for a long time. They had wanted to know why he had not taken all of them to meet God as well. They wanted to meet Him too.

'They are okay. They are too young to understand the passing away of their father. They are treating his absence as something temporary and are pretty much normal. That is making me worry more. What will I tell them a month later, three months later ...' she trailed off.

This meeting was difficult. There was a bomb going off wherever I stepped. I decided to try a direct course.

'The EPF, gratuity monies have come in. We need to invest them in line with your future needs,' I ventured.

'Yes, yes. You can invest them wherever. I don't understand these things,' she said.

'Preeti, you need to take a bit more interest in these things now. We need to first discuss the plan. Based on that, we can deploy the money.'

She looked disinterested.

'Preeti, you cannot disconnect yourself from life now,' I started. 'By doing so, you will be more miserable. The more you disengage with life, the bleaker it will seem. You know your responsibilities, and I'm sure you would want to discharge them in the best way possible.

'You both had so many plans for your children. These innocent children cannot be pawns sacrificed at the altar of your grief. Why do you want to make life ahead harder for yourself?

'Life is like a movie. It has its dull moments and moments of joy. It has ups and downs. It holds many surprises—some pleasant, some nasty. We need to evaluate life as a whole, like we evaluate a movie.

'We cannot walk out after the first twenty minutes because it is slow and boring. The director may be taking his time to build the story. If we exit early, we might miss the wonderful parts that come later, once the pace picks up.

'Also, each event has something to teach us. If we look at life positively, instead of being cynical, we will realise that we have slowed down at certain points but not completely derailed.

'That happens to us when we drive. We need to slow down at the bends, or when we come to a speed breaker or a pothole, but at certain stretches of the highway we do floor the accelerator. None of us complains that the entire drive was not possible at full speed. Life is very much like that.

'Some of us can be broken and accept defeat at the first sign of trouble … we can be fragile like a twig that breaks when stepped on, never to come together again.

'Some of us can face the stressful event and bounce back after the flood waters have ebbed. This happens to the reeds on the river bank, which bend when the river is in full flow and straighten up when the water has receded. They are resilient.'

'Very few treat troubles as opportunities to hone themselves and come out much better than what they were earlier. A forest fire rages even more fiercely if there is a wind blowing, instead of being put out.

'The demons in Hindu theology have this boon of sprouting more demons if their blood falls on earth. These are examples of a property called antifragility. Those that are antifragile emerge stronger after a catastrophe or stressful event.

'The antifragile concept is explained by Nicholas Nassim Taleb in his book, *Antifragile*.

'Everyone experiences problems, even calamities. It is how one treats them and then moves ahead that is important.

'During the Kurukshetra war in Mahabharata, Arjuna was racked by remorse and loathing because he had to fight his own kith and kin as well as his acharyas, to get the kingdom back.

'He felt that a victory like that would be a hollow one, devoid of meaning. Hence, Arjuna was prepared to cast away his bow and arrow and relinquish the rights to the kingdom, even before the fight started.

'Lord Krishna laughed at him and reminded him of his duties. He pointed out that he was a warrior and had to discharge his duties on the battlefield. His duty was not to rationalise the right and wrong but rather to fight the good fight against people who had taken up arms and were ready to annihilate them.'

'Lord Krishna reminded him that posterity will see him as a coward, one who shirks duty, if he were to turn away from the war now. Moreover, he said that the other Pandavas were pinning their hopes of victory based on Arjuna being there at the forefront. You cannot disappoint them, he had chastened Arjuna.

'The entire Bhagavad Gita followed and it is now a guide for all of humankind.

'What Lord Krishna told Arjuna then applies equally to you today. You have to act responsibly and discharge your duties towards your children in the best possible manner. There is no room for shirking and sinking into self-pitying thoughts.

'Life has a way of delivering its share of joys and sorrows. We all need to be prepared for both, the rough and the smooth.

'It is all in our attitude. We can keep crying about how unfair life is. Or we can take charge and make the life ahead meaningful. There are countless examples of people who have been handed lemons and have made lemonade.

'Think well and choose wisely. What is it that you want to do with your life ahead? How do you want to take it forward? Think about it. I can help you once you have some thoughts about this.

'As far as finances are concerned, it is not going to be difficult to learn what is needed. I'm here to guide you. Hence, you do not have to worry. However, I would like you to be fully aware of all that we are going to do, and why we are doing it.

'I cannot take decisions on your behalf. You need to be in the driver's seat as far as your life is concerned and need to tell me the direction in which you would like to travel. I can always assist you and guide you on that journey. If you want, you may involve Naina and Raj. That's just a suggestion from my side,' I concluded for the moment.

She was listening to everything.

She took a sip of water and said, 'You are right. I cannot sink into despondency. God has created this situation for me, for some reason. The same God will also give me the strength to overcome this difficult phase, and even excel.

'That is what Vishal would want for the family. I'm going to make efforts to not get into a negative spiral. Let me start looking ahead and see what can be done.

'I do not want to involve Raj and Naina. I would like to handle this myself, with your guidance. It's my opinion that it would be better that way.'

That sounded good to me. It meant that she was intending to take control of the situation, which was excellent news. I told her that she could think about it for a while and that we needed to meet the day after tomorrow to set a fresh course and take appropriate action with the money that had come in.

I told her, 'I'm going to immediately move the money to a liquid fund, except for about ₹5 lakh.' She did not say anything.

I just explained to her that this was a temporary parking spot for the money, until we figured out the way forward. A liquid fund would offer a bit more than a savings account and the money could be cashed out at will. Since the amount is large, it made sense to move it right away.

I put some forms before her and explained what they were. She needed to go to the bank to transfer the money the next day. I filled that form out and handed it to her with the instructions that she needed to complete.

She nodded. She seemed fine now; in any case way better than what she seemed when she came.

Before leaving, she said, 'I was despondent when I came here, resigned to my fate and to exist only because I have to. Thanks for putting some sense into me. Thank you very much indeed.'

She smiled. I was seeing that after a long time. Then she was gone. I was happy to have made the Arjuna in her come to the fore, rise and shine forth. I hoped that this awakening was permanent and would bring out the best in her.

It was a short but productive meeting and I was happy that it produced an excellent outcome.

15

THE SCEPTIC COMES AROUND

Psychology plays a major role when dealing with people. It plays a big part in their perceptions about money, the correlation between money spent and satisfaction they derive, their buying patterns, which schools they send their children to or where they vacation and so on. People believe they are rational and think that the decisions they take are well thought out.

However, the basis of most decisions is emotional—only that people do not accept it. A financial adviser knows this and many times struggles with the emotions of the client and the decisions borne from them.

I was to face another emotional problem that day. It was regarding the fee the client needed to pay to an advisor.

Ajay and Arundhati had fixed up another meeting with me. They wanted some clarifications, I asked them if they were ready with the information we had discussed about previously. They said they were ready with almost everything, except for some bit about EPF, gratuity and the insurances that their respective employers had got for them. I told them that if that was all that was missing, it would be fine to start off.

They came around 1.45 p.m. Once the pleasantries were over, they took out their notebook where they had jotted down the questions they wanted to ask me.

'We wanted to know if the plan that you would be making will also be implemented by you,' Ajay started. 'We get busy and, left to ourselves, we may not follow through on the plan.

'We need ongoing advice, constant monitoring of the portfolios, review of the plan, advice from time to time, etc. Would that all be included in the services you had explained last time?'

This Ajay was a smart cookie, I thought. He was plumbing the depths to find out what all he would get within the fee I had mentioned last time.

I took charge now. I told him that I would be explaining the planning bit in detail, what we will be doing now and what services will be a part of that. I started explaining to them.

Financial planning and life planning

'Firstly, we need to do the financial plan based on your individual requirements and personal and financial situation. The plan will be a blueprint for achieving the important goals in life, while at the same time taking care of all the expenses and near-term requirements.

'During the planning process, we will also examine your investments and insurances, ascertain the risk profile, come up with appropriate asset allocation and suitable suggestions.

'I had mentioned about life planning to you earlier. To jog your memory, this is an exercise to find out your true values and motivations in life, based on which you can design your life itself. All the choices and decisions will be borne out of that.

'A financial architecture in the form of a financial plan would then be made to support the new life envisioned. This portion, which we call life planning, needs to be done before financial planning. Some portions would also be going on concurrently, along with financial planning.

'You may opt for financial planning alone, or you could choose to do this along with life planning. These are one-time assignments, after which you can either take over the implementation or engage us for ongoing advisory and implementation services. The choice is yours.

'We will charge a fee for the one-time assignment of financial planning and life planning, as chosen. The ongoing services will be charged separately, if opted for.' I stopped with this.

I knew why he asked that question, and what he wanted to know. But I wanted him to broach that topic specifically. And I wasn't disappointed.

Ajay asked, 'The one lakh fee you quoted was for the financial plan and the life plan?'

I said that it was a ballpark figure. 'The exact fee can be determined once I have all the information and am able to estimate the amount of work needed.'

Ajay's next question was: 'Are you charging for your time or expertise or both? Sorry for asking this but how come the fee is so high?'

I had to explain in detail now.

'There are differences between a product distributor who is offering some advice and a true adviser who has the client's best interest at heart.

'Many of the things I would talk about would apply to us and to any good fee-only advisor.

'There would be differences in the process of engagement, service breadth and, consequently, the fee charged. But the fundamental premise of a fee-only adviser and the benefits such an adviser will be able to deliver will remain across such advisors.' With this preamble, I started.

The fee charge rationale

'The fee we charge will be calculated based on the time spent in your case,' I continued. 'But, as can be expected, it is also for the experience and expertise, and, consequently, the level of maturity of planning and the advisory process itself. We also charge a premium for the quality of our advisors, who are well-trained and have all the necessary qualifications and certifications.

'In our planning process, there are three planners involved, which lends depth to matter and offers the wisdom and perspectives of three planners. Also, compared to most other planners, we spend much more time on a plan, about sixty hours.

'We keep upgrading and qualifying ourselves constantly, in our endeavour to offer high-quality advice. This involves time, effort and money. These will be amortised over all clients we have, as they are the direct beneficiaries when we burnish our knowledge and acquire new qualifications.'

'Do we charge the same fee to all clients, you may ask. The work we do for every client is different, though the overall planning process may be the same. Every plan we create is tailored to suit the needs of that client. The emphasis can be different in different cases based on the client's stage in their life, family dynamics, dependencies, goals, problems to be addressed, potential alternate scenarios and so on.

'Two people in similar situations may be charged about the same. But, even in such cases, it can be different based on the complexities and nuances of the concerned case. Hence, what we quote from client to client can vary. It is based on the estimation of the time we will be spending, the complexity and consequent efforts as well as the special purpose work we need to do for that client, etc.

'The work we do can be compared with that of a lawyer or an architect. Every case they handle would be different and they would estimate and charge each one of their clients differently, according to their situation.

'One thing we can assure those who come to us is that we do not change the fee or charge extra, once we have quoted our fee after the estimation exercise,' I explained.

The next part of the question was about the fee being high.

I had already explained to them, in the last meeting, about how much someone would be paying their driver and maid over the lifetime of their service. I reminded them again that the figure would be over ₹3.2 crore. The figure was astronomical and yet, even after knowing it, we would not dream of discontinuing their services.

I went on to other significant aspects that Ajay needed to know.

Representation and conflict of interests

'We are fee-only advisors and derive our income only from the clients we work with. We do not distribute any product of a fund house, insurance company, stock broking house, etc., and so we don't collect commissions from them. Hence, we are independent.

'This makes us conflict-free as we represent only the client's best interests and are not hampered in our judgement or by any kind of endorsements from product providers, as we don't have any commercial arrangement with them at all.

'Distributors of products represent their principal and seek to sell those products to the clients. They receive commissions from their principal and from the charges deducted for products sold.

'Commissions go against the fiduciary standard of care. Every person rendering a service will need to get remunerated. Commissions are a way of getting remuneration. However, indirect, embedded remuneration like commissions along with the fact that they now represent a principal, while at the same time claiming to represent the client, brings in conflicts of interest.

'When intermediaries represent some principal, they may be beholden to their directions, guidance and targets. When their principal is paying them, there is a natural allegiance to them, which clearly would not be in the client's best interests. Such intermediaries are also prone to offering products that give them the best commissions or incentives.

'Such a conflict of interest compromises the independence and objectivity of the advisor. This takes away the intense client-centricity that otherwise a fiduciary is supposed to have. A true adviser needs to represent only their client and no one else, and get paid only by them.

'We are SEBI-registered investment advisors with a fiduciary responsibility. We are subjected to higher standards in education, experience and certification. SEBI is responsible for regulating, developing and promoting the security markets in India.

'Such advisors also need to follow proper processes right from onboarding to advisory, and beyond. Higher compliance and record maintenance requirements are also imposed upon them. They need to get themselves audited for process and compliance every year. These are the high standards that advisors should be remunerated for so they can be maintained.

'Also, such advisors need to act in a fiduciary capacity for their clients. Fiduciary standard of care is one where the adviser puts the client's interest ahead of everything, including their own interests. This means that the clients can implicitly trust such advisors, as the model under which they operate itself would be verifiably conflict-free.

'In the case of distributors, they follow a lower standard called the suitability standard. Here, they need to suggest products that are broadly suitable to the use case.

'For instance, if the client is looking to invest for the retirement phase, they just need to suggest a pension product of the company they represent, even if the product they suggest may be costly and may have lesser benefits when compared to other similar products.

'In contrast, for advisors following a fiduciary standard, they need to check all available options that can help satisfy that requirement and recommend the most suitable product for funding retirement. They cannot just look at the pension products alone. Even products like Public Provident Fund (PPF), mutual fund schemes, National Pension System (NPS), etc., can be used for retirement funding and they need to look at all these options holistically, before recommending them to the client. Then they may suggest an optimum blend of these products so that the client's retirement planning objective is met in the most optimal manner.

'The investment world is plagued with conflicts of interest, obscure disclosure and an overall lack of transparency.

'Surprisingly, even among those calling themselves fiduciaries, there can be issues. What you need to determine is whether the adviser is truly a fiduciary for you, or is the adviser just checking the fiduciary box from the regulation point of view? Confusing, isn't it?

'Under the SEBI's Investment Adviser Regulations, 2013, advisors who have registered under it have taken a fiduciary responsibility. This means that such Registered Investment Advisors will always need to act in the best interest of the client, in every way.

'But, SEBI, as a regulator, oversees only certain products in the financial services space. There are three other regulators who have different jurisdictions—like the Insurance Regulatory and Development Authority of India (IRDAI) for insurance, the Pension Fund Regulatory and Development Authority (PFRDA) for pension products and the Reserve Bank of India (RBI) for banking-related products.

'If an adviser who is registered with SEBI sticks to the fee-only approach with regards to providing advice on products coming under the capital markets regulator and deals with other products outside SEBI's ambit on a commission basis, they would still be following investment adviser regulations. They would, however, be abusing the spirit of the regulation.

'In the above case, they are a fiduciary as per the SEBI IA Regulation, but not from the client's point of view.

'That is the reason why a true fiduciary should not represent anyone except the client, and not accept remuneration from anyone except the client, even if the regulation permits it,' I concluded.

I pointed out to Ajay that he needs to understand these things while hiring an advisor, and not blindly sign up someone based on what they say.

Disclosures by themselves do not reduce conflicts

'Some advisors registered under SEBI's IA Regulation may also be distributing products not under its jurisdiction. Other advisors could have tie-ups with third entities to distribute products through them and have a commercial arrangement with them. At other times, the advisor's suggestions may directly impact their fee (like when they suggest that the client square off the loan by redeeming investments to pay off).

'All these result in conflicts of interests. Such actions may also violate the spirit of the regulations, though they may still not violate the regulation in letter. As per regulations, advisors need to disclose such conflicts of interest to let their clients know that it is there. However, just disclosing this to clients does not reduce the conflicts of interest which the client would just learn to live with. Such information is largely meaningless.

'For one, the clients may not be able to fully understand the import of some of these conflicts. For another, they may not have the time or ability to understand, evaluate and take a decision based on such disclosures.

'Also, disclosure documents are long-winding and in small print. No one really goes through the voluminous submissions. Disclosure documents have hence become a tool for obfuscation and not telling the truth, rather than clarifying and conveying.

'Disclosures, along with disclaimers, are ironically permitted to paper over conflicts of interests. These are used by some advisors to hide behind and feign compliance with the regulations.

'Clients need to question their advisors and ask them directly if there is something that is important for them to know. Clients should ask for a one-page synopsis of those that may be important for them to know.

A true fiduciary to the client

'Fiduciary is an abused word today. Different people give different definitions for it.

'Fiduciary is one who puts the client's best interests ahead of everything, including their own interests. It should be that way, irrespective of regulations, if they want to act as true fiduciaries to their clients. As seen earlier, that would be possible only if they are truly independent and do not receive indirect remuneration from some principal whose product they are dealing in.

'There is no immediate solution to this problem. Some of it (especially the regulatory arbitrage) will get sorted only when a super regulator that regulates the entire financial services space comes up.

'Till then, the advisors will need to set themselves to the higher standard in true fiduciary spirit, to only represent the client and be truly independent. They need to act with ethics and integrity and uphold the fiduciary standard from the client's point of view.

'Clients may find it hard to know this difference. They need to ask their advisors about the nature of their fiduciary position. They should hire them only if they are true fiduciaries.

'I would like to state that we are a true fiduciary to the client. That should mean something to you, especially after knowing who a true fiduciary is, I suppose,' I said and looked at Ajay and Arundhati. They nodded in acknowledgement.

Advisors spend time to understand clients

'True advisors spend a lot of time understanding the client's present situation, their goals, finances, their family situation, etc., so that they may be able to create the right financial architecture to help their clients achieve their goals and live a well-funded life.

'Good fiduciary advisors can make all the difference, especially when their clients' means are limited. The margin for error in such a case would be slim. Hence, an adviser can craft a plan and offer advice that helps the client walk the tightrope and achieve the agreed goals by deft financial management.

'For the wealthy, the stakes are very high. They cannot afford to make mistakes when the errors in absolute terms can be quite large. Hence, a good fee-only adviser can be invaluable to them to ensure that their portfolio is well-positioned in terms of risks and rewards. They will also need someone they can trust and ideate with.

'So, in almost all situations, a skilled financial adviser will be able to make a telling difference. Their counsel will be extremely useful because they fully know the client's situation and, therefore, would be able to suggest solutions that completely align with the said situation.

Good advisors save a lot of money for their clients

'As fee-only advisors, we recommend only commission-free products, so that our clients save on costs, and we as advisors are able to stay conflict-free.

'In case of mutual funds, there is a class of commission-free products called direct plans. We recommend only that to our clients. In case of other products, where commission-free products do not exist yet, we talk to the product providers and ensure that they pass on what they would give a distributor as commissions to our clients by way of reduced charges. We do this in a transparent way by informing both—the clients and the product providers—about this.

'This statement by itself does not do justice to the enormity of savings that this one act engenders. The savings can be in the tens of thousands of rupees to a few lakhs per annum.

'The other savings come from suggestions that bring in tax efficiency. We would use our understanding of the client's situation and our domain expertise to come up with the right portfolio constituents that also optimise the tax incidence.

'Efficient management of available resources to meet the objectives is another major benefit. Through this, good advisors will ensure that money available is managed well and invested in a manner as to be able to offer the required benefits of liquidity, income generation, appropriate risk management as well as better tax-adjusted returns for clients.

'The other thing is that investors invest up to the potential level of surplus they have only when there is an advisor. Else, they invest some money, and the rest stays in the bank account, yielding low returns, and sometimes gets spent as well. This is what we call the adviser wealth effect.

'If all these savings and positive enablers are taken into account, the fee we charge will be much less than the savings in most cases. That makes our advisory offering a compelling value proposition.

You won't commit those huge mistakes

'Left to themselves, most people are prone to making huge mistakes. Some of them are major blunders, which cannot be easily undone without corrosive financial implications.

'Buying a holiday home may be one such blunder. Buying land somewhere because a highway is expected to come up is another such blunder. This is speculation, not investment, and is best avoided.

'Another blunder is buying unwanted insurance policies. People get locked into such unsuitable products for years that end up yielding low returns. Or it can simply be investing in FDs and taking no risks at all. That is in fact a huge blunder—one committed by too many people.

'Taking the appropriate amount of risk in one's investment is the way to boost returns at the portfolio level. Some don't want to take any risks and blame the government for the poor returns they are making.

'A good adviser helps in putting together an appropriate portfolio, taking the level of risk appropriate to their situation.

High-quality advisory services

'A good adviser offers comprehensive advisory services that take care of the various needs of the client.

'In our case, we offer financial planning, review and recast of the plan, periodic portfolio reviews, scheduled client discussions, financial consultations on matters that have implications, life planning, etc.

'A trusted adviser can greatly help in turning around the fortunes of their client by ensuring the right asset allocation, disciplined and regular investments of the surpluses and ensuring that they have resources to meet the expenses and goals that come up from time to time.

'In short, a good adviser can deliver financial freedom, clarity on the way ahead and peace of mind.'

I paused and looked at Ajay. He said, 'Wow,' which I had now come to expect from him. What I understood from him was that his 'wow' was a mixture of—it's a good story to edify the high fees being charged and impressive in its breadth of justifications with elements of truth in it.

That 'wow' still had scepticism. I resolved to tackle it head on.

I looked at him directly and told him, 'You don't seem to fully appreciate what we could do for you and the major difference we could bring about in your life. You seem to be concerned only with what we charge and not the value we would bring to your lives.

'I suggest that you check out others who charge much less, if paying an appropriate fee for fiduciary advice is a concern to you. Please bear in mind that when someone charges a low fee, they may have other sources of earnings such as commissions or they may not have our experience and expertise, or even a full team to support their clients and they may not be able to offer detailed and comprehensive plans and advice that we offer.

'Take your call, Ajay,' I said, rather hotly.

Arundhati, who had been silent all this while, sprung to life. She started talking to Ajay.

'What Suresh is saying makes sense. He is fee-only and plays a fiduciary role. He has a model we can trust and has about two decades of experience. He needs to be remunerated properly for his services. After all, don't we receive higher salaries when we have more experience and develop good expertise in our areas of operation?'

'So, whatever he has said was all right and cogent. The only area which I would like to lean on is that we do not know yet the benefits that will accrue from the engagement. Hence, we should be able to pay some money now, and the balance fee on achievement of certain milestones. That would be fair, I suppose,' Arundhati said, and looked at me.

This was a nice way to negotiate, I noted and admired. But I had to dash their hopes.

I paused for a few seconds, after which I began.

'The financial planning engagement is a one-time assignment that is expected to take about forty-five days. The objective of this exercise is to understand your situation well, look at the expenses, goals and other financials and check the feasibility of achieving the various objectives and outcomes, arrive at an appropriate asset allocation in line with your specific situation, sort out and reconfigure the existing portfolio, introduce the right investments, channel savings properly into the right investments, etc.

'This will sort the chaos that may be there in your finances and deliver clarity about the road to tread to attain financial freedom. This process delivers peace of mind, as you would then have a financial blueprint to back you up.

'The effect of the financial plan will be felt over time, as one implements the suggestions and recommendations. It will be exactly like a blueprint created by an architect. The building, bridge or whatever the blueprint was made for will come up over time.

'The architect does not wait till the subject of the blueprint is brought to life. The architect expects to be paid in full for rendering professional services from his side, though it may take years for the blueprint to come to life.

'The comparison can also be with the work of a surgeon. An operation done by a surgeon removes the problem one may have. It may take weeks and months for the person to recover to normalcy. The surgeon charges for the procedure he does on the patient, and does not wait till the patient completely recuperates.

'It is the same in our case too. We charge the financial planning fees in advance, before taking up the work.

'The patient may go to the doctor for ongoing consultations, which are charged separately. We also have ongoing financial advice after the financial planning exercise, which you may opt for at your discretion.'

I looked at Arundhati, and asked her if my analogy gave her the answer. She nodded. But still she wanted to know why the full financial planning fee had to be paid in advance.

I told her that it was a fair question that had an easy answer.

I told her that I had no intention of running behind clients for our fee after we completed the plan.

'Surprising as it may sound, some clients have behaved unprofessionally, kept raising frivolous questions just to delay payments and only paid after much follow-up. This process leaves a very bad taste and sours the relationship.

'Hence, we have decided that our prospective clients will have to pay up fully after they are completely convinced about our credentials, our ability and intention to deliver a robust plan that would help them.

'To assure you, we offer references of our existing clients who have availed our services. Our prospective clients can talk to them and make up their mind.

'I would like to do the same with you. You may also mull over all the information I have given you, talk to a few other advisors and understand what they have to offer, before taking a decision.'

I had finished.

Ajay and Arundhati looked at each other. I thought that they were signalling to each other about leaving. But a strange thing happened. They were apparently struggling with something, and I did not understand what that was.

Arundhati was the one to break the silence.

'We have been doing a bit of research about financial advice and the kind of financial adviser we would like to engage. We have met seven till now, and have read and analysed probably two dozen advisors.

'We came to you after proper due diligence. It so happens that a relative of someone we know had done a financial plan through you, and is also availing your ongoing advisory services. There are a few more in his company who have taken your services and are your ongoing clients.

'We talked to all of them and got very good feedback. They also told us that you are costlier than the rest and that you expect their full trust, compliance and cooperation. They advised us to go with you. So, that part has already been done.

'We have more or less decided to go with you and were hoping that you would give us a lower fee quote,' she smiled.

I was digesting the information she had given. I was mentally scanning who these references might be. We have several clients who worked at the same company and there were several such companies. Hence, it could be anyone. It was good to know that our clients were happy and recommending our services to others.

I asked her why she had questioned me so much if they already had done the due diligence and had decided to go with us.

She said that the references' positive reviews had helped her more or less make up her mind, but she still wanted to know many things from me directly.

'I'm glad that we asked all those questions. Your answers were revealing and very helpful. Your fees are quite high and was one more reason why we wanted to know how you are really different from the rest. Now, I have almost got all the answers,' she concluded.

But then she wanted to know whether we would be ensuring a better return on investment than what they were getting now. This was also a fairly regular question.

I wanted to answer that at length, as this was an important matter to be clarified.

Would we ensure better returns than what they were getting now?

'To put it another way, should a client come to us expecting better returns? As advisors, we are not looking for such clients. Our role is not that at all. Our role is to help our clients achieve their goals and important outcomes in their lives.

'What we do to ensure that is to analyse their specific situation and create a financial architecture that will be suited to them based on their unique needs. Hence, if their needs require that we allocate more in debt, we do that. The portfolio return will reflect the proportion of allocation to various asset classes.

'Returns are also a function of risk. In fact, risk and return are two sides of a coin. One cannot get returns without assuming a certain level of risk. So, if one is obsessed with high returns, then one may have put together a portfolio of riskier instruments to achieve that. This could make the portfolio unsuitable for a person, based on their risk profile.

'This is happening to people today. Many have put together portfolios of small-cap and midcap funds, sectoral funds, thematic funds, etc., which are inherently risky. Many have invested in them because they were doing well at one point. Worse still, those who are conservative in their investment intent have been lured into equity assets, tempted by high returns.

'This is a major problem. Investors want to invest in schemes which are doing well at that point. Typically, people want to keep switching to schemes and products that are doing well at a certain point. It is virtually impossible to get into the product at the right time and exit at the right time. It can happen sometimes, but that is like predicting heads or tails in a coin flip.

'Most investments would perform over their cycles. It is important for the investor to be positioned well in a product, to the extent required, before the upward move starts. This is what is feasible in real life.

'Getting the asset mix right in line with the goals, liquidity, taxation, tenure requirements, etc., is really the important aspect of a portfolio. This will ensure that the portfolio is positioned to meet the goals one may have.

'Achievement of the goals is important, irrespective of the market performance or investment returns that various assets offer. This is what we focus on achieving while we create a plan.

'We generally provide for goals coming up to three years and provide for them in low-risk instruments. The products of choice would be arbitrage funds and shorter tenure debt funds. Both these products have low-risk profiles and can be offered in a manner so that the tax incidence is minimised and the post-tax return is maximised.

'We also provide for up to three months of expenses for liquidity needs. In cases where there is a risk of income irregularity, we may provide between six months to a year of expenses as liquidity.

'Apart from this, we may also have to provide for contingencies. Some of the contingencies we provide for are medical emergencies, provisions for assisting a family member monetarily and so on.

'Contingencies are events that one may face at some point, but the timing is uncertain. Hence, the investment should be done in a way as to account for the indeterminate nature of the requirement of funds. So, even in the case of contingency provision, it would have to be in arbitrage or shorter tenure debt funds.

'If we are going to invest a good amount for short-term goals, liquidity and contingencies in arbitrage and short-term debt funds, this portion of the portfolio is going to offer low returns, which will affect the overall returns of the portfolio. But this is very much required to ensure that goals are met and all situations are covered.

'Ultimately, this is what is most important. We take care of this in our plan and that is why our advice can be invaluable for a client, even though we are not seeking to maximise the returns,' I concluded my explanation.

'Have I answered your question?' I asked her. She nodded.

I told her that I could send her a final fee quote once she shared all the information. She said she had all the information with her, and handed me a file. This was again a pleasant surprise. They had come well-prepared.

I went through the contents—goals, incomes and expenses, insurances, investments as well as an explanation of their personal situation and what they were intending to do going forward. It was a fairly elaborate document. I was impressed with their thorough work and went through it completely. But I had to give them some more disappointing news.

From the information given and the scope of work that I was able to assess, the fee would go up substantially. I told them this now. I quoted the fee. There was a sharp draw of air from their side, indicating profound surprise.

I suggested that they think it over carefully, and get back to me in due course.

'You are sure that this is your best quote?' Arundhati wanted to know. I confirmed that it indeed was.

She looked at Ajay, and signalled to him. He took out the cheque book. Arundhati wrote a cheque for the entire amount and handed it over. This was a pleasant surprise. I had thought that they were sceptics who would want more time to get convinced.

I thought they may resort to pleading for a lower fee. But the last thing I expected was for them to finalise the planning engagement then and there.

Life is full of surprises, and here was one more instance.

16

PLAYING THE ROLE OF A SARATHI

It was five days since I had met Preeti. She had transferred the money the very next day, and the investments had been done. She wanted to come over to discuss the further course of action. I had given her time at 2 p.m. today.

I had worked out what we needed to do, and was ready when she came in. She seemed quite normal now. It was almost like the Preeti of yore!

We got talking a bit about her home and the changes she needed to make to welcome her new child. She said she already had most of what would be required. Ashitaa was born just three years back and the cradle and pram were still with her, in good condition.

Preeti wanted some changes in one of the rooms for the baby. She was also going to do some work in the other room, as the children were growing up. The estimate she had got was about

₹4 lakh. She said the contact was reliable and was given by her sister.

I suggested that we keep aside another ₹5 lakh, over and above what I had already suggested for liquidity.

Now, I got down to what we would be doing regarding investing the money in such a manner that she could receive a regular income. Out of the ₹1.5 crore, ₹5 lakh was for liquidity, ₹5 lakh for home renovation work and another ₹5 lakh for contingencies.

I wanted to explain how we were going to set up a regular income for her.

I started. '₹1 crore invested can offer an average of about 7–7.5 per cent a year. When we set up this income, you will have an income that will attract a tax. That cannot be avoided. You had mentioned that your regular monthly expenses were about ₹65,000.

'That would include some portion of the children's tuition fees, but not entirely. Most of this requirement can be set up with this ₹1 crore that you have got. There was another ₹4 lakh approximately by way of other expenses coming through the year.

'Since it is almost certain that your income will attract taxes, we will also need to use the available tax-saving sections for this purpose. One of the sections that you can use to save taxes is 80C, under which you may contribute up to ₹1.5 lakh, using certain specified investments.

'Under the same section, you can also show the basic school tuition fees you would be paying for your children. You will need to invest only the balance amount to meet the ₹1.5 lakh target. We can invest this anytime during the year.

'Once you get the balance amounts due to you from insurance claims, we can estimate how much more you will have to invest for setting up regular income.'

She nodded. 'Where are we going to invest?' she wanted to know.

I had some explaining to do.

'We need to set up regular income that will take care of the monthly expenses. We are going to do that with a combination of products.

'We will invest in corporate FDs, non-convertible debentures (NCDs) and perpetual bonds. Apart from this, we will also invest in debt mutual fund schemes. In case of debt funds, we can set up an income by systematically withdrawing the desired amount at regular intervals. Usually, one may want to receive a steady sum on a monthly basis. However, setting up an income on a quarterly or half-yearly basis is also possible.

'In case of the FDs, bonds and NCDs, the one who has issued the financial instrument will pay an interest or a coupon.

'For the debt mutual funds, one will need to set up a regular income by withdrawing the amount of money we may need.

'Even though you can set up the income amount you want, it does not mean you will be able to withdraw whatever you want from the scheme. We need to set up a withdrawal amount that is sustainable considering how much the scheme is expected to earn. For instance, if the scheme is offering 8 per cent a year, setting up a withdrawal below that would be a good idea, for long-term sustainability of income.

'There are many advantages of setting up income via debt funds.

'You have the flexibility to set up precisely the level of withdrawal you may need and can decide the period as well. You can stop and restart whenever you want.

'Debt mutual funds are subject to capital gains treatment. Here, tax would be levied on the capital gains, that is, the amount received on the sale of units over and above their cost price. We have discussed earlier that debt MFs are subject to STCG treatment irrespective of how long one has remained invested.

'Even under STCG, the effective tax would work out to be much lower than the typical income tax slabs one may come under. Hence, the effective post-tax returns will be much higher than the post-tax returns from the FD, NCDs and perpetual bonds.

'I'm telling you all this, as it is my duty to communicate to the person I'm advising why I'm suggesting certain actions, even though you may fully trust me as your advisor. There is one thing we need to keep in mind. In case of a debt fund, the value of the investment can be volatile. It may not be as volatile as an equity fund. But it does exhibit some level of volatility, since all underlying instruments in a debt fund are traded in the market.

'This can deliver capital appreciation or depreciation in the portfolio. So, the returns from a debt fund would be the sum of the underlying returns of the papers along with the capital appreciation or depreciation.

'We need to choose the debt funds we invest in skillfully. I will take care of that. For your information, we would be choosing funds that invest in shorter tenure, high-quality papers. This would work best in a rising interest rate scenario.

'We would be choosing a mix of all these instruments whereby the effective post-tax yield can be near 7 per cent annually. That would largely take care of your monthly expenses.

'The rest of the income set up will have to be done from the ₹3 crore that is expected shortly. The annual portion of the expenses will also need to be set up from this.

'You need to keep your expenses in check as the corpus available needs to meet all your goals and expenses. We need to invest properly to ensure that the corpus grows, and comes handy to meet future goals,' I concluded.

We discussed a bit more on this and completed the process needed to make all the investments. She seemed relieved.

I printed out a listing of the investments already done as well as the amounts that were being kept aside for contingencies and liquidity purposes for her record. I also gave her the timetable of when what amounts would come in. Again, this seemed to be comforting for her.

Before leaving, she told me apologetically that she had not understood many of the things I had patiently explained. But, she optimistically added, she would learn as we go along.

17

PLANNING FOR RETIREMENT

I had received a call the previous day from someone called Kala. She said she had been following my blogs for a long time.

She wanted to meet me and asked if I ever came to Pune, for that is where she lived. I explained to her our remote model through which we served clients, wherever they were, from our office in Mumbai. She then said that she was retiring in another eight months and wanted to plan her retirement phase well. She was a senior professional in an automobile company in Pune in the HR department. She wanted to come over and meet me once. I told her that she was welcome at our office.

She had informed me that she was single and her mother lived with her. I understood from her that she had a sister residing in the US, who had two children. Her sister had been living there for over twenty years.

Today, Kala was expected in about fifteen minutes. I was polishing a blog post I was writing. A new angle became apparent to me in that almost finished blog. How come it had not occurred to me earlier, I thought to myself. I was engrossed in giving shape to the piece, when Kala walked in.

I welcomed her and ushered her immediately into my office. She seemed a bit tired. I offered her water. After ordering some juice for her, we settled down.

I invited her to tell me about herself in more detail and exactly what she looked forward to getting from the engagement. Sometimes, planners assume that the client may want something and we ultimately find out to our surprise that they are indeed looking for something quite different. Hence, it is best to allow them to talk and clearly tell us what they are looking for in terms of planning, and what specifically they are expecting from us as advisors.

Kala started. 'I was born in Pune, grew up there, did my college education—all in Pune. As luck would have it, I got a job in Pune and my entire working life, I have been there. Except for brief travels outside the city, I have been a faithful Punekar.

'I have not been able to travel much these days as my mother is quite old now, about eighty-five, and finds it difficult to travel. Hence, my travels have reduced considerably in the past five years.

'Regarding finances, I have been investing on my own. I would not call myself financially savvy. But I'm not as bad as some of my friends, whose knowledge of financial investments starts and ends with FDs and PPF. Having said that, I do acknowledge my limited knowledge in this area and see the clear need for a professional to guide me.

'This has been a niggling worry, especially as my retirement is due now. Till the time the income flow is on, there is no worry. I worry about the time when the income will stop and I will have to dip into my savings. My savings, I reckon, are decent given that my lifestyle has been quite modest and I have been single.

'I would like to understand first whether the wealth I have created is enough to see me through post-retirement comfortably. I do not have any significant pension income in retirement, except for the superannuation pension amount that is expected to come.

'I would like you to take a look at my investments and see what needs to be done so that my retirement phase can go through without a hitch,' she said and paused.

That was my cue. I asked her if, after eight months, she may be asked to continue to work. She said that was a possibility, and she may work as a consultant for a couple of years.

This happens a lot in organisations, and I was not surprised at all. I asked her whether she would be interested in taking it up.

Kala said that she had not really thought about it. But if they wanted her to continue for a couple of years, she might.

I asked her, 'You have come to me to ensure a well-funded retirement period. While that is very important, have you figured out what you will be doing after you retire? This is very important as you have been busy with your corporate life all through. Suddenly, when you stop working full-time, there may be a lot of time on your hands.

'Many people view this positively since free time is hard to come by when one is actively employed. While there will undoubtedly be a lot of free time after retirement, you will need to see how you will keep yourself occupied.'

Kala replied without skipping a beat. 'I have been working continuously for almost thirty-seven years. I think if I stop working, I will enjoy it.'

I used a different tack. 'Let us assume that you retired a week ago. What would your daily schedule look like?' I queried.

She thought about this a little bit. She said she might sleep a bit more in the mornings, go for a long walk, freshen up, prepare and have breakfast, read the paper and relax a bit. She would also take care of her mother and cook some lunch. A bit of relaxed reading, some TV, some music may follow lunch. A siesta after that. In the evening there would be tea and some snacks. Then again, she might go for a walk, visit some of her friends once in a while and come back by 7 p.m. or so. Then prepare some supper, watch TV, have dinner and go to bed. This would be her typical day, she said.

She mentioned that during the year, she might also travel a bit. She reiterated that due to her mother's advanced age, it would be very restricted. But it could still happen. For instance, she had gone to Mahabaleshwar for a couple of days about six months ago, which even her mother had enjoyed, she said.

'Well, it looks like you have mapped out what you might be doing,' I said. 'That's very good indeed. But what looks good for one day may not be so great, day after day, for the rest of one's life. I'm not saying this in a judgemental way.

'When they retire, people do all those things they had always dreamed of—travel, go on morning walks, meet friends, read, watch TV, movies, go to the occasional concert, parties—the works. But many tire of this routine fairly fast. It gets boring after a couple of months.

'There are only so many friends to meet. The walk and scanning the newspaper may occupy a couple of hours. The household chores make one dream of office again! Time looms large on the horizon.

'TV therapy is the inevitable outcome. After some time, the shouting matches on TV and the laboured soaps also lose their allure. The retirement bliss that one was anticipating morphs into a long, boring vacation.

'It is important that you understand how you would spend your retirement years. These years are a significant portion of one's life, and it is important one makes them vibrant and enjoyable. You may be wondering now why I'm talking about your life in the retirement phase when you have come to me for planning the finances for your retirement.

'We have found that planning what you will do in retirement is much more important than planning your investments. Retired life should be happy, peaceful and contented, and not boring, monotonous and an aimless drift till death.'

I then asked her if there were any hobbies she had, any pursuit that interested her that she may want to take up, any activity or vocation that might engage her productively in this phase of life.

This set her thinking. She was silent for about a minute. I did not want to disturb her train of thought.

Finally, she said, 'It is interesting that you raise this. I had not thought through this aspect. I now understand that this is something I need to give more attention to. Sorting the money question is something that you may be able to handle. I'm sure of that. Veer had talked highly of you.'

Now this was new information for me. I always thought that she has been following my blogs, and that's how she contacted me. Now she said that Veer had referred me.

'Are you referring to Veeraraghavan?' I asked. She said no. She was referring to Bharat. He was popularly known as Veer amongst his friends and colleagues. I also knew that, but I called him by his real name Bharat, and hence was not able to make the connection.

Bharat had been a client for about eleven years now. She then told me that it was Veer who had forwarded some of the blogs I had written and nudged her to keep reading them so that she could get financially aware.

She said, 'Veer has been telling me to sort out my finances, get a financial plan done and take ongoing professional advice. I have been postponing it, as I have been busy with my work. I have delayed it quite a bit. I have approached you virtually at the eleventh hour. But as they say, better late than never.' She smiled.

I explained the process that we would follow and told her to fill out the information sheet, which would be the basis of the plan. She told me that her case was quite simple, and she took out a printout that contained all her investments.

I glanced through it. Some things were missing. I told her that my team would put those things in an information sheet and send it to her so that she could provide the missing details.

She was fine with that. She wanted to know the fee. I quoted a ballpark figure and told her that I would wait till I took a detailed look at the information before I make a determination about the amount of work involved and the complexity. Based on that, the fee would be charged, I informed her. She was fine with this. She took leave and was gone.

I had touched upon the topic of what she should do in retirement. One of the things I keep saying to those who are about to retire is to make some meaningful contribution to society after retirement. I wanted to introduce this topic to her, as this was directly relevant and contextual for her.

Taming boredom and making a difference during retirement: At retirement, many are in good health and still productive and would be able to contribute. It would be a shame for such people to just stop working one day. Retirement at fifty-eight or sixty is an artificial finish line which was set in an era where the human life expectancy itself was in the sixties.

Today's retirees, who were busy till the other day, are suddenly deemed too old to work. Till retirement, they would have been leading very busy lives.

Suddenly stopping work creates a huge void. Time seems to stand still. Many experience the feeling of worthlessness, being unwanted. This kind of feeling brings a strain on existing relationships and hangs like a pall of gloom. They begin to wonder why the retirement they had been romanticising is so starkly different. But it need not have to be like this.

There are things which one has always wanted to do, which got relegated to the background while working. One can pursue those—be it music, spirituality, yoga, travel, etc.

Again, many people have the intention to contribute to society. And many people contribute to philanthropic causes with money. People in their retirement can contribute their time as well. They would have a wealth of experience, which they can lend to any organisation or activity they want to be a part of.

Identifying causes: Each person may have an area that interests them—be it environment, spirituality, social, political, consumer causes and so on. One needs to identify these first. There could be more than one area one may be interested in. The next step is to figure out the areas to focus their energies on, and how much time one would want to allocate to it.

Once the area is identified, one needs to find the right platform and people to do that work with. Once that is identified, one will be able to channel energy and time to worthwhile causes, making a difference to society. This is one important way to contribute.

Lighting the torch: There are other ways as well. Each one of us has worked all our lives and might have some specialised knowledge that will be useful to others. We need to seek to pass that on, instead of just killing time.

An automobile production engineer, for instance, would have a wealth of expertise in that domain. Instead of teaching children in a school after retirement (lot of people want to do this, which is not bad at all, but not the best use of their knowledge base and their potential to make a difference), he would be doing society and the industry a great service if that knowledge and skill can be transferred properly.

It would be like one lamp lighting another. Unfortunately, this is not happening in a large percentage of cases, which is a considerable loss. Even business organisations are not systematically capturing the knowledge that walks out of the door at retirement.

In the book, *Die Empty*, one of the things that the author, Todd Henry, deals with is passing on knowledge or ideas before we wander into the netherworld. This seems simple. But if we all end up doing this, it will make a world of difference. The impact that this can have on the society would be transformational.

Enlightened altruism: After retirement, we all want to spend our time meaningfully, want to contribute and be a part of the mainstream. Philanthropy, in terms of just donating money, is one way to give back to society. Engaging in heartfelt passions is another way.

Apart from this, giving back one's accumulated knowledge, ideas and wisdom enriches societies and communities much more and leaves a legacy.

Lighting the torch by being a mentor and guru is the ultimate way to pass on Aloha—passing on a blessing without expecting anything in return.

I resolved to send all these thoughts to Kala as they were very relevant to her, considering the stage she was in.

18

GETTING THE NUTS AND BOLTS OF RETIREMENT RIGHT

Retirement is a point when we see many people getting jittery. This is certainly understandable since it is a significant phase change.

After working for thirty-five years or more, one abruptly stops work. People crib about their work, lack of work–life balance, they are also fed up with the humdrum work routine, the 'yes sir' culture that inevitably becomes a part of life, the stress that comes with today's high-pressure jobs, the toll it takes on one's health, office politics which are disempowering and other reasons.

Many people hence publicly claim that they look forward to retiring. But when the time for retirement comes, they demur.

For many, their work identity is the one they have built over the years and are known by. The set routine of going to the office is well-established and comforting, the work is well-defined and, for many, it is a vibrant and stimulating environment, despite what one may choose to say about their workplace.

It is only when one retires that one understands how much they had identified themselves with their work, how absorbing and engaging it was or at least helped in productively deploying one's time, despite their complaints.

Retirement is a sudden vacuum in one's life. Unless one has properly thought through what they intended to do in retirement, it will get difficult.

Those are the real challenges one faces in retirement. Most are not prepared for this and assume that the retirement period will be enjoyable.

Let us come back to retirement planning in financial terms.

Those of us who are working will need to understand and appreciate that we all have to retire one day. And on that day, we need to have enough wealth to take care of all the requirements in retirement.

During youth, one would need to rein in the excesses (with relation to money) and remember that we all have to retire one day—just that it is somewhere beyond the horizon for now. We will all get there one day. We need to make the choices necessary to ensure a fully funded retirement.

Coming to terms with retirement funding

Chasing the chimaera of early retirement: Retirement planning is serious business, even if one retires at the normal superannuation age of sixty.

I see this emerging trend of early retirement. Many want to retire as early as forty-five! Early retirement can be challenging financially and tough to plan, unless the family is willing to make adjustments in their lifestyle.

If one retires early, the survival period is longer, and one also needs to provide for many goals like children's education, which would not have got completed.

Hence, one needs a bigger corpus to retire. However, since one is retiring early, they need to build a bigger corpus much earlier in life, which is a tough task.

Retirement corpus illustration: Let us take a typical case and run some numbers. Amey is a forty-year-old and his family is spending ₹60,000 a month today. Assuming an inflation of 6 per cent, that would be ₹1.92 lakh per month after twenty years.

Age (years)	Expense (per month)	Inflation assumed	Expense at age 60 (₹)
40	60,000	6%	1,92,000

Normally, expenses do come down after retirement, as children's education would be over, lifestyle expenses would moderate, local commute would come down, etc. Due to this, we can reasonably assume a 25 per cent drop in expenses. (See table on page 186.)

Despite taking that into account, the monthly expenses would still be ₹1.44 lakh, adjusting for inflation of about 6 per cent. Assuming a twenty-five-year survival period and investment returns of 7 per cent per annum, the corpus required would be ₹3.85 crore. If Amey wants to travel or indulge in any way or leave an inheritance, the corpus would need to be much higher.

Now, if Amey retires at fifty, he would need to provide for children's education too, from his corpus. Let us say the amount needed for that in today's terms is about ₹50 lakh. A rough calculation of corpus required at fifty (assuming expenses remain same till sixty and then drops by 25 per cent) would be about

₹3.14 crore (adding about ₹50 lakh of education goals, which most likely would come after retirement). (See table on page 186.)

You see, the corpus needed at fifty is still a massive one, but it is needed ten years earlier.

Early retirement is not that easy as people think it is. Many believe that since they are earning very well, they can retire early. But most of them also build a lifestyle and goals to match their income. Hence, they may be able to build a good corpus early in life, but that still may not be enough to support their lofty lifestyle and goals.

Very few can make this work—I would say just 1 in a 100 can retire at fifty and still be well funded.

Saving potential peaks between fifty years and sixty years: The other thing that people have to understand is that the saving potential between the ages of fifty and sixty is very high.

Most people would have paid off all their loans, their incomes would be quite high, most things are well-settled by this time and further new expenses one incurs when young (for instance, setting up a home) are not there.

Due to all this, a rough calculation indicates that one will be able to save in the years between fifty and sixty what one has saved in life all along till that point, maybe even more! Hence, this is an important period in life from a financial standpoint, and one should think properly before retiring prematurely.

Fuzzy and fancy ideas: Let's say it were possible. Most people have not figured out what they want to do after they retire. When asked, they give vague answers—pursue their passion, teach in schools, travel extensively, start something and work at a leisurely pace, etc.

Retirement age	Inflation assumed	Expense at age 60 (₹)	Age till survival (years)	Yield assumed	Corpus required at 60 (₹)
60	6%	1,44,000	85	7%	3,85,00,000

Retirement age	Expenses till age 60 (₹)	Corpus at 50 to take care of expenses between the ages of 50 and 60 (₹)	Education goal expense required at the age of 50 (₹)	Expenses from age 60 (drops by 25%) (₹)	Corpus at the age of 50 to take care of expenses from the ages of 60 to 85 (₹)	Total corpus required at age 50 (₹)
50	60,000	68,68,236	50,00,000	45,000	1,95,71,448	3,14,39,684

These don't stand scrutiny. For instance, travelling extensively involves a lot of cash. If they do that for five years, their corpus will start dwindling sharply.

Teaching in schools is not a walk in the park. It requires real interest and total dedication, and nine out of ten would chicken out within the first six months. Most end up filling up the time watching TV and wondering what to do with those hours weighing on them.

The howler is the one where they want to start something and work at a leisurely pace!

When one starts up a consultancy or any venture, one needs to put one's heart and soul into it to get it off the ground, work endless hours—keeping the cock company as it announces the day's arrival and be at it to hear the owls toot in the stillness of the night! If this looks like a leisurely pace, all the best!

All one can say is that it's a fad to want to retire early and do one's own thing. It sounds cool—certainly. But it is difficult to make it fly. If properly examined, it's not even desirable. If all one wants is to work, why not continue working where one is currently engaged? Why resign and then struggle at the end of the career, when one can enjoy the fruits of one's work till that point?

Some say that they are fed up and want to retire to a restful life. But that is precisely what one is going to do after sixty—for decades. Why advance that?

Getting the basics of retirement planning right

Planning for retirement should start early: We have already tackled the early retirement bit. What should be done early is planning for retirement and saving for it right from the beginning.

For young people, retirement is something that's a long way off. So long that most don't give a thought to it. But it is the single biggest goal that we all have. Yet we neglect it and make it subservient to the flimsiest of desires, like going on a vacation or buying a fancy gaming laptop. Most people will have no qualms dipping into the retirement corpus for fulfilling such desires.

We do not understand the enormity of the goal. This goal is very important.

As we saw in Amey's example, if he were to retire after twenty years, at the age of sixty, and were to live to the age of eighty-five years, he'd need ₹3.85 crore (assuming a 7 per cent return on it) at his retirement only for his expenses in the post-retirement period, with nothing left to leave as inheritance.

We see that the amounts involved are astronomical and we cannot take retirement lightly. There is no need to get worried and deflated though, diligence and regularity will help scale this summit too.

Saving for retirement: Let us look at how to get to such astronomical numbers. The first way to tackle this is to start early. It becomes a lot easier when one starts saving for retirement funding early in life.

That also presents an opportunity to invest in assets like equity, which can offer the best long-term returns, though they may be volatile in the short term.

The earlier one starts investing for retirement, the better is the benefit of compounding and higher the possibility of reaching the desired corpus. Even modest amounts put aside early on and increased slowly over time for retirement will eventually accumulate to a big amount.

Here is an example—Ashok (twenty-five years) starts saving ₹2,000 per month via mutual fund SIPs and keeps it at the same level till twenty-nine. At thirty, he increases it to ₹5,000 per month. Every five years, he increases the amount by ₹5,000 per month till he is fifty-five years old, and he contributes at this level till he is sixty years old. Sounds unremarkable, right?

But this would swell to ₹1.83 crore (assuming a 7 per cent return) at his retirement, when he is sixty.

ASHOK'S EXAMPLE

Yield assumed: 7% per annum

Age (years)	Contribution (monthly, ₹)	Till age (years)	Corpus (₹)
25	2,000	29	1,40,000
30	5,000	34	5,60,000
35	10,000	39	15,10,000
40	15,000	44	32,10,000
45	20,000	49	59,82,000
50	25,000	54	1,02,70,000
55	30,000	60	1,83,00,000
Retirement corpus @ age of 60			1,83,00,000

Now, let's say Ashok missed investing from the age of twenty-five to the age of thirty-four and spends the amount of ₹4.2 lakh, which he would have otherwise invested in this period. But from age thirty-five onwards he invests as in the previous example. The corpus at the end would be lower by ₹34 lakh, even though the amount he missed investing was only ₹4.2 lakh!

ASHOK'S EXAMPLE

Yield assumed: 7% per annum

Age (years)	Contribution (monthly, ₹)	Till age (years)	Corpus (₹)
35	10,000	39	7,16,000
40	15,000	44	20,90,000
45	20,000	49	43,95,000
50	25,000	54	80,20,000
55	30,000	60	1,49,00,000
Retirement corpus @ age of 60			**1,49,00,000**

Let us say Ashok realises the need for a retirement fund accumulation much later in life and starts saving only from the age of forty-five. The amount to be invested to reach ₹1.83 crore would be a whooping ₹52,000 per month.

Compounding is called the eighth wonder of the world. Now you know why. Allow it to work for you.

Never touch this corpus: Since retirement is seen as something far away in the future, most people withdraw money from their retirement funds. They dip into them for celebrating anniversaries, birthdays, vacations, children's education, home renovation, loaning to relatives, etc. The result is that the retirement corpus at the end of the period tends to be a rather small number, which would mean a life of penury in the golden years.

I had read a while ago that about 80 per cent of EPF corpus at retirement has ₹20,000 or less. Can you believe that?

If there were ever a live example of people drawing down on their retirement corpus, this is it.

It's difficult to mend it later: Most goals can be reworked or even done away with. Education goals can be scaled down, and children can borrow money. A foreign vacation can be dropped, if warranted. The type of car to be bought can be purchased in line with one's cash flows.

But in the case of the retirement goal, it obviously cannot be dropped. At best, some amount of scaling down and adjustments can be made. Beyond that—nothing. Importantly, one cannot borrow to fulfil this goal.

Hence, retirement planning needs to be approached with all the respect and caution it deserves.

No loans for this goal: Think about it—this is probably the only goal for which you cannot borrow money as a way out of the problem. For a home, car, education, vacation, etc., one can always borrow and pay later.

So, this is a goal that calls for a significant corpus. It is hence imperative to save from the very beginning for this goal.

Some people nonchalantly think that their kids might take care of them in their old age, since they have invested so much in them. But that can be a serious mistake, as how the future will pan out is not known.

Things have changed substantially from the time when this was the popular thought and begetting a son was the only retirement planning that was needed.

Gargantuan amounts of water have flowed since then and things have changed. Now, we should all be prepared to fend for ourselves. It is possible that children may support their parents in the future as well, but one's retirement strategy cannot be that.

That makes this goal a unique and a critical one to plan for. We need to give it the mind share it truly deserves.

Put the security nets in place: One needs to have the right health insurance in place. Many have group medical insurance until they are employed. All the same, they should take adequate cover several years before retirement so that any pre-existing illnesses, too, will get covered from the time they retire.

Ideally, one should get a personal medical insurance policy, apart from the company-given policy, before attaining the age of forty itself. This is suggested as getting medical insurance would become difficult as one's age advances and illnesses or adverse medical conditions manifest. In such situations, it is difficult to get past the medical tests and get a policy.

The other important thing to keep in mind is the requirement of a good medical contingency fund, which could come in handy if the medical insurance is inadequate or does not cover certain portions of the expenses.

The other fund to keep aside would be a liquidity fund that one may use for any spikes in expenses or other unplanned expenses. Expenses themselves should be kept in check, the portfolio reviewed from time to time and adjustments should be made to the asset allocation, as necessary.

When these security nets are in place, half the battle is won. The remaining half is in putting this advice to action.

Living too long: Paradoxically, this is going to be a major problem for many. The survival period post-retirement has now increased to decades, and is not just a few years long as it had been earlier.

People tend to joke that they may live for just a few years after retirement and then get a one-way ticket to meet the maker. The number of breaths we have in retirement is not in our hand, and we cannot blithely ignore the peril of living long and not having the financial resources to sustain ourselves.

Having said all of this, many people still reach the finish line called retirement without sufficient funds.

What can one do if the retirement corpus is not big enough?

Continue work after superannuation: This may be a stupid idea from my side. I agree. For a vast majority, this may not work. Getting employed after sixty is going to be challenging, with a capital C. Also, one's health might not permit such work. The easiest is to seek to extend one's tenure with the current employer itself. That may probably be the best option for continued employment in retirement.

Some very skilled people may offer their services as consultants. But then, this is not going to work for everyone. Others who need to work for a few more years may look at internet-based jobs which do not require them to travel and can be done from home. This could probably be a very easy option for professionals like doctors, lawyers, architects, CAs, etc., who can continue working for as long as they want.

Relocate: One can always consider relocating to another town to bring down costs. Selling off properties in big towns or cities may free up some money, even after buying a home in a smaller town. Also, the cost of living could be lower in a smaller town, which can help. But here, one may have to leave behind a known place and friends—which may make it a difficult decision.

Cut down on expenses: One can cut down on expenses by scaling down one's requirements. This may mean a comedown in terms of lifestyle, which could be an option where none other exists.

Reverse mortgage: There are many senior citizens who are asset-rich, but cash-poor. For these people, their home is their biggest asset. Such people can borrow against their home equity.

A regular income which is typically referred to as an annuity can be set up for up to fifteen years, which can help greatly. Also, they can continue to live in their homes for as long as they live.

But reverse mortgage is not all that popular in India, as the house should not be more than fifteen years old, the annuity will be calculated on a lower value compared to the value of the home, the interest rate charged is high, etc. Hence, it may be a better idea to simply sell the home, instead of doing a reverse mortgage.

Let's hope we don't have to resort to any of these. Let's give fiscal prudence the pride of place in our lives and avoid Grecian tragedies.

Where do you invest for retirement planning?

Now that we have looked at pension plans in detail, and have concluded that these are at best secondary supporting options, we need to look at options that help create a good retirement corpus which can be used to set up an income during the retirement phase.

There is no single product that we would recommend. We need a bouquet of products that together would help in retirement funding.

This may be desirable as asset allocation may need to change over time, which can be easily accommodated if one is investing in a bouquet of products.

Laddering option with insurance plans

Insurance agents offer laddering as a solution. They may suggest twenty endowment policies which will mature every year in retirement, ensuring that there is some inflow every year.

While that looks fine on the face of it, there are problems with that. Firstly, endowment policies tend to offer 4.5–6 per cent returns. The returns are low, though tax-free.

The problem is present from the start. One would be getting into low-yielding insurance products and would invest continuously for a long period. Investing in a low-yielding product for the long term would create a much smaller corpus at the end.

For instance, if one were contributing ₹10,000 per month for twenty years and one product yields 6.5 per cent and another 10 per cent, the corpus at the end of twenty years would be ₹49 lakh and ₹76 lakh, respectively. The difference is of ₹27 lakh. The corpus in the latter case would be 55 per cent more. (See table on page 196.)

Also, when one is putting money into insurance, there is no flexibility. One needs to pay consistently for a very long period, which can be a positive too. But with life situations being as fluid as they are today, we need the flexibility to change investment amounts as we go—or even skip payments, if necessary. The other problem is that all investments here are in debt products, which is the reason for low returns in the first place.

To sum it up, it is better to avoid setting up an income stream through insurance plans for they are rigid, inflexible, low yielding and without the possibility of diversification and hence a concentration risk.

A bouquet of investment products may be the way out. In this case, we will be able to rejig the portfolio of products as per the

Monthly contribution (₹)	Investment period (years)	Yield	Corpus in hand after 20 years (₹)	Difference in corpus (₹)	Difference of corpus (%)
10,000	20				
Product 1: Yield		6.50%	49,00,000	27,00,000	55%
Product 2: Yield		10%	76,00,000		

unfolding future and the changing asset allocation requirements over time.

Relying on fixed income products alone: Many make this classic mistake. They want all their money parked in FDs, bonds, small savings schemes and the like, which are low on risk. But these instruments offer returns that are subject to income tax. Hence, the wealth build-up is rather slow and eventually low.

Post-tax returns hardly beat inflation, and there is no real growth of money after accounting for inflation if one is dependent predominantly on such fixed return products. There needs to be a proper mix of fixed return products that offer lower returns with low risks and other products like equity and equity mutual funds which may carry higher risks but also offer much higher returns. Getting the asset mix right in one's portfolio at various points is what becomes critical.

If people are wary of investing in growth assets like equity-oriented products in the run-up to retirement, they are even more scared to invest anything in growth assets during retirement.

These people wrongly believe that in retirement, they should not take any risk. The biggest risk in retirement is not taking the required level of risk, so that the corpus lasts through one's lifetime.

Income from real estate: Many people invest in real estate to fund their retirement. There are many ideas here. Some people buy land, which they would like to sell for a handsome profit later to fund significant goals, including retirement. While this is fine on the face of it, there are problems here too.

Land appreciation is overhyped. While some land parcels appreciate very well, it is not true across the board. Also, land is prone to encroachment, as many people do not keep close tabs on their property.

Residential and commercial properties are better in that respect. But again, the appreciation is not good across the board, and one can get caught on the wrong foot. For instance, in the past several years, properties in many areas in Hyderabad, Bengaluru and Delhi NCR have given poor returns and, in some cases, negative returns, which would come as a surprise to many. And these are not isolated cases. Several areas across India have offered negative or anaemic returns, making property investments not such a great option.

In the case of properties, one may spend on interiors, upkeep, taxes, registration and stamp duty, brokerage, etc., which are generally not factored in the final returns. Also, most people do not count the interest paid on their loans, which adds to the cost of property. After factoring all of these, the final returns may not be all that great when the property is sold. Further, there are taxes to be paid on the sale.

The other intractable problem is the illiquid nature of property. One may not be able to sell property when needed, making it a difficult asset class.

If one keeps the property for rental returns, residential property offers about 2–3 per cent returns on the market price, and commercial property offers 4–8 per cent, all of which is taxable. Then there are maintenance costs, property taxes and income taxes on rent earned that need to be paid too.

This makes the yields drop to half of the gross rental yield.

Which fixed return products are suitable? As per the tenets of asset allocation, we need to invest a portion in fixed return products at every point. Hence, during the accumulation phase, when one is earning, some allocation will be there for fixed income products.

Choosing the right instruments to invest in is important. For retirement, one will have to invest in products that are tax-efficient and are essentially long-term products suited for a goal like retirement funding, as well as somewhat difficult to access.

EPF and PPF are right fits for the retirement goal. These are long-term instruments, which are not very easy to dip into and are tax-efficient.

NPS is also a good choice for retirement funding. It ticks almost all the boxes—good diversification within the product itself, can normally be accessed only at the age of sixty, offers tax deductions for contributions as we have seen earlier, has no restrictions on how much one could contribute, etc. The annuity coming from this is taxable, but that is a small negative, one which I'm hoping will get negated in the future as this is a long-standing demand from the financial services fraternity.

One should contribute to these funds and forget that one has invested in them. One can dip into the above mentioned products under certain conditions; but it is not easy to just redeem like in the case of an FD or mutual fund schemes. This inbuilt rigidity is a plus, as it stays out of bounds.

FD, NCD, bonds, etc.: For a lot of people, FD is the weapon of choice for all situations. For the short term, they will invest there; for children's education they will invest there; for retirement too, they will invest there.

The problem with FDs is that the interest rates are modest and become far more modest as they go through the shredder called income tax. Most bank FDs are offering just about 6–7 per cent a year now. A person in the 30 per cent tax bracket would end up with less than 5 per cent returns. These returns would not even beat inflation.

However, I'm not against FDs just because they offer low returns but because they are low-risk instruments as well.

To push up the returns, one may look at high-quality corporate FDs, which have the potential to offer an extra 0.5–1 per cent annual return, though the risks involved even in high-quality corporate FDs are somewhat higher than in bank FDs.

Perpetual bonds and NCDs would be available from the secondary market. They may be available at around the same rates or at slightly more attractive rates as compared to good quality corporate FDs. One could look at these as a part of the overall debt portfolio.

One could even consider zero-coupon bonds, if available, as these tend to be long-term products and are suited well for the long-term goal of retirement. Not currently available, but would be good products to consider when they do become available.

Tax-free bonds are long-term products again which one can look at. Current yields are low and hence locking in on the returns now may not be worthwhile.

Debt funds: Debt mutual fund schemes are the other product category suited for inclusion in one's debt portfolio. When investing for the long term, one could choose medium to long-term duration debt funds.

Debt mutual fund schemes also lend themselves to setting up a stable income during retirement. We can set up systematic withdrawals from debt funds. Systematic withdrawal plan (SWP) is drawing down a specific amount on a regular basis (say monthly) for a period of your choice.

This is like setting up an annuity as per your convenience and drawdown requirements. If we set up a withdrawal which would be less than the annual interest, it can be sustained in perpetuity.

Some people are not comfortable with debt funds because the returns are not fixed. The reason is that there are many underlying debt investments in a debt mutual fund scheme, which are all traded and hence the net asset value (NAV) can fluctuate.

But they will largely mirror the interest rate in the system and hence will revert to the mean, even if it deviates in between. Debt funds are open-ended, and can be liquidated if there is an urgency, which is a great positive.

These schemes no longer enjoy the LTCG tax treatment, after three years from April 2023. Any redemption is treated as STCG now.

Even so, they are tax-efficient as withdrawals are treated as redemptions. One needs to pay taxes on the difference between the purchase price and sale price of the units. Hence, if one withdraws the returns one has got from time to time, the tax amount is very low and the effective tax is in single-digit. SWP is, therefore, a very useful and effective retirement income set-up tool.

Equity-oriented products: Till now, I have only mentioned fixed income products. But we need to invest some money in growth-oriented assets, like equity mutual funds, to ensure that your portfolio grows and can offer returns above inflation.

For that one needs to take risks early on and think long-term. We need to allocate resources to equities and equity-oriented funds early in life. They may be volatile. But they perform over time.

Starting monthly investments in good equity mutual funds would be a good place to start. The kind of equity funds that may be suggested for someone depends on their risk tolerance levels.

For those who are conservative, large-cap-oriented mutual funds, hybrid schemes (which have a mix of equity and debt investments) and index funds would be good fits. For those who can stomach a bit more risk, multi-cap or flexi-cap funds, value funds, thematic funds and international funds are suggested for the long term.

For an aggressive investor, small-cap and midcap funds, sectoral funds and a higher preponderance of international funds can also be suggested.

As time goes by, these allocations need to be reviewed and appropriate changes need to be made. Changes should be made only if it is essential.

Getting the asset allocation right is what is important to ensure financial well-being—not chasing returns. Seek professional help, where necessary.

Equities have delivered over the long term—the Sensex has given more than 16 per cent returns in over forty years. There have been periods when the returns from the stock market have been low—for three, five, seven, even ten years. That's precisely why you need to give it time. Investing early and staying invested for long periods really helps.

The much vaunted property investments work just for that reason. Just because price discovery is difficult, it is illiquid, there are taxation issues, etc., people keep it for a long time—and then they gloat that they have got great returns from their property. Equities, if held for such long periods as properties often are, would beat the daylights out of them, eight times out of ten.

Retirement funding through pension plans

Buying pension plans is not retirement funding

The other common investment that people make for retirement is a pension plan. Many times, pension plans are seen as the best way to save for the retirement years. However, doing it through pension plans is inefficient. For one, pension annuities are taxable.

If one goes for a traditional pension plan, the corpus grows at a measly 4–6 per cent, ensuring that the corpus build-up is glacial. Unit-linked pension plans (ULIPs) can potentially give better returns, but the risk in the underlying investment is with the investor.

Commutation of pension is possible between 25 per cent and 33 per cent, without tax. In case of the National Pension System (NPS) from the Government of India, the amount that can be withdrawn is 60 per cent, pre-tax, at the time of vesting (when the annuity or regular income will start). The balance amount will have to be deployed so that it may offer a regular income in the form of annuities. Annuities are taxable as income, making them a poor choice.

Traditional plans can offer annuities of between 5 and 7 per cent return on the corpus accumulated. But in all cases, annuities are taxable. Also, annuities remain the same throughout life, making them less meaningful as time goes by.

Hence, if your predominant vehicle for retirement funding is through annuities, you can never hope to hold your head high (unlike the *Sar uthake jiyo* pitch of pension plans). Annuities are at best a secondary option—not primary.

When do pension plans make sense?

Pension plans may be fine in certain situations.

For those whose incomes are modest and may not come in the higher tax slabs, pension plans may still make sense. This may also be suited to people with a modest risk appetite.

Also, if the person concerned is not very financially savvy or is profligate, a pension plan may be a good fit, as it gives a steady annuity income for as long as that person lives.

There is nothing much one needs to do in a pension plan, once it has commenced. This makes it a good fit for those who want a simple product that does not need any interventions like renewing or reinvesting in another instrument.

However, the person receiving an annuity will need to produce a life certificate at certain intervals to prove that they are alive and hence can continue receiving the amount. This is the only thing the person receiving an annuity needs to do.

We have already discussed the merits of going in for a retirement home. Buying one in advance and putting it on rent till retirement may not be a great option; also, the house weathers down and may require repairs by the time one retires and moves in. Our thoughts about where to settle down itself can change over time and hence one should consider it closer to retirement and not too much in advance.

National Pension Scheme

NPS is an annuity plan from the Government of India. There are several advantages that NPS offers over a regular pension plan.

Let us first understand the features of NPS and what is unique about this pension plan that is getting a lot of attention these days.

Firstly, there are three funds into which one can contribute. There is an equity fund (E), government securities fund (G), corporate bond fund (C) and alternative investment fund (A).

One may exercise an active fund choice where one can choose the funds to invest in. One has the option to select the funds, subject to certain limits. For instance, in the case of E, one can invest a maximum of 75 per cent of one's assets there. In the other two funds, C & G, the investment can go all the way to 100 per cent. However, for the A fund, which is a new asset class, it is limited to just up to 5 per cent.

There is also a passive investing option called Auto Choice lifecycle option where the proportion of investments in the funds is predefined. As per one's age, the equity portion in the portfolio will keep coming down.

Even in the lifecycle option, there is an Aggressive Lifecycle Fund (LC-75), where the equity allocation can be up to 75 per cent till the age of thirty-five, and then will start going down slowly. This is well suited for young investors in their twenties who want to invest aggressively.

There is a Conservative Lifecycle Fund (LC-25), where the starting equity exposure itself will be 25 per cent. This may be more suited to older, conservative investors.

Then, the original Automatic Lifecycle option (LC-50) is also available where the equity exposure can be no more than 50 per cent. This was the one that was available originally.

Lifecycle funds are good for those who do not want to get involved in choosing the funds, monitoring their performance, and changing the constituents as one goes along.

The flexibility does not end there. Currently, there are eight pension fund managers. The subscriber can choose the one whom they want to manage their funds.

On attaining the age of sixty, the subscriber can choose an annuity service provider to receive the annuity from.

One of the major talking points of NPS is its extremely low charges. The total charges, including fund management charges, asset service charges, etc., would come to about 0.1 per cent a year, which is comparable to charges in ETFs and low-cost index funds.

The very low charges in NPS translate to better-retained earnings in the fund and work in favour of the subscriber, over time.

Account type and contribution

You can invest a minimum of ₹1,000 in a year. There is no upper limit to one's contribution, unlike in a PPF or Post Office Monthly Income Schemes (POMIS) and so on.

There are two kinds of accounts that one can open in NPS: Tier 1 and Tier 2.

Tier 1 is a pension account in which money contributed accumulates until sixty years of age after which one can receive an annuity. One has the option to defer receiving the annuity until seventy.

During the contribution period, money invested in NPS can be withdrawn for specific purposes like a child's education or wedding, home construction and onset of a critical illness, if the account is at least three years old. The amount that can be withdrawn would be 25 per cent of one's contribution up until that point.

However, if one wants to exit NPS before sixty years, one can take out 20 per cent of the corpus. The remaining 80 per cent will be annuitised when the subscriber turns sixty years old.

Tier 2 account is an investment account where one may contribute and withdraw any amount at will. The investment returns from this account are fully taxable.

Taxation benefits available from NPS and other pension funds

Contributions to the tune of ₹1.5 lakh in a pension fund (including NPS) come under section 80C. The following two special provisions are available only for NPS.

Additional ₹50,000 contribution to NPS is available as a deduction under section 80CCD (1B).

Employers can contribute up to 10 per cent of the basic salary to NPS, and the whole contribution would be tax deductible (under section 80 CCD (1A)), without limits.

When should one opt for NPS and pensions plans from insurance companies?

NPS is a good tool for creating a considerable retirement fund over time. Hence, this will work well if one has time on one's side. The low cost, special tax eligibilities, choice of fund managers, etc., are positives for NPS.

NPS is a pay-as-you-go product. There is no commitment amount that needs to be necessarily paid every year, unlike in the case of pension plans where there is a commitment to pay the premium amount every year. NPS is very flexible in that sense and hence can be beneficial for many for this very reason.

If one wants to set up an immediate annuity from the retirement proceeds, then life insurance companies have pension policies to take the lumpsum amount and start offering monthly annuity amounts. These are called immediate annuity plans.

Plans like NPS where one needs to contribute for a long period of time and then start getting an annuity at some point in the future are called deferred annuity plans.

Pension plans from insurance companies, especially ULIPs, may offer even more fund choices as compared to NPS. This can be attractive for some.

Overall, NPS scores handsomely over pension plans from insurance companies on most parameters.

What are the life annuity options available?

There are various options to receive annuities and finally get back the amount accumulated by a person before the annuity starts (usually at the age of sixty). The total amount accumulated just before the annuity starts is referred to as the vesting amount, purchase price or notional cash option. There are various life annuity options which one can opt for.

One of the common options is life annuity with return of purchase price. In this option, the annuitant will get annuity for their lifetime after which the purchase price is returned to the nominee.

It is important to note that most pension plans just pay a portion of the interest they generate from the purchase price, and that is how they would be able to return the purchase price at the end of life of the annuitant.

There are other variants too. There is something called a joint life annuity with return of purchase price. In this, the annuity will be available to the annuitant and then the surviving spouse, after which the purchase price would go to the nominee.

These options are good since the annuity will be available for the entire lifetime and the vesting amount will also be returned to the nominee.

There are other options where only the annuity will be paid but the vesting amount will not be paid back.

The annuity for life option offers annuity throughout the life of the annuitant. On death, the annuity will stop, and the vesting amount will not be returned.

Similarly, there is an option called annuity-certain where the annuity will be paid for a certain period like five, ten or fifteen years. In this too, the annuitant or his nominee will receive annuity for the period chosen, even if the annuitant passes away.

If the annuitant survives the period, the annuity will be available till he is alive, after which it will stop. In this case too, the vesting amount will not be returned to the nominee.

When the vesting amount is not be returned in some of these annuity options, it would be higher when compared to options where the original accumulated amount needs to be given back to the nominee on the death of the annuitant.

If a person were to pass away just after few years after the annuity has started, they would have received but a small amount and the entire vesting amount which they had painstakingly created would go to the insurance provider.

In the other case, the original vesting amount will come back to the nominee if the annuitant were to pass away. Hence, in this case, though the annuitant has not received annuity for a long time, at least the original vesting amount will come back to the nominee.

Life annuity with return of purchase price or joint life annuity with return of purchase price are the best options to go for.

I again thought of Kala, who had triggered all these thoughts which I had now captured in my blog. This would certainly be useful to her, I thought, and sent it across to her as well.

19

THE MILLENNIALS RETURN FOR MORE MONEY LESSONS

Malvika had called me the other day to see if she could come over that day itself, towards the evening. Since it was not possible for me that day, I suggested that we meet three days later. And today was that day.

She may be coming any moment now. I was going to talk about a few other areas that may pique her curiosity and interest. I had already talked about risk earlier. I wanted to give her a download on many other areas today. I wanted to talk to her about consumer behaviour, an essential area for all of us to know. It is a critical area that needs understanding to ensure compliance, and ultimately get good outcomes.

Risk compensation, additional risk assumption and risk misperception when the risks come down are some rather puzzling behaviours that we see all the time.

Risk mitigation is an important part of ensuring a steady life. It is important to cushion against shocks in all areas of life.

However, whenever a risk-mitigation measure is taken, we have also found that people overreach and end up taking more risks. They get into the risk-compensation mode.

For instance, it has been found that those wearing helmets while riding bikes tend to be rougher riders as compared to others. That is because those wearing helmets tend to feel safer and are willing to take more risks. Seat belts similarly make the drivers speed and take tighter turns.

So, risk-mitigation tools are not always as effective as they should be when it comes to outcomes. And that is the paradox. It works like this in many areas of life.

The other thing that happens when the risk in one area comes down for a person is that they don't seem to be happy there. They invariably assume more risks. Additional risk assumption hence is the other important consumer behavioural paradox.

Also, a lot of times, we do not perceive the risks that are very much there. That is risk misperception.

We will be dealing with these three paradoxes as they apply in real life.

Children: Parents want to do everything for their children, give them the best and cushion them from the harsh realities of life. This is a classic risk-mitigation mechanism. But what really happens?

They accompany their children everywhere, robbing children of initiative and inhibiting their learning by doing everything for them. The children operate in an environment where they pretty much get everything, without so much as lifting a finger.

Their social interaction skills are stunted as they are exposed to a carefully curated audience. They are not in touch with reality and tend to develop elitist attitudes that work against them in their interactions with the real world.

The children get used to fancy schools, air-conditioned classrooms, private tuitions, access to pricey learning aids, fancy toys, branded clothes, etc. Many children do capitalise on the advantages conferred on them, score well and rise up. But does this prepare them for the real world? Hardly.

They are, in fact, unfit to operate in the real world of grime and hard work. They want sanitised environments like their parents provided them. But that is nowhere to be found. The outcome is that the children find themselves unsuited in most areas of life—work, relationships, money, etc.

Parents' risk mitigation behaviour makes the child maladjusted and creates problems for their wards in the future.

Work: When things are going well, people tend to do certain things that jeopardises everything they have. Is it boredom, hubris, search for challenges—we don't know.

Here they may be assuming unwanted risks, when the risks go down.

We have seen people at the height of their career taking unwarranted risks. For instance, they gamble by moving to another firm even though they are doing fine, are well-regarded and rewarded in the company they work.

Some want to push their luck by embarking on an entrepreneurial venture with huge risks and uncertain payoffs. There are others who indulge in an ill-fated fling with a colleague that can jeopardise their careers.

It is almost as if they do not want to enjoy the good life that they have been endowed with!

Money: A similar thing happens with money. When a person invests somewhere and makes money a few times, the person gets a feeling of invincibility and their perception of risk becomes skewed. This is risk misperception.

This is what happens in a rising market where someone invests in equity and makes money. They tend to think that they are the latest rodeo riders in the market and put in increasing amounts of money, only to find themselves thrown to the ground at some point in the future.

Apart from this, people also indulge in some money-maximising tactics and invest aggressively, without considering their risk profile. This is a combination of greed, risk misperception and unnecessary risk assumption.

They decide, for instance, that they are through with the middle-class routine of investing in mutual funds and now want to invest in Portfolio Management Services (PMS), structured products, alternate investment funds (AIF), private equity and so on.

Most people don't understand the risk–rewards inherent in their investments and simply invest based on returns it has given in the past. This adds tremendous risks in the portfolio and is an example of unnecessary risk assumption.

Again, when things are going well, the heavens seem to be smiling and one is well set to achieve their goals, people feel that urge to stretch things a bit. They want to achieve certain stretched goals, now that the going is fine. This is a voluntary risk assumption. A high-end car, grand home in a tony neighbourhood, world tours, lifestyle upgrade, etc., are some of those. There is nothing wrong with these new goals as people earn to enjoy. But some of these increase the overall risk quite significantly.

For instance, an expensive home bought on loan increases costs significantly and reduces headroom for manoeuvre. If the loan is so high that the couple needs to work for a long time, they lose their flexibility. Also, today there is the possibility of a job loss for any number of reasons, which can land them in a jam.

Then, there is this goal of educating kids abroad, which is quite common these days. The only issue is that this is by far the costliest exercise a parent can undertake. Children's education is moreover an emotive issue and parents want to fund the whole binge, costing crores.

These things individually may not upset the overall life trajectory. But a few of these together can exert tremendous financial stress.

Health: When people are on medication and things start looking up, people loosen up a bit and start becoming free-handed with starches and fats. The effect of this is not immediately evident. But it does have a delayed impact.

This is the same effect as when a person wears a helmet, he rides more rashly than he used to. Again, an example of risk compensation.

To summarise, when risk reduces in the natural course or is perceived to reduce, we get into the mode of assuming more risks.

When risks are high and we take steps to mitigate these risks, the reduced risk again compels us to take on more risks, which is risk compensation.

At certain points in life, the risks reduce and things may be going smoothly. For some people, the decreased risk makes them take up more risk, which is an example of risk assumption.

A person wearing a helmet riding more rashly is risk compensating. When a person throws away a job when everything is going well, they are assuming unwanted risks.

Many times, we perceive less risk than there is. This is risk misperception due to which we end up taking unwanted risks.

This happens quite naturally in many facets of life. It is for us to recognise and avoid taking unwanted risks. Managing risks well is a fundamental part of wellness—whether it is with money, health, work or in other areas.

I thought someone was at the door and surmised that it must be Malvika. Nor was I mistaken. But in thinking that it would only be Malvika who came, I certainly was mistaken. There were four people with Malvika. I immediately recognised Urvi and Priya. There was another girl and a boy, who were new faces for me.

Malvika sheepishly came into the cabin and told me that she had brought four of her friends this time. She said she was very sorry to impose upon my kindness and magnanimity but could do nothing as, apparently, she gave such a rousing account of my session last time that her friends certainly wanted to be there.

I told her that there was no problem. I told her that at this rate I would be conducting college classes in my office! I saw that her face had become clouded after this comment, and I realised that I might have been a bit offensive.

I told her that I was just joking and would be happy to have them here. This instantly cheered up Malvika. She waved her friends into the cabin and introduced the two I did not know. The girl Dipanjana and the boy Vignesh. With the introductions out of the way, I was ready to start.

I asked whether there was anything specific that they wanted to know. No one answered. I looked at Malvika. After a short pause, she said that maybe I could throw some light on the systematic withdrawal option of a debt fund. She said she had read up about this since the last time we met. She said she came across this concept when she was reading about debt funds and how they can be used to set up a stable income, in a tax-efficient manner.

I looked around and wanted to see if this was okay with them. Their faces were mostly inscrutable. I then actually asked whether I could take this subject up for discussion. They agreed with the plan and so I started.

Systematic Withdrawal Plan

'Systematic withdrawal is an option that can be used to good effect in a debt fund to set up an income. Systematic withdrawal is redemption of a certain amount from the debt fund in which one has invested, at a predetermined frequency.

'You might wonder what is so hot about redeeming from a fund in which one has invested in? But it does have its merits.

'For one, the tax treatment, in this case, is of capital gains, and hence the effective returns are higher. Also, one can set up the amount required as regular income, which can be done for the period of one's choice.

'Hence, this would be a good tool in the hands of someone who is looking to set up a regular income. Retired people are the ones who need regular income, and this could be a handy tool for them.

'Most retired people dip into their savings accounts or turn to bank fixed deposits to meet their regular income needs. At a time when interest rates are down, turning to bank FDs can expose a person to a significant risk called reinvestment risk.

'When the money matures, if the prevalent interest rates are down, and one needs to invest at those lower rates, it is a risk, right? This is reinvestment risk.

'There is also the taxation angle to worry about, especially if such a person were to fall in the highest tax bracket.

Benefits

'Debt mutual funds can be a better option for setting up a regular income for retirees. By opting for a systematic withdrawal plan in a debt mutual fund, investors can withdraw a pre-fixed amount from a scheme at regular intervals. SWPs are flexible and can be stopped whenever required.

'The primary benefit of using SWPs is significant tax savings vis-à-vis bank FDs. Not just bank FDs, SWPs in debt funds can also be a far superior alternative to pension plans of insurance firms. And it's not only retirees who stand to benefit.

'Anyone who wants a regular stream of income—be it those on a sabbatical, those looking to start their own business or even those simply wanting to augment their cash flows—can benefit from this option.

'Let's say one invests ₹1 lakh in a debt fund and wants to withdraw the entire 7 per cent earning on a quarterly basis (₹1,750 per quarter). The amount can be arranged by setting up an SWP. As long as the fund is growing at a rate above the level, it can sustain these regular payments for an indefinite period.

Tax advantage of SWP

'In SWPs, the units are cashed out based on the amount of money required in each instalment. In the above example, the amount cashed out is not interest income. It is just the number of units which would offer ₹1,750 per quarter.

'For tax purposes, short-term capital gains are calculated by taking the difference in NAV from the time of investment to the time it is withdrawn and multiplying it by the number of units cashed out. The gains are taxed at slab rates.

'SWPs started after investing in a debt fund leads to STCG. But even for a person in the highest tax bracket of 30 per cent (with additional cess and surcharges), the capital gains arising out of such withdrawal would be minuscule.

'Let us take the example of someone who invests ₹1 lakh in a debt mutual fund and a bank FD. For an apple-to-apple comparison, the returns from both the debt fund and the FD are taken to be 7 per cent.

'Assume the withdrawal from the debt fund is at the rate of 1.75 per cent per quarter, which is approximately what one would expect as interest income per quarter from a bank FD. Also, assume that the person falls under the 30 per cent tax bracket and no exit loads are paid. (See table on page 219.)

'The tax to be paid in the case of the FD on an interest income of ₹7,000 comes to ₹2,184. In contrast, the STCG tax for debt mutual funds on withdrawal of ₹7,000 comes to just ₹143.

'So, for FDs, the incidence of effective tax is 31.2 per cent, and for debt mutual fund the effective tax comes to just 2.04 per cent.

'In the current interest rate scenario, an FD offers a fixed return for the tenure of the investment. When interest rates go down, FD rates also decline. While reinvesting in the FD, the new rate applies.

'In case of debt funds, the underlying debt instruments go up or down in value based on the rates at which they are traded. The uncertainty in returns is something that unnerves people, but it is not as bad as it sounds. And it is nothing like the volatility seen in equities.

'The rate at which the debt instruments are traded depends on

Withdrawal option	Amount invested in debt fund (₹)	Frequency	Interest rate (assumed)	Yearly payout (₹)	Taxation (₹)	Excess tax paid in FDs (₹)	Effective tax paid
Debt SWP	1,00,000	Quarterly	7.00%	7,000	143	2,041	2.04%
FD Interest	1,00,000			7,000	2,184		31.20%

the interest rate cycle, among other things. In a falling interest rate scenario, debt funds will be positively impacted depending on the kind of debt instruments the underlying scheme holds.

Scoring over annuity plans

'An SWP in a debt fund is a far superior alternative to a pension plan. Most people invest in pension plans of insurance companies for a stable income stream. But annuity payments are taxed as income, just like FDs.

'Annuity payments also have other disadvantages. For instance, the disbursal rate in an annuity plan is typically 5–6.5 per cent per annum, which is very low. The returns are even lower when taxation is considered. What's more, annuities once started cannot be stopped, which can be a big handicap when a person wants to access their principal for an exigency.

'In contrast, SWPs in debt mutual funds can be started and stopped at any time. Also, there are a variety of debt funds to choose from, so the underlying corpus can be invested in funds that have the potential to offer much higher returns as compared to annuity plans. That's not all. The amount required from SWPs can be adjusted over time to suit one's individual needs,' I concluded on systematic withdrawals and related discussions.

They were all quiet. Vignesh was the one to break the silence. He wanted to know why people invested in bank FDs even today when debt mutual funds were a better option in terms of post-tax returns, income setup, liquidity, etc.

That was a good question, I told him.

'Debt mutual funds don't promise a certain return, unlike an FD. This is unnerving for some even though they do understand that what debt funds deliver will be similar, or better than an FD.

But the fact that the returns are not certain dims the attraction of debt mutual funds for a lot of people.

'Also, people are used to investing in bank FDs and getting interest income. Mutual funds are a new concept by comparison and hence the trust levels have not caught up yet.

'The third factor is that people still do not know much about debt mutual funds, and don't really know that they are a viable alternative to FDs.

'Since FDs can also be liquidated when needed and there may be some reduction in the interest rate in line with the tenure while withdrawing, they don't consider the debt mutual fund liquidity proposition as a big deal. In debt mutual funds, one can get the return fully without any penalties, after the completion of the early exit periods, as specified.'

Having answered this, I looked again in their direction for any further questions. There were none.

I thought I would steer to a subject which may be useful to them. I wanted to cover active versus passive investing and launched forth on that.

'Active investing is where an asset or fund manager will choose the investments from a universe of financial instruments, based on a specific mandate that a particular scheme has.

'For instance, an active equity fund manager will pick and choose the equities that they want in the portfolio. The asset manager will choose an index to benchmark the portfolio to. Now the asset manager will seek to beat the benchmark by bringing to the fore their stock-picking acumen.

'While this can work, the active fund manager also charges for the work and that pushes up the cost charged to the fund. Hence, to beat the index, the active fund manager will need to first bridge the gap of the higher cost being charged vis-à-vis the index, to just come on par with it. The gap can be as high as over 2 per cent annually.

'Also, the information availability is much better than ever before, and price gets discounted either way, based on the nature of the information. There are many more analysts covering an ever-increasing list of companies. The potential for a fund manager to cash in on privileged information has become scarcer now.

'SEBI has recategorised and streamlined the way funds are defined, making it difficult for fund managers to move beyond their focus category or theme and opportunistically bring in others into the portfolio that have the potential to perform in the short term.

'For these reasons and others, it is going to be difficult for fund managers to beat the index, at least in the large-cap category. In the other categories like mid- and small-cap categories, there may still be opportunities that an active fund manager can pursue and may have a chance to beat the index, after all charges.

'The concept of passive investing is borne out of the realisation that stocks are priced in a way which captures all the information that all market participants have been able to glean. It is the collective wisdom of all participants, who may react in different ways to the information they get to know. Also, when some new information comes in, the markets adjust to that, based on how all the participants react.

'The stock market index which captures a certain portion of the market (like large-caps that the Nifty 50 captures) becomes a good passive investment tool. The index is generally chosen based on market capitalisation of equities in a certain market segment.

'An index fund or an ETF replicates the index composition and tends to offer a return similar to what the index offers. Here, there is no skill involved. Someone just needs to replicate the index and rebalance it, when the index constituents change.

'The market capitalisation of a company is a good representation of the value of the business, after considering all the information there is to consider. The index is revisited periodically and after evaluation, some existing equities may exit from the index and some new entrants may come into the system.

'This means that the index will always capture the ones with the highest market capitalisation in the chosen market segment. These are hence the companies that are most valued at that point.

'This ensures that the index will always have the right kind of companies by design. That is the major attraction. When one invests in index funds or ETFs, there is no chance of the fund manager bias and subjectivity coming in, which is the main advantage.'

I looked around to see if they were listening. They seemed to be. I asked if there were any questions.

Vignesh shot one in my direction. He wanted to know why the index fund return did not precisely match the index returns. He mentioned that he had seen this disparity and was always puzzled by it.

I complimented him on the question, as it would bring out many more aspects with respect to index fund investing.

I started again. 'The deviation of returns of the index fund or ETF as compared to the index is termed as a tracking error. It is so called as the index fund returns are supposed to track the underlying index, and any deviation in the positive or negative direction becomes a tracking error.

'Tracking error creeps in due to many reasons. One of the reasons may be that the time elapsed before the index fund or that the ETF is adjusted before it reflects the index constitution. The second reason is that the index fund will charge a certain expense to the fund, which reduces the returns to that extent. The third reason is that the fund has to maintain some cash to take care of redemption and to meet various charges that the scheme needs to pay.

'However, the fund managers try to keep this to the minimum by investing the cash in index futures or fixed income securities as well as doing stock lending to generate some income. These help in narrowing down the tracking error. However, it cannot be fully avoided.'

It was Urvi's turn now.

She said, 'It's all fine to extol the virtues of passive investment. But the fact is in India, active funds are doing well in comparison to passive funds. That's what my limited experience with mutual fund investing and my reading on the subject tells me.'

I was pleasantly surprised to hear that Urvi had been investing in mutual funds and knew the Indian situation regarding where active funds stood verses passive ones.

This was a bunch of bright young kids. I congratulated Urvi on her knowledge on the subject and for her foresight in investing in mutual funds so early in life.

I told Urvi that as per the SPIVA India Scorecard (a research report published by the S&P Dow Jones Indices) index funds, especially of the large-cap kind, were able to beat over two-thirds of the actively managed funds over a ten-year period.

'Over shorter periods like one and three years, a large-cap index like S&P BSE100 is able to beat even a higher percentage of actively managed funds. However, the number of active funds outperforming the index is higher in the midcap and small-cap categories.

'This study eliminates survivorship bias (funds may be liquidated or merged over the period of study; this study accounts for the entire set at the beginning of the period, making the study truly represent the real picture). It compares funds with their representative benchmarks to improve authentic comparison.

'There are other ways in which the data is cleaned to represent a true comparison of active funds versus the index. Hence, the case that active funds outperform the index is not particularly strong. Over time, this will weaken further, due to reasons we had discussed earlier.

'One can undoubtedly say that there is a case for having a mix of active and passive funds in one's portfolio. For now, passive funds tracking a large-cap index like the S&P BSE100 may be a good candidate to have in the passive space. In the midcap and small-cap space, active funds may still have some juice left.

'That is what we do when we put together a portfolio for our clients. Advisors need to build diversified portfolios that are the best fit in each situation and offer the best return for the level of risk they are willing to take at the portfolio level.'

The clock on the wall told me that it was closing time. I realised that we had been at this discussion for close to two hours. I looked at the kids. They seemed to be as fresh as lilies, and seemed eager to absorb new knowledge. It was I who was going to throw in the towel.

'That's all for today, folks! Hope today's session was useful.'

They made all the right noises. Dipanjana thanked me for the session. I was surprised all over again by the enthusiasm this bunch of kids had for learning. These millennials were a savvy lot. Whatever they did, they did it with full dedication.

20

THE RISE OF THE SCION

Preeti was now very near her time of delivery. I was in touch with her and her sister, Naina.

I had even visited her about ten days ago, just to see how she was doing. She seemed absolutely fine.

Yet, today I got this call from Naina who sounded worried and wanted help with insurance for Preeti. I quickly got to know that Preeti was admitted to a nearby hospital as her labour pains had started. I told Naina that I would come over right away.

On reaching the hospital, I found Naina looking very grave. I asked her if there was a problem. She said that there was indeed a problem, one that could threaten the child, and could be dangerous for the mother as well.

What I heard was that it was a breech presentation of the foetus (instead of the head positioned to descend into the birth canal, it was the buttocks which would present first during childbirth in breech presentation) and the umbilical cord was wrapped around the foetus. This problem was apparently known earlier, Naina mentioned.

While these conditions were relatively rare, they were not unheard of. Doctors had opined that normal birth might be dangerous for the baby as well as for the mother, and caesarean section would probably need to be performed.

But Naina told me that another complication had cropped up. Known as umbilical cord compression in medical terms, it meant the foetus was feeling the stress and they may need to perform the C-section right away. Doctors may come out any moment and tell us this, Naina said.

I understood the issues now and quickly explained to Naina that the medical insurance that Preeti had did not cover childbirth. Very few policies covered childbirth and that too after a long waiting period (usually four to six years). The money then needed to be arranged, which I understood would be about ₹1 lakh.

Preeti should have had ₹4–5 lakh in the bank account. But now, there was no way to ascertain that. I asked Naina if she knew the user ID and password of the bank account. She replied in the negative.

I immediately called my office and gave instructions to arrange for up to ₹2 lakh from her investment. The problem was that the money redeemed would again go into the bank account. I told Naina that she might have to transfer the required sum to the hospital, which Preeti could reimburse when she was out of the hospital. Naina had no problems with that.

As Naina had foretold, a doctor did come out and announced that they were wheeling Preeti in for a C-section. They wanted Naina to come in as Preeti seemed terrified and the doctor felt that the presence of Naina by Preeti's side would help. Naina went in with the doctor.

I was left to sit outside and ponder over the goings-on in the life of Preeti and her family. It had been a tumultuous time of late. This complication in her pregnancy was the latest upheaval in their lives.

To my limited understanding, this pregnancy problem was no longer a major problem as the doctors had chosen to do a C-section. This would help in circumventing the complications that had arisen.

I went into a reverie and was transported to a place far, far away.

I was standing in a forest. It was dark and forbidding. The shafts of sunlight that penetrated the thick canopy of trees were like golden strands coming down to the forest floor. The gentle sway of the branches made the sunlight streaming from above dance playfully, forming kaleidoscopic patterns on the forest floor.

I was transfixed while witnessing nature's art, which it was rendering so effortlessly with light and shadow in brilliant hues, on the medium of the forest floor, across time. This was a performance painting over the space–time continuum.

The gentle breeze that was wafting through the forest was cool and moist. It looked like it was going to rain, which happens quite frequently in tropical forests.

There was some screeching and rustling in the branches. I saw a troop of monkeys jumping from branch to branch, and moving higher up the canopy. Then it occurred to me that there may be a predator somewhere nearby. My guide suggested that I get into the SUV.

The chatter of the monkeys subsided, and there was just the rustle of the wind, which had now gained speed. The light had dimmed a bit. The visibility levels on the forest floor went down even further.

The guide who was sitting beside me told me that the chatter of monkeys and the fact that they were going to the top of the canopy indicated that a predator like a panther was lurking in those parts. He pointed to the general direction in which the panther could be found. What I saw was a dark patch of forest. Then it happened.

There was a streak of something up in the air. It landed near us, and in another two leaps, it was gone.

There was a deep roar to the rear. My heart skipped a few beats—or so I felt. The roar signified anger, disappointment and resignation at the same time. I did not know whether to feel good about the deer having escaped getting killed or whether I should feel bad that the panther would now have to go hungry. I was unsure what my stand was.

My guide told me that it was a spotted deer that the panther must have laid in wait for. Now, the prey had escaped and the panther was roaring with anger and frustration at the prospect of having to go hungry that afternoon.

The guide suggested that we drive to the nearby river. He mentioned that on the trees along the riverside, there would be a lot of hornbills. That sounded good. We went near the river which was in full flow.

The guide parked the car at a vantage point and told me that the river had crocodiles, and that we needed to be careful. There was something about this guide that was very familiar, but I could not put a finger to it. We looked around and stepped out. He was now pointing to the branches yonder, and sure enough, there were hornbills. He handed me a pair of binoculars for a closer look.

Wow. There were so many of them, squawking, flying around, sitting next to each other, jostling for space. They were so pretty, and looked happy. The huge yellow beak contrasted beautifully with their black and white bodies. My guide explained to me that they preferred silver oak trees and needed those trees to raise their young ones.

It was wonderful to behold a hornbill in flight—the black wingspan was fringed elegantly with white accents, and the tail had a black centre and white feathers at the extremes. The fantastic visual symmetry was accentuated by the elegance with which they were flying.

I was moving my sight from branch to branch and was rewarded with even more hornbills. I kept shifting my gaze till I came to the ground ahead. There were a group of hornbills on the ground, scratching and rolling. They were having a mud bath.

The guide showed me the bend where the river narrowed and the water seemed to be descending with great force onto the rocks below, forming a white froth due to the churn.

He told me that many people did white water rafting there and this point was one of the most difficult to negotiate. His very words were: '*Vishal Kali nadi mein rafting karnewalon ko yehan par apni pehchaan dikhati hai aur sakshaat Badri Vishal ki yaad dilati hai.*'

We were rooted to the spot for maybe a couple of minutes and were taking in the sights of the river, the forests, the variegated green cover in a multitude of hues. Just mentioning that it was beautiful would be trivialising the sublime spectacle that it presented. I felt one with nature. A cool breeze was wafting now, bringing with it the fresh smells of the forest.

He asked me to get back into the SUV immediately. I complied. He explained that he saw some movement in the undergrowth to the extreme left and he figured it might be a crocodile. We kept watching that area. Nothing came out, however. All the same, his caution was understandable.

It started raining, somewhat mildly to start with and then it intensified rapidly. It was now raining in sheets, and the visibility was low, as the clouds obliterated the sun. There was a giant thunderclap and a huge flash of lightning, which made me leap.

I saw Naina standing beside me and I was agape.

Where did she come from, I wondered. I then saw the surroundings and for a second was confounded. Then it became clear that I was dreaming, and had been transported to the sanctuaries and forests of Dandeli. I had been there before. But the sights I had seen so vividly today were new. I was wrestling with my thoughts when there was a tap on my shoulder.

'Are you alright?' Naina wanted to know. I straightened now and confirmed to her that I was.

For the first time I noticed the worried expression on Naina's face.

'How is Preeti and how is the child?' I wanted to know.

Naina did not answer immediately. She was clearly wrestling with her emotions. This did not look good to me.

'Preeti's C-section is over. The baby is fine. But there is excessive bleeding in Preeti's case, and the doctors are trying to stanch that blood flow. Preeti is weak and is sleeping. She is said to be out of danger. But the doctors have said that they will have to keep her under close observation for at least forty-eight hours. She is in the ICU now,' Naina poured out her concern.

This was a bolt from the blue. I had hardly expected any problems during childbirth. This was really a rough bunch of cards that the Almighty was dealing to this family. I was now worried about Preeti and her three kids.

I did not know what to tell Naina or how to console her. I asked her in whose care were Shreyan and Ashitaa. She told me that they were at home with the maid and that she would go and take care of them at night.

I asked her whether I should stay there during the night as it was generally expected when someone was in the ICU. She told me that Raj would be there tonight. That sealed it. I asked her if I could drop her off at Preeti's home. She nodded.

On the way, I asked her about her daughter Ritika. She was a young girl, and she would probably need her mother too at night. Naina had asked her to come over to Preeti's home for the next few days. She said that she had anticipated that Preeti would need to be in the hospital for a couple of days, and had made arrangements accordingly.

'It now looks like it may be a longer stay than that,' she said.

I dropped her off and was on my way home, immersed in thought.

At home, Madhu asked me something. It did not even register. She came closer and asked if anything was troubling me. I then told her the entire episode about Preeti. She was concerned now. She knew Preeti well. Their family had visited us several times, and Madhu was on very friendly terms with Preeti. She did not know Naina though.

I wanted to go have a bath and refresh myself. After about fifteen minutes, I emerged cleaner externally, and somewhat calmer internally. The extreme anxiety that I had felt had subsided a great deal.

After a while, I sat down for dinner and was almost through. My mobile summoned me; it was a call from Raj.

'What is it, Raj?' I asked.

'Is your blood group O negative, Suresh?' he asked. I confirmed that I was. He was asking me if I could come over immediately as they required at least two units of blood right away. The blood bank did not have this blood type at the moment, he mentioned.

I assured him that I would be there in fifteen minutes. I told Madhu and rushed to the hospital.

Raj was pacing up and down the corridor, visibly agitated. He was relieved to see me so soon. He immediately put me on to the nurses concerned. Before long, the process of harvesting my blood began.

Once they had their two bags full, they let me go. They asked me if I was feeling giddy. I confirmed that I was not. They told me that I would need to lie down for another fifteen minutes as a precautionary measure.

After they released me from their clutches, I went over to Raj.

'What has been happening, Raj?' I wanted to know.

Raj clearly wanted someone to talk to. He started off by saying that there was profuse bleeding still and they had been giving Preeti blood all along. She was still unconscious and the doctors themselves were worried, as her condition was not stabilising at all and her parameters were still erratic, several hours after the C-section.

'I am worried, Suresh,' Raj said simply. I nodded. I told him that everything would be alright and by morning we would feel really silly that we had worried so much. I don't think I said this convincingly. But he nodded and kind of indicated that it was reassuring.

In the meantime, my heart was aflutter. I started worrying all over again about Vishal's family. The problems were coming one after another like tsunami waves, and it was overwhelming, coming so close to each other like this.

I had by this time joined Raj in pacing up and down. We were not walking together. He had his beat and I had mine. We were too immersed in thought and bent down by woes that it was not allowing us to sit down. We were too agitated.

My health app was surprised that I had walked so much that day and congratulated me on my heightened level of perambulations. It also told me how many calories I had burnt and where I can reach if I kept this up on a day-to-day basis.

The nurse came out and asked me if I was fine. I said I was. She told me in confidential undertones that they had started giving the blood to Preeti. She said that even the two units from me would be insufficient. They wanted another three units, and asked us if there was anyone else who could donate the O negative blood type. I looked at Raj. He gave me a helpless look.

I told the nurse that I could give maybe one more unit if that was safe. I also assured her that we would send across an SOS message for donors of this blood type. I asked Raj if he knew anyone with O negative blood type. He shrugged to indicate that he had no idea.

The nurse said that they could not take more than two units from a person. They were willing to do it this time, as this was an emergency. She wanted me to wait for a couple of hours after which she said she would take one unit from me. I agreed to that.

I immediately sent a request to all the WhatsApp groups I was a part of about the blood requirements on an emergency basis. I sent it to Raj as well and asked him to suitably modify and forward the messages.

I got many responses to indicate their sympathy but none which said they would be able to donate blood. That was somewhat expected, as O negative is a rare blood group and these problems do occur.

After about an hour and a half, one of Raj's friends had responded that he was of the same blood group and indicated that he would be able to donate blood. He was asking if it could be done tomorrow morning.

I asked Raj to talk to the nurse and find out before responding. The nurse was insistent that the blood might be required during the night and hence the need was now. Raj was hesitant, as it was 9.45 p.m.

But there was no choice. He called Vinit. Vinit answered the call immediately. Raj explained the situation to him. Vinit agreed to come over as soon as possible.

Raj heaved a sigh of relief. We told the nurse that there was another person who was coming to donate blood. She also seemed relieved.

Conversation wore thin between us. We were both lost in thought. Vinit landed up soon. It had just been twenty-five minutes since Raj had called. This was a pleasant surprise.

Raj made the introductions. Vinit was a strapping guy of six feet two inches and had the body that could have tackled a bull with nonchalance. Raj took him in to tell the nurse that her quarry was in.

The nurse lost no time in preparing to take her two units from Vinit. It took about forty-five minutes, which included fifteen minutes of rest for him. He came out strutting like a proud alpha male, which he very much was. Then, the nurse came for me. I went inside, and my job was done in about thirty minutes, which included the fifteen-minute resting period.

When I came out, Vinit was still there, chatting with Raj. I thanked Vinit for coming at this hour and helping us. Vinit protested that this was the least he could do for someone in need.

A cosy banter followed, and we were at it for about another fifteen minutes.

I wanted to go home and retire for the day. I told Raj and Vinit. I also told Raj that he could call me anytime during the night, if required. He nodded.

While driving back, I thought that it was providence to have encountered Vinit at the right time. I sent a silent prayer and thanked the Lord for his timely help.

At home, Madhu wanted to know what happened. I filled her in on the details. I told her that I would turn in for the day as I was feeling bushed.

I was lying down and the entire day's event unspooled like a movie. Sleep eluded me. Madhu came after me and slipped into a deep slumber almost immediately. She had settled into a nice rhythmic breathing.

I was tossing and turning and could not get a wink of sleep. Finally, I got up and went to the living room. I thought I could read the newspaper for some time, which probably would bore me enough and make me sleepy.

I was flipping the papers for a while without interest. It was about 1 a.m. Still, I was wide awake. I tossed the paper aside and was immersed in thought. Today was the day of ruminations.

Again, I was sorry for the trials and tribulations that Vishal's family was being put through. I cupped my hands, covering my face and thinking these thoughts. Why is Preeti being put through such problems now? I shuddered to think what would happen to the family if she were not around. I felt sick even to think of such a possibility. It was depressing.

When I sat up, I saw my Lord sitting on the opposite sofa. This time his entry had been unobtrusive—no Om intonation in the background, no smells of chandan, camphor, tulsi, etc. While I was thinking this, the Om chanting started and a strong whiff of chandan, camphor, tulsi, flowers, etc., wafted to my nostrils. The smells and sounds elevated my mood.

I fell at his feet and gave my pranam. He motioned that I should sit on the opposite side, which I complied.

Like before, he was asking me directly in my mind what was agitating me so much. I did not feel the need to talk and conveyed my thoughts directly to him. 'Lord, you know the problems that have overtaken Preeti today.

'The latest is that her condition has not stabilised and the bleeding continues. I was very worried, as all the three children are very young and need their mother. When they wheeled her in for a C-section, I was not worried. The fact that she is still bleeding and doctors themselves are concerned is upsetting for me.'

There was silence. The Om chanting was going on in the background and the strong smells of camphor and tulsi were soothing. I have heard that the aural and olfactory stimuli can control the mood itself. I was experiencing the soothing effect of these sensory stimuli working on me and calming me.

Finally, the Lord was forthcoming.

'I understand the concern you have and your interest in the family's welfare. You are certainly going beyond the call of duty here, and that is exemplary.

'I told you yesterday that every atma chooses the kind of sadhanas they want to do in this life. It is hence Preeti's choice that dictates the events that are about to unfold. While Preeti wants to surge ahead and take some difficult paths, her decisions would be tempered by the realities of her current life and the people in it.

'Preeti clearly realises that three lives depend on her. She cannot act cavalierly and throw the three vulnerable babies to the vicissitudes of fate and the charity of sundry others. This is a troublesome period for the family. Even this will pass. Preeti will pull herself through for the sake of her children.

'This is all the comfort that I can offer you. The three children will have their mother. She will start recovering rapidly and regain good health. The infant who is born will be an illustrious son who will achieve big things in life and will blaze a trail for all to see. He will be a Yashasvi.

'He is the blessed child that Vishal always wanted. He has the blessing of none other than Badrinarayanan, whom Vishal used to revere. Ask Preeti to name the child Badri Vishal. Badri would be the child's name and Vishal as the father's name would anyway follow it. That is the name by which the deity at Badrinath is known. Vishal would have loved it,' the Lord concluded.

Something was churning within me. This Vishal-Badri name play somehow seemed familiar. And then it struck me.

The guide who was with me had made a curious remark in Hindi, which at that time did not stand out, but now it did. He had said: '*Vishal Kali nadi mein rafting karnewalon ko yehan par apni pehchaan dikhati hai aur sakshaat Badri Vishal ki yaad dilati hai.*'

I looked up at him.

The Lord said, 'I wanted to show you the exact point Vishal was swept away. I had just done it in passing. Vishal remembered Badri Vishal even in the moment he was being swept away. Even those who have controlled their senses completely find it difficult to keep the Lord in view, when their time to leave the mortal coils arrives. Vishal did it. It is only right that his child goes by that name.'

There was a serene expression and a beatific smile on his lips. As I was watching, his countenance changed to Lord Krishna.

This again made me prostrate before him. The Om chanting had stopped, and a mellifluous flute music was playing. It was divine and otherworldly.

The Lord was still there in his enchanting, divine form—in his yellow brocade silks, intricate and wondrous ornaments, his body effulgent, with his trademark peacock feather in his crown. He was resplendent and stunning. Even while I had him in my sights, he vanished like mist that evaporates when the sun comes up.

I was happy for more reasons than one. The Lord has assured me that Preeti would regain good health and the three cherubs would be well cared for.

The newborn was fated to be an illustrious child, which would be like music to Preeti's ears. I was smiling to myself. Preeti would love to hear this.

I was happy that this illustrious scion was to be called Badri Vishal.

21

THE CALM AFTER THE STORM

The next morning, I was my peaceful self again. The assurance the Lord had given me at night regarding Preeti had put a spring in my step. I was humming while I was shaving and playfully tapped on Madhu's head.

She saw that I was in a good mood and asked me the reason. I just said I got up on the right side of the bed and the day had started on a happy note.

She looked askance but then let it go.

I got ready and headed for the hospital. Naina was there, looking well-rested and bright. Was she really looking like that or was it just my elevated spirits viewing everything with rose-tinted optimism? I greeted Naina gaily and asked how Preeti was.

'The nurse has said that she is absolutely fine now,' said Naina

I said, 'Of course, she had to be.'

Naina looked at me, to see what I meant and to see if she could decipher the source of my optimism.

I said that I was always optimistic about her speedy recovery and this did not come as a surprise to me. She was mollified by this and let it go.

'Can we go and see Preeti?' I asked Naina.

'The nurse told me that they would be shifting her from the ICU to a normal ward within an hour. She had said that we can see her then,' said Naina.

This deflated me a little bit. But the fact that Preeti was fine enough to come to the normal ward was great news.

I took off and started loitering along the corridors. Then I found a lawn and a bench in a shady alcove, which was perfect to spend an hour in quiet contemplation.

I sat on the bench in padmasana, closed my eyes and did some pranayama. I wanted to do it in the morning but had not found the time. It was a pleasant twenty-five minutes I spent like that, undisturbed. The place was wonderful. There was no disturbance and very little sound. It was a nice retreat within the bustling confines of the hospital.

I thanked the Lord and sent him my prayers for the good tidings that were now coming the way of Preeti's family. I got a call on my mobile phone from Naina. She asked me where I was and informed me that Preeti had been shifted to the regular ward. I told her that I was very much in the hospital premises and would be there in a minute. I rounded the corner and saw Naina sitting on the bench.

When she saw me, she got up. She indicated that we could go to the ward to see Preeti. We reached her room. There she was propped on the bed, with thick blankets drawn till her chest.

She was awake and seemed fine. Her face was clear, and she looked like she was at peace. She smiled as we entered.

Naina went up to her and hugged her. There were tears in Preeti's eyes instantly.

She asked about the children. Naina said they seemed to understand the situation and behaved with a maturity beyond their years. Preeti's eyes moistened again.

I asked, 'Where is Badri Vishal?'

Preeti peered at me intently. All she said was—'So you know!'

Naina who was standing there could not make head nor tail of this cryptic exchange. Preeti and I seemed to have connected at some deeper level, where a few words were enough to convey our profound understanding, and Naina could make nothing of it.

Preeti came to the rescue. She said that she had had a very vivid dream during the early hours of the morning. She was visited by the Lord himself who conveyed to her that her troubles were over, that she would recover fast and regain her health.

The Lord had also asked her to name the child Badri Vishal after Vishal's favourite deity. The Lord had also prophesied that Badri would go on to become an illustrious scion, be an achiever and would be quite well-known.

Naina then turned to me and asked how I knew.

I just said that I had also had a similar dream. This was not in the least convincing, I confessed. But at a moment's notice, this was the best I could come up with. I could not possibly tell her that God visits me and talks to me from time to time. Not just Naina, but almost anyone hearing this would think I'm off my rocker.

Preeti smiled at me, and I smiled back. It was a conspiratorial smile which Naina caught but could decipher nothing from.

Naina must have let it go as she was relieved that her sister was fine now and, ultimately, that was what mattered. We spoke for another five minutes when the nurse came with some medicines.

She made Preeti have them and requested us to leave her alone to rest. She said that it was crucial for Preeti to regain her strength for which she needed lots of rest.

We were not about to contest that. We bade goodbye to Preeti and went out. I asked Naina about the baby boy. She said he was being kept in an incubator for the moment. He would join his mother in a day or two, she said. That was good enough for me.

While we were in the car, Naina said that Raj and she had been thinking a bit about what I had said about education, life planning as well as budgeting their expenses. She mentioned that they wanted to come over and discuss further in my office.

I told her to come after two days at 6 p.m. She was fine with that.

I was still in an elevated frame of mind when I dropped her off at her place. I was humming a gay tune till I reached home.

Madhu was immediately able to make out that I was in a good mood. She followed me to our room and wanted to know how Preeti was. I appraised her of the situation. She was relieved.

Madhu also wanted to come over to the hospital to meet Preeti. It so happened that Preeti had chosen that moment to call me. I was a bit surprised as I was with her till about half an hour back. It brought some wrinkles on my forehead.

I picked up the call. Preeti seemed fine when she talked. She came straight to the point.

She mentioned that some payments needed to be made to the hospital and that she needed my help to arrange that. She mentioned that she had already called Naina and told her where her cheque book was. She said that she would like to sign the cheque and hand over that to me so that hospital bills could be cleared. This was a relief, and the tension relaxed.

I asked her to sign at least three cheques so that they could be used as necessary. I asked her if she used internet banking. To my relief, she said she did.

I told her that she could take the cheques from Naina first thing tomorrow morning and hand them over to me when I came to meet her. She assented. I gave the phone to Madhu who talked to Preeti and enquired after her health. She told Preeti that she would also come the next morning to visit her. She signed off with a cheery 'get well' message.

All seemed to be fine, finally, with the world the Lord had created!

The next day was a busy day with many activities that included a meeting with Ajay and Arundhati who were coming over to my office for a plan discussion.

In the morning, we went to the hospital to see Preeti. Naina had visited her quite early before going to her office. Preeti had the cheques, which she handed over to me. She requested me to coordinate the payments at the hospital. I assured her that I would do that.

Madhu was talking to her for some time. I got a call from Anshuman, a client of mine, out of the blue. He had taken my advice a few years ago. We had not been in touch after he had gone abroad.

On the call, Anshuman narrated his story and brought me up to speed on what had happened in the past few years. He was asking if he could come over that day to meet me. I asked him if it was urgent. He said it was not urgent in that sense, but was keen to meet me as soon as possible.

I told him that I would probably not be free till 5 p.m. and asked him whether he would be fine coming over at 5.30 p.m. He said it suited him.

I then stepped into a meeting with Ajay and Arundhati. I explained to them that the initial feasibility study had indicated that meeting their goals and objectives would be a breeze. They had already gone through the sheets I had sent them. They had understood what I was trying to convey. There was no real problem in their case in terms of meeting their goals and objectives. They were a high-flying couple, and most of the things they wanted in life seemed to be well within their ken.

The discussions were about other things.

ESOPs: Ajay had some ESOPs (or employee stock option plan) that were vesting in the next few months. He wanted to know what to do about them.

His company was listed on the Indian stock exchanges and was doing well. I asked him what he felt about the prospects of the company and the industry, as he would know more about it than anybody else. He said that he was optimistic about his company's prospects, its relative position within the industry, its competitiveness and the unique success factors that it enjoyed.

Companies allow employees an option to buy company stocks at a certain price (grant price), that is generally lower than the market price, thereby conferring a monetary benefit to the employee. The employee can buy the shares during a certain period called the vesting period.

When the employee buys the shares during the vesting period, they will need to pay tax on the profit, which is the difference between the current market price on the exercise date and the grant price at which they bought the shares. This tax is at one's income tax slabs.

If they choose to hold on to the shares, then capital gains tax as it applies to Indian equities will apply on the difference between the sale price and the exercise price, when they sell the shares.

I learnt that for Ajay the options had vested and he would be able to exercise his option to buy ₹3.5 lakh worth of shares, whereas his grant price would come to ₹2 lakh. So, he would have to pay ₹2 lakh to buy the shares, and would have to pay income tax on ₹1.5 lakh, as per the slab he falls under.

He wanted to know about the capital gains tax applicable on these shares.

If an employee chooses to retain the stock further and sells before the completion of one year, then 15 per cent of STCG tax will apply on the difference between the market price on the exercise date and the market price at the time of sale of the stock.

If the employee chooses to sell after twelve months of vesting, then LTCG taxation will apply. For Indian stocks, LTCG of up to ₹1 lakh in a year is tax-exempt. Any LTCG after that would be taxed at 10 per cent. Surcharges, as applicable, will also be levied.

I told him that he should probably buy the shares and keep them, as the prospects of the company seemed to be good. I also told him that I would be able to spell these things out clearly at the end of the plan.

Arundhati also had ESOPs, but they were shares that were listed abroad. She, too, wanted to know what she should do. I asked her the same questions.

She told me that the stocks had already vested in her case. The value today was ₹18 lakh. What she may have to pay as per the grant price would be ₹10 lakh. She mentioned that there would be new vesting of about ₹4 lakh every year, for the next three years.

She said that she was also contributing to an Employee Share Purchase Plan (ESPP), and they, too, would be available for sale.

I told her that in her case, it might be a good idea to sell some portion of it. What portion of it to sell and when was a determination we would make when we completed the plan itself.

She was hazy on the taxation of foreign shares and wanted me to clarify.

'Equities listed abroad are subject to STCG taxation at one's income tax rate until twelve months after the exercise date. If the investments are held for longer than that, they are taxed at 10 per cent without indexation benefit, and 20 per cent with indexation benefit,' I began.

I then told them that I had assumed two children in their case, even though they had not specifically told me anything. They said that they noticed that and were okay with the assumption. I then specifically asked them if they had given any thought to this.

Arundhati said that they were indeed planning one baby in another two years. She said they were not sure about the second child, though they may have one.

I asked them if they had seen the child-related expenses I had provided in the plan. They said they had seen it but had no questions about it yet. They said that this was still hypothetical territory for them and would go by our opinions and assumptions at this stage.

I quickly briefed them about the child-related issues like raising them into well-adjusted individuals who would be able to navigate and function well in the real world.

I talked about the considerations while choosing a school, the extremes to which the parents stretch themselves and their wards to ensure that their children are well-rounded, earning the moniker of 'Tiger-moms' as the mantle of child-rearing most often falls on the mothers.

We talked and discussed a bit more on this subject before

moving on. They said that they found some of these perspectives useful, and would keep them in mind.

Ajay wanted to know what they could do about saving taxes.

This is again another question we field quite regularly.

Tax-saving possibilities: I quite understand the sentiment behind tax-saving, as tax payers rarely get the benefit from taxes paid. In our country, under 2 per cent of the population pays income tax. What honest taxpayers see is a legion of self-interested groups who are cornering the benefits, and are leaching into tax payers' funds.

Even agriculturists and farmers who earn very well do not pay taxes but corner lots of benefits like loans at concessional rates and many times full waivers, low-cost or no-cost electricity, subsidised inputs like fertilisers, seeds, pesticides support prices for crops, etc.

Politicians ensure that the tax they pay is small or nil by showing agricultural income as well as routing their ill-gotten gains into real estate and front companies, routing money abroad and stashing it away in safe havens, round-tripping and investing back in India, etc.

These people are well-aided by the bureaucracy, law enforcement machinery like the police, our legal system, media participants, etc., who all benefit from the corrupt system they are part of and nurture. Then there are extra-constitutional players like thugs, dons, mercenaries who all work with many of the above people to enforce a gamed, corrupt system to siphon off tax payer money.

Business people are beating the system and are paying less tax than they should, they siphon off the money in the company through various means, get loans which they don't pay, etc.

These are some of the major ones. There are many other parasites who suck the vigour and vitality out of the system. We see a venal, corrupt system which has been set up to systematically siphon off our money.

We keep witnessing the frauds being perpetrated on us without being able to do anything. Many times, we know who these people are but are powerless to do anything, and they continue to occupy positions of power and continue sucking the vital energy out of the economy.

In such a situation, we feel miserable that we are paying lakhs of rupees as taxes, which these people are misappropriating. We feel sorry for the state of the infrastructure we have, the lack of civic amenities like parks and playgrounds, are bogged down by endemic pollution of all kinds, open drainages, dirty environs and so on.

No wonder we feel sorry for ourselves and want to pay as little tax as possible.

Tax-savings sections: There are a few sections under which a normal citizen can make some tax savings legitimately. You will be aware of Section 80C, where you save ₹1.5 lakh overall, and get that as a deduction.

There are multiple investments one may make under this section—PPF, NPS, EPF, five-year bank deposits, National Savings Certificate (NSC), life insurance premium, etc. Then there are others like basic tuition fees that one pays for their children as well as the principal component of home loans, which come under the same section.

Medical insurance premiums of ₹25,000 per annum can be claimed as a deduction by normal citizens, and ₹50,000 per annum for senior citizens as a deduction under Section 80D.

Further, if the senior citizen does not have medical insurance, they (or their children, if they are dependent) can claim a deduction for the medical expenditure incurred. Another ₹5,000 a year can be claimed as a deduction for preventive medical health checkups for one's family, including dependent parents.

An additional ₹50,000 for contributions into NPS can be claimed as a deduction under Section 80CCD(1B).

The interest paid on a home loan can be claimed as a deduction up to ₹2 lakh under Section 24. This is available for more than one home.

Education loan interest is fully exempt without limits and comes under Section 80E. This, of course, would apply only if one has such a loan.

If one stays on rent, a person (who is an employee) can claim a deduction under Section 10(13A) based on the least of HRA received, 50 per cent of basic pay for metro cities (40 per cent for other cities) and rent paid above 10 per cent of basic pay.

Apart from this, charitable donations to eligible organisations are covered under Section 80G. Normally, 50 per cent of the amount donated is available as a deduction.

These things keep changing from time to time, and one needs to keep a check on any changes during the next budget presentation or even in between.

As I finished explaining these things to them, they nodded and were fine to go to the next item they wanted to discuss.

Ajay gave tongue to his thoughts. He wanted to be an entrepreneur in about four years in the IT field. He wanted me to consider that in the plan.

I asked him the reasons for wanting to be an entrepreneur.

He posed a rhetorical question to me: 'Don't we all want to work for ourselves at some point in our lives?'

I did not say anything. He had to break the silence. He said he had been having such thoughts for the past two years. He was fed up with office politics and intrigue. Also, he said, he was fed up with working for somebody else and wanted to work for himself and make money.

I asked him if I could give my perspective on entrepreneurship. He welcomed it. I started.

'We all have someone we envy. It may be someone with a fancy car, or a home in a tony neighbourhood, or it could be another who does those foreign vacations every year, or that guy who owns a business and whizzes across the country or abroad incessantly.

'These days, the guy who owns a business—the one who sits in the corner office in a glass and chrome building—is the cynosure of all eyes. He is that guy who has broken out of the rat race, the stud who has achieved glory by doing his own thing.

'He is the ultimate achiever and role model—never mind if his start-up has been kept alive by oxygen pumped in periodically by angel investors. He has not made any money yet, but he is living his dream and has a 25 per cent stake in the company. If it goes public, he will be a very rich man.

'I find such adulation and envy among a lot of people I deal with. People are fed up with their day jobs. It's staid, predictable and, to a great extent, linear. It's not that they don't earn well … many are earning very well indeed!

'But the grass seems greener, much greener, on the other side. But that is not the whole picture.

'**The risks involved:** Though business may appear exciting, it comes with a large dollop of risk. Though there may be start-up capital coming from angel investors, most people still invest significant sums of their own money as well.

'Many businesses, especially at the start-up stage, may appear to have some very unique business models, with a unique solution to a problem. The business potential may seem insanely exciting.

'But however bulletproof the business model may appear, it needs to be tested in the real world. Like the Yankees say, we will know only when the rubber meets the road!

'What looks great on paper may not actually have demand on the ground. An example of this is the shoe cleaning business. Based on the rates they quote for this I'm forced to conclude that their target is someone who buys a pair of shoes that cost more than ₹5,000.

'While there are people like that, the market becomes quite limited. Even among the target set, many may not want this service and many who would never hear of such a service, which is again a challenge.

'For the regular shoe buyers, the typical range is ₹1,500–3,000 a pair. For them, it may make sense to just cast away the shoe at some point and purchase a new one, instead of paying for such services.

'Hence, for many new innovative services, it needs to be seen if there is a big enough addressable market at a price where it will make business sense, and if it can be viable at all.

'Another prosaic and straightforward reason why businesses struggle is due to the lack of efficient execution capabilities. Many even fail just for this reason.

'There are so many other gears which need to engage and perform seamlessly—like people, production, service delivery, efficient management of capital, sales and marketing, technology, etc.

'Competition is another problem. Every business or idea can be copied, and differentiating one's offering becomes difficult. When service offerings are similar, the businesses start competing on price—which depletes everyone.

'If one is starting a business in an existing area, then there will be strong, entrenched competition. It will be challenging to compete against established names.

'Many do not appreciate the brand equity of the organisations they were working for. They think they are getting the business on their own steam. They do not understand that many will not even meet them, but for the significant brand equity of the organisations they work for.

'It is not individual brilliance that customers are looking for; they want an organisation that is able to deliver what they need and support them over the entire product cycle.

'**Starting a business for the wrong reasons:** One of the reasons people start a business is to get rich quick. People who think like this always have some anecdotal evidence. But that does not make it universally applicable.

'Many businesses look great from the outside, but it is a lot of hard work to run them well as profitable businesses. Every business needs to make money and every business has the potential to make money, if run well.

'Good businesses happen when someone establishes an enterprise that they are passionate about, and have deep knowledge and insights. Also, they need to be realistic about all aspects of their business, keep their ears to the ground and be willing to keep trying and refining it, have tremendous patience and fine-tune the business over time.

'These things take time. But such businesses have the best chance of success. There are many who pursue this course. These businesses have a high probability of success. How much money the business makes is a factor of how well it is run.

'The chances of success come down when people start businesses in entirely different fields, the service or its delivery is completely novel (hence how successful it might be is not known in the beginning), when the business is capital-intensive, when the business is not self-sustaining, needs cash infusion at regular intervals, etc.

'In spite of all this, we find people regularly talking about starting businesses in unrelated fields, and some end up doing it.

'There are others who start a business with the idea of just starting up something, getting it going and selling it after a while. No wonder, many start-ups today do not have a business model which can make a profit at all. They are stuck in maximising client acquisition and the topline, with scant regard for the bottomline.

'The model itself depends on just building a business (albeit without any profit which is the raison d'etre of a business) and selling it off to make money.

'**Getting away from the rat race:** When someone is in a corporate job, they get fed up with it for various reasons. It may be the boring routines, the cantankerous bosses, the business pressures to deliver performance, poor growth prospects, etc.

'That is when disillusionment sets in and the job that they have been doing seems like drudgery or even meaningless work. That is when they decide to get off the treadmill and do something on their own.

'Also, people form the impression that they are working too hard in their jobs for someone else's benefit and they deserve to do their own thing and earn all the profits—for some, this is their other reason for getting out of the rat race.

'But there are things they will realise only when they are no longer in the job—like the certainty of a pay cheque every month, the many perks which their job was offering, holidays and leaves which they could avail, the fairly high remuneration for the time they were giving, the insurances which were available for them and their family, etc.

'So, getting away from the 'rat race' is not always easy, especially when one has EMIs and lots of commitments, and a fairly good lifestyle that needs to be sustained. This becomes all the more pronounced when the prospect of taking any money out is a long time away. It creates all kinds of stresses, which they have never experienced before.

'Also, in a job, there is an entire organisation that one can bank upon. There is so much deep knowledge and support infrastructure in the organisation that assists a person in doing their job. This is seldom realised. Only when one is an entrepreneur and is trying to do everything on their own does this become evident.

'**Flexibility and timing:** People want to get into business as they can be their own boss and because it offers flexibility and freedom to pursue what they want on their own time.

'Being one's own boss suits people who are disciplined, not all. While flexibility and freedom would be there, with it also comes the onus of shouldering enormous responsibility.

'Some people think that they will have more time, which is a common delusion. When one starts a business, twenty-four hours are not enough. There are no leaves, no holidays and there is a lot of back-breaking work.

'The other aspect is that in a corporate job, there are people and systems to take care of almost everything, as discussed earlier. When one starts a business, one may have to do virtually everything—from strategy, composing the marketing brochure, client pitches, admin work to even paying bills! Even if one has staff, it will only be for some basic admin and accounting work. This would be very trying for those who are used to a corporate lifestyle.

'Not everyone is going to like doing all of this, and only someone who has a fire in their belly and is ultra-passionate about their vision for the business and has the patience that Lord Krishna had with Sisupala will get past this.

'**The lesson to keep in mind:** While one may have rants about the current job, one needs to evaluate whether leaving the job and entering a business is really suitable for them.

'Inexplicably, many want to give up their well-paying, enviable jobs and start a business, despite the enveloping uncertainties.

'This is what I would call the black widow spider syndrome (a male black widow spider offers itself to be eaten by the female during copulation) as one wants to throw away everything that they have for a chance of a potentially glorious but uncertain future.

'So, dear Ajay, you need to think this through properly before you venture out on your own.'

Ajay probably had not expected this sermon from me. I told him that I was sorry for pouring cold water over his enthusiasm. Ajay was silent. Arundhati came in strongly.

'I have been telling him that we are currently in a very nice place and have excellent prospects going forward. I have been cautioning him that we should not rock this by foolish flights of fancy, which could end up virtually anywhere. I'm happy that you have explained this in detail. I'm so happy that this discussion happened,' she chimed in.

With that, they stood up. The meeting for the day was over. I told them that I would need about ten days to send them their next version.

22

BRINGING SUNDERED HEARTS TOGETHER

I got a call from Anshuman around 4 p.m. He told me that he was on his way. He was slated to come in by 5 p.m.

Anshuman was not an ideal client. He was someone who did not easily trust other people. He was fidgety and unsure of everything. He would run every suggestion that we would offer by his friends, bankers, colleagues, etc., and keep coming up with multiple ideas, sometimes diametrically opposite to what we were suggesting. This made things challenging for us.

The number of explanations we had to offer were much more than what we would have liked. We had spent thrice the amount of time on his case than we had on any other financial planning client. This was five years ago.

After giving him the plan, we had encouraged him to execute it on his own as we felt that this relationship was going to be challenging to keep up. He was also fine with it. We did not hear from him much after that.

We just knew that he had gone abroad six months after the plan was made. Incidentally, there was no mention of going abroad while we had made the plan.

Anshuman walked in. The time was 4.58 p.m. This was one great trait he had. He was always on time for meetings and calls.

We settled down after pleasantries. I just looked at him. He averted his gaze and looked down. I did not understand this.

It looked like he was wrestling with some emotions. Finally, he looked at me and said that he had gone abroad and had returned from there for good. I did not sense rancour there. But the next sentence removed any doubt that his sojourn abroad was tumultuous.

'I had worked and started a business in South Africa. The business was doing well. But as an outsider there, I was subject to a lot of problems and faced a lot of discrimination. I had to virtually give away my business and come back. I landed in India just five days ago,' he said.

I remained silent.

'You had done my plan about five years back. I had implemented it only partially. As was my usual style of operation, I had consulted my friends and others after the plan had been completed,' he continued. 'I took disparate suggestions and implemented what I felt was right. I freely admit that many of those have come back to haunt me now.

'I had purchased a PMS product, which after four-and-a-half years is offering a paltry 5 per cent return. I had bought a real estate product in which the minimum investment was ₹25 lakh. I had put in about ₹40 lakh there. It is still on. It will take me another three years to get out, I hear. It is currently giving a return of 1 per cent. I hear from them that it will improve from here, but that remains to be seen.

'I bought a clutch of mutual funds with suggestions from my friends and my distributor. That portfolio is offering a 6 per cent return. I also invested in real estate, which is stuck.

'I had advanced money to a builder through my friend, who was paying me an interest of 30 per cent per annum. I got the interest for the first year. After that, the builder has been incommunicado. My friend and I lost a lot of the money advanced to him. I lost a good sum of money I had invested in South Africa too.

'You had suggested some investments at that time. I should have stayed with them. I did run some calculations on where I would be now had I stuck to your advice. I would have done quite well had I simply stuck to your advice.

'These are some of the issues. But the major issue is that divorce proceedings are going on, and they are putting some pressure on me. The financial mess I got into took its toll, and the impending divorce is the result,' he concluded for the moment.

I was taking in the information and did not react.

He said, 'I also got into a whole lot of insurance policies which my agent insisted were good for me. That was another blunder. The problem in my case is that my money is all stuck or lost. Some portions like the mutual fund investment can be salvaged. But that amounts to only ₹13 lakh.'

I was silent. He also did not speak further.

I asked him what he intended to do now and what he wanted from me specifically.

Anshuman said, 'I am not sure what I'm going to do now. Maybe I should start working. I do not have too much money to start anything. Also, I do not have the mind or the appetite to start a business now.

'I have circulated my resume to some friends as of now. I have not started applying yet. My mind is aflutter. That's why I thought I could come to you for counsel,' he said.

It was my turn to be flummoxed. Though he had shared his situation, I saw very little I could do.

I started cautiously. 'Why are you considering separating from your wife? What about the children?' I asked.

That seemed to have stirred him to the depths. He was gulping and I could see his Adam's apple go up and down, a sign that he was experiencing some major emotions.

He came to the surface now. 'I really don't know what is going to happen, Suresh-ji. Both my children are young, and a divorce at this point is bound to affect them. I have been talking to Krupa, my wife, trying to convince her that we should not walk down this path.

'She was dead against us going to South Africa and starting a business there. She was all for staying in India. When that unravelled and she came to know that my other investments were disasters as well, fights ensued. You know what happens in a fight. One thing leads to another and soon the scale of the war escalates.

'She came back about a year ago. She is staying with her parents, and has found a job. She is kind of settled into her new routine. She doesn't even want to talk to me. Her parents have also reconciled to the fact that we may be divorced before long. Hence, even they are not doing anything to help us patch up,' he said.

He asked me what he should do.

I was at a loss for words. Though he had given more information, I was struggling to think of ways to assist him.

Events seem to have run ahead of him, and he was feeling overwhelmed. That was clear. He was unable to think of what to do.

I knew that I had to give him some solace and some direction as well as I could with my limited understanding of his situation.

'Krupa is probably peeved that you did not pay heed to her advice and acted recklessly. She may be feeling that you don't care about anybody and will do what you want. She may be feeling that you are an egotist. She may be feeling that you are not caring enough for the family and are gambling away everything, much like Yudhistir,' I said.

His eyes widened.

He exclaimed, 'This is exactly what Krupa had said! She, in fact, calls me a Yudhistir! You seem to understand this very well. Please tell me what to do in this situation.'

It was not my intention to dash his cup of joy prematurely. But it had to be done. I told him that the situation was complicated and that I could only give some broad guidelines. I told him clearly that in the matter of their marriage and interpersonal relationships he would probably need a marriage counsellor.

He said sadly that his wife would have none of it. She just wanted a divorce.

I told him that he should probably write out a crisp letter stating his intention and making it clear that he had erred in the past and would like to make amends. He should also state clearly what he wants to do going forward, and what he would do for his family.

I told him that his wife might be craving security, and that is something he should focus on providing. This appealed to him. He said that he would try his best to convey to her his seriousness.

He now asked me whether I would help him if Krupa warmed up to his proposal. I was noncommittal. I was not sure how this was going to go. This was unfamiliar territory for me. I told him that we would take it as it comes. He did not push me further. His spirits seemed much better now than when he had entered the office.

After he was gone, I was pondering about the implications of one's financial actions. This was not the first time that I was witnessing a relationship coming off at the seams due to financial stress. Financial security is the glue that keeps the family together—we need to accept that. It is certainly not the only ingredient but definitely one of the main ones. I hoped that he would be able to get his life back on track.

I was slated to speak at a conference the next day. I was going over the presentation that night, just so that my lecture would pan out well. I had not talked to Preeti in a while. I checked for any WhatsApp messages. There were none.

I had presented her cheque to the hospital and had cleared a big portion of the bills. Preeti was to be discharged some time the next day. I had told Preeti and Naina that I would not be there, but someone from my office would be present to assist them at the hospital.

There was a message from Naina. It said that Preeti had been running a fever and that she may not get discharged even the next day. I was wondering about this sudden development when there was a call. It was from Anshuman.

What now? I thought. Anshuman was on the line. He profusely apologised for calling after 10 p.m. He said that he had immediately composed and sent an email and a message to his wife. He called her and pleaded with her to read it and give him an audience.

Apparently, his wife had read the message and agreed to meet him. He had met her and said that the meeting had gone well. He was talking with the excitement of a college guy having found a girlfriend.

I was happy for him. He wanted to meet me along with his wife tomorrow. I was not sure in what way I could help. I told him that I was not qualified, and may even be ill-suited for the job.

He pleaded. 'Krupa seems to know you. She has been reading your blogs and follows you in the media. I can say that she is your fan. When I said that you are my financial advisor, she was taken aback.

'She thought that I got into all this financial mess due to your advice. I quickly cleared her misconception and told her that I got into a mess because I did not follow your advice.

'I also told her that I met you and you had advised me to write this note. Her respect for you has gone up manifold now. She feels that things can work out if you get involved,' he stopped.

I was very happy that he finally had something to cheer about. But I was apprehensive that I may have inadvertently raised his expectations sky-high.

I told him this. I also told him that I have no expertise in counselling couples and bringing them together. It was much better for him to seek a marriage counsellor. Once that part has worked out, I told him, I could work with them on the financial part.

He would have none of it. 'I do understand what you are saying, Suresh-ji. It is right that you say this. But you have to give us one chance. Krupa and I want to meet you tomorrow itself,' he said.

'I am in a conference all day tomorrow, Anshuman. It will not be possible to meet tomorrow,' I said.

There was a yelp of pain at the other end. He was pleading now. 'Please, Suresh-ji. You have shone a small ray of hope in my life. Please give us some time tomorrow. Even if it is late, give us a dinner appointment. We can go to any hotel of your choice for dinner, which will be my treat. I'm sure Krupa will come, however late it is.'

I told him that tomorrow was a busy day. But I could accommodate him at the end of the day. I suggested that we could have a meeting at 6.30 p.m. at my office.

He was elated. He thanked me so many times I felt embarrassed. I was seriously feeling the weight of his expectations and wondered as to how I was going to meet them.

The next day's conference was a fairly regular affair. My presentation was well-received. I came back to the office around 4.30 p.m. I had some work to wrap up before my meeting with Anshuman and Krupa.

Anshuman called me around 5.30 p.m. to confirm the meeting. I told him that I was at the office, which elicited a cheery response from him. It was funny. I was once again assailed by my doubts about how I could help them at all. I finally reconciled to meeting them and doing what could be done.

Anshuman walked in with his wife at the stroke of 6.30 p.m. I do not know how he did this, but he did it almost every time. You could set the watch by his arrival.

I ushered them into the cabin immediately. Krupa was a very beautiful young woman. Anshuman was a well-built, handsome man himself. So, this was a strikingly good-looking couple.

Krupa seemed familiar. I could be mistaken, of course.

I asked Krupa whether we had ever met before. She was also not sure. Then it came to me. I had lectured in a city college years before, and one of the coordinators had been Krupa herself. I told her that and she immediately remembered.

'It was eight years ago,' she said. The ice was broken, and Anshuman realised that.

He started by thanking me for guiding him the day before. I started protesting that I just suggested something which may have worked but hastened to add that I was in no way qualified for the job they may want me to do.

'Sir, it was very kind of you to have advised Anshu,' she said.

The use of the pet name, Anshu, signalled some warmth. Anshu sitting beside her was pleased as punch.

'The letter that you asked Anshu to write to me had all the right things in it. I was disillusioned with him as I felt he was willing to throw all of us to the whims of fate with his reckless actions. He said that you have a plan that will set our house in order. We have two children—four years old and two years old. Not just our future but even their future is at stake.

'I have been following you for a year now, since I came back to India. I wanted to put my finances in order and hence started reading up. I see that you are extensively quoted in the media.

'I have read many of your blogs and even articles you are quoted in. I can say that I'm your fan. You write very well and have a balanced and sane approach to most issues. That is why when Anshu said that you are our financial planner, I was thrilled,' she stopped.

I was able to sense that her anger was circumstantial, and was based on the wrong path that Anshuman had stubbornly chosen. It now looked like she was interested in mending ways and was looking forward to a new future together. This was promising, but the mess he had created would take quite some undoing.

I started. 'I want to be candid, Krupa. I told Anshuman yesterday that I may not be the right person to counsel couples on the trials they are facing in their marriage. However, Anshuman insisted that I should meet you both and help you. I hasten to add that I'm in no way qualified to advise on matters of marriage and bringing couples together. In the matter of finances, I'm more at ease,' I said.

'Always the fiduciary, sir!' she smiled. I smiled too. She must have read the many articles I had written about being an adviser with a fiduciary responsibility.

'I heard about the financial situation from Anshuman last evening. It is not in great shape,' I sent a trial balloon.

Krupa was a smart lady. She immediately caught on and was able to sense that I was testing the waters about how much she knew.

I complimented her quicksilver intellect. I looked at Anshuman, and he clarified that he had made a complete disclosure.

'Anshu has made a complete disclosure of the mess we are in. I hope he has told me the whole story. So, you can go ahead,' she said.

'Anshu had come home last night after the message and the long call and stayed over. We talked into the night about all of this and more. That's how I'm clued in,' Krupa said.

That was good news. I told him that he could make a list of the financial assets, including the ones which were problematic and may even be difficult to recover.

Anshuman said that he had already made that and had even sent it to me earlier in the day. I saw that mail and opened it. True. It was all there. I saw that he had marked Krupa as well. I asked her if she had seen it. She said that she had.

This was a huge relief for me. I started by saying that the current position they were in was unenviable.

I told them that there was no easy solution out of this. To extricate from them, surgery may be needed, and that may mean some pain and some losses as well. They were past the stage of grieving about losses.

Before coming to the finances, I wanted to know whether the reconciliation had been effected. I asked this to Krupa. She nodded her head. I was amazed—all the bad blood sorted out in a night.

My surprise must have shown on my face.

'Anshu came across as an honest guy who wanted to leave the past behind and build a new future. I hope he did not speak about all of that because of some boost that you had given. It was essentially a financial blunder and nothing else. I figured that all of us make mistakes and we should give a bit of leeway, especially if one is repentant and has learnt their lesson,' Krupa said.

I told her that it was fantastic to hear this. I told her I was a mere instrument in the process of reconciliation, and it must have been God's will all along.

'I told him that from now on, we will need to take every financial decision only after consulting you. I told him I am fine with a reconciliation only on that condition,' said Krupa.

This was getting curiouser and curiouser by the minute.

'So, what are you going to do now, Anshuman? Now that you have won your family back?' I asked him.

He was beaming. 'I'm planning to find a suitable job at the earliest. I have already met my earlier boss. I spent some time at my erstwhile company this morning. Things look promising. They have certain openings in my field of expertise. So, it may work out as early as next week,' Anshuman chimed.

I was impressed with Anshuman. He may have his faults, but he was a man of action who did not believe in half measures. I was confident that he would land the job.

His last job had been with an auto major in Mumbai, in the product development area. He confirmed that my recollection was right and that he was poised to get the position of a DGM—R&D. He informed me that the pay would be in excess of ₹2 lakh a month, that would see the family to reasonable affluence. I agreed.

'I will also be working for sure. I wanted to give him a hand at this juncture. I will talk to my parents about helping us out with the children while I'm at work. I'm sure that they will oblige. They just adore the kids. Besides, they had given up hope of a reconciliation. If they come to know that we have patched up, they will be thrilled,' Krupa said.

'It is settled then. I will go over the data. We will meet after Anshuman gets his offer. I do not want to start anything till the income sources are secure and where you live is finalised,' I said.

Krupa said, 'In our parents' building itself, there is a flat on the floor above. It is not occupied. We know the owners who also stay in the same colony. We can fix that.'

Things were falling in place much faster than I had expected. I told them that they needed to know about my fee, which would be higher than most, since we were fee-only planners.

'You may want to hear me out on this,' I said.

'I agreed to the reconciliation only because you are involved, and we will sort out the finances with your guidance. If Anshu is not able to hire you as a financial advisor, everything is off,' she said and smiled.

They invited me to dinner. I declined, saying that my wife Madhu would be expecting me.

'Also, you people should celebrate such a day in each other's company. Go ahead and enjoy,' I said. They nodded and smiled.

I called Preeti after Anshuman and Krupa had taken leave. She was cheerful. She said that she was feeling fine and was looking forward to getting discharged. Badri Vishal was by her side now. She was super thrilled about it.

Badri Vishal was doing well. At that moment, he was sleeping. She informed me that the discharge would happen by noon the following day.

The next day dawned. I was in the office very early that day, as I had some writing work to complete. I completed that and was waiting for the call from the hospital about the time of discharge. Naina and Raj were both at the hospital. So, I did not see the need to be there.

The call came at 11.30 a.m. that Preeti will now be discharged. When I went to the hospital, my colleague was ascertaining the bill amount and settling it. It would be completed in a few minutes, I was told.

Preeti was still in her room. I saw Badri Vishal for the first time. When babies are very young, one can hardly make out any resemblance to their parents. Badri Vishal was a sprightly infant. He was wide awake, and when I whistled to him, he grinned his toothless grin and his legs cycled and kicked while his hands were up in the air. It made for a happy picture.

The process was completed, the payments made and the discharge card was given. Preeti was wheeled to where the car was. Raj was at the wheel. When Preeti had seated herself comfortably, with Badri Vishal by her side, the car was on its way. I followed them.

In fifteen minutes, we were at Preeti's place. There was now a new bundle of joy in Vishal's household. Both Shreyan and Ashitaa were there, waiting for their mother and their baby brother. They came and caught hold of her legs. There were tears of joy in Preeti's eyes. She embraced both children and kissed them copiously.

She then showed them Badri Vishal. There was a squeal of joy from Ashitaa. Badri Vishal was frightened and began to cry. His mother comforted him.

Preeti put Badri Vishal in the cradle and asked Ashitaa to rock it gently. Ashitaa did so with loving care. She peeped into the cradle from time to time to see if her brother had slept. Badri did not sleep. He found Ashitaa's peeping amusing and smiled every time her head bobbed into view.

Shreyan was sitting beside his mother, holding her hand. He seemed visibly relieved that she was back home. Preeti gave him a peck on his cheek at which Shreyan looked up at his mother, smiled and hugged her. She gave him another kiss.

Time went on pleasurably. When I understood that things were in order, I wanted to excuse myself. They asked me to have lunch before leaving. I was not hungry at all. I bade goodbye and was off to my office.

I had hardly started working when the phone rang. It was Anshuman.

23

ANSHUMAN AND HIS FAMILY FIND THEIR MOJO

Anshuman informed me that he had got the job. His salary in hand was expected to be ₹2.35 lakh per month. Apart from this, he would also get a bonus and other perks, he mentioned. This was wonderful news.

He said he would be joining in ten days. He wanted to know if I could meet him and Krupa the next day. This time, I said yes unhesitatingly. We fixed the time for 11.30 a.m. I invited them to have lunch with me, which was wholeheartedly accepted.

The next day brought the couple to my office. Both were fantastically attired. Anshuman was in a peacock blue kurta and a spotless white churidar.

Krupa wore a dressy kurta and a churidar, and was looking very beautiful. I figured that she looked that way as their problems were getting sorted now and this was showing up in her disposition. I was very happy for them.

I had done some very basic calculations to show them how things could look like for them. I had prepared two scenarios—

one in which only Anshuman would be working and another in which both were going to work.

The first scenario was working out fine and the second was working wonderfully. Krupa was clear that she would be working and she wanted me to plan as per the second scenario. She told me that financial security was very important for her. She mentioned that, in her childhood, she had seen some very rocky financial situations that were indelibly etched in her memory. She wanted a rock-solid financial foundation for her family, and would do what it took to get that. I was impressed with her steely resolve in this respect.

I told them that they needed to fully trust and cooperate with me. Only then would the results show. I looked at Krupa and told her somewhat sternly that she needed to ensure this and that I would work with them only on that condition. They were a bit taken aback.

I explained that the first time around, Anshuman had not followed the plan and landed himself in trouble. This was version two, and I wanted the best for them. They had recovered and nodded.

Anshuman said, 'Sir, you have brought us together. I will now follow anything that you say, even over what Krupa commands me to do.'

We all laughed.

I wanted to cover some preparatory work for them today, before we got into the planning process.

They had a whole lot of insurance. I wanted them to understand insurance a bit, especially because they had waded knee-deep into a busload of insurance policies.

I started.

'**The concept of insurance:** Insurance is based on the law of large numbers, and the risk of a catastrophic event is borne by everyone in the group. The premium is paid to the insurance company by a large group of insurance policyholders in the pool, which takes on the risk and offers a cover to those suffering a catastrophe from that pool.

'We would want to retain the risk if the event is a mere irritant and not catastrophic. For instance, loss of baggage while travelling may be an irritant but not crippling. We would like to farm out the risks that are big to an entity (an insurance company is one such entity) that will assume the risk for a certain payoff (premium).

'Insurance companies will want to cover risks that are essentially unpredictable and have a comparatively low frequency. The higher the frequency, the higher would be the premium that would be demanded.

'No insurance company would insure a very high-probability risk. That is why one may find that insurance companies may decline covers for people who have suffered major illnesses or conditions (like those with a history of heart, lung, liver ailments, etc.). They do this, as the premium they would be getting would not justify the risk they shoulder since there may be a high probability of hospitalisation.

'Life insurance is to essentially cover the risk of an income earner not being around, the income suddenly stopping and affecting the lifestyle as well as the goals that the family had. Life cover should hence be sufficient to cover the regular expenses of the family as long as necessary and should be enough to cover all the goals of the family.

'The problem in most cases is that the insurance premium is high, but the life cover from the policies taken is insufficient, as the insurance has been bought as an investment. In such cases, the premium is high, and the life cover component tends to be low.

'Almost all the policies that you people have taken are of this type.

'Please understand the fundamental objective of insurance is to offer financial protection and security to the family in the event of the death of the policyholder.

'This is the reason why insurance should be taken where there is a payout only on death. The insurance company sets the premium based on the probability of death of people in a particular pool.

'In the case of pure life insurance, there is a payout only on the death of the policyholder. These pure life insurance policies are called term insurance covers. This is what we recommend to our clients. The things to look out for while selecting these term policies apart from the premium amount is the organisation itself, its claim settlement ratio, the ease of dealing with the organisation if there were a claim, etc.

'These policies are available at low premiums and provide an excellent safety net for the family, in case of the unfortunate death of the life insured. There is no payout if the person survives the tenure of the policy.

'Most other policies are a combination of life cover and an investment component. There are endowment policies, where the policyholder gets a certain life cover for the tenure of the policy as well as a certain return at the end of the tenure.

'There are other policies called money-back policies which return a certain amount at regular, specified intervals. There are whole-life policies where the life cover will be for the life of the policyholder, and the proceeds will go to the nominee after the lifetime of the policyholder.

'These policies are popular because most people are not able to digest the fact that they would get nothing in return in a term policy if they survive the entire term.

'What they are missing is that a term policy is covering the risk of income interruption and goals getting short-circuited, and offers a massive payout in case of death—all for a small premium. This is to be seen as a security net that a person throws around a family to ensure their continued well-being, even if the income earner is no longer around.

'The policies with an investment portion will offer some returns at the end of the tenure. But the point to note here is that to give back those returns, the insurance company is taking the money from the policyholder itself, investing it and returning that money.

'The returns from insurance policies are low. They are tax-free though, except in the case of pension policies where the annuities are added to the taxable income. If one is channelising a huge amount of one's surplus into insurance, then one is committing ongoing surpluses for a long time into low-yielding instruments. This hampers the process of wealth creation.

'A better option is to take term insurance to the extent required, and to make the investments in various assets as dictated by one's personal situation, risk profile, tenure, liquidity needs, taxation, etc.

'**Stopping insurance policies:** Many people realise their mistake of buying the wrong insurance policies much later. In such a situation, what does one do?

'There are two courses of action. One may continue the policy without paying any further premiums. The proportionate benefits of the policy will be payable at maturity. This is known as making the policy 'paid-up' in industry parlance.

'The advantage in making the policy paid-up is that further premiums need not be paid. This will free up the sums going into paying premiums for other productive investments.

'In the case of traditional (non-unit linked) policies, one may be able to stop paying after three premiums.

'The other option available to a policyholder is to surrender the policy and get paid a certain sum and close the policy. If one surrenders the policy, they pay the proportionate benefit for the period paid in today's terms. Usually, on surrendering the policy, there would be losses in the initial several years.

'Surrender and paid-up are related, and if you look at them carefully, they are the same thing. In a situation where the policy has been converted to paid-up status, the proportionate benefit is paid at the end of the tenure. If a policyholder is demanding the money now, that is, they want to surrender the policy, then the paid-up value is discounted at a certain annual rate (like, say, 7 per cent) and the amount is paid now.

'The other way of looking at it is that if the surrender amount is allowed to grow at 7 per cent as in this example, one will get to the paid-up amount at the end of the tenure of the policy.

'We always suggest that one should surrender the policy and clean up the portfolio rather than having the policy alive for the entire tenure. However, many people are not comfortable with this idea as it involves 'losses'.

'There is going to be a loss while getting rid of a wrong insurance policy. There is nothing much one can do. It is best to clean and move on rather than continue with past mistakes.

'**Medical insurance:** Medical insurance is very important to have today as the cost of hospitalisation and the treatments are high.

Hospitalisation can potentially drain a person's wealth. That is precisely why having a good medical insurance cover that covers hospitalisation becomes important. Medical insurance policies are reimbursement policies in that the policyholder will get what they had spent on the treatment and nothing more. This is unlike a life insurance policy which is a benefit policy, where the payout to the tune of the sum assured is paid out on the death of the policyholder to the nominee.

'Unlike life insurance, which is triggered only on death, medical insurance can get triggered multiple times in one's lifetime. So, this policy is even more critical to have and get right.

'In a medical insurance policy, one needs to look at various features and benefits as part of the selection process. Premium is just one aspect and not such an important one at that.

'We need to look at the pre- and post-hospitalisation coverage periods in terms of medicines, investigations, consultations, coverage or exclusion of pre-existing illnesses, etc. We need to check whether there are any limits in terms of room rent, ICU charges, etc., in the policy. One also needs to ascertain whether domiciliary hospitalisation is covered and under what conditions.

'Organ donor coverage is another important feature to check. The number of hospitals in their network where one would be able to make cashless claims is an important criterion too. Also, one may need to check if there is some co-pay option, if one gets admitted to a non-network hospital. One needs to check the level of bonus that the medical insurance policy offers.

'These are some of the important benefits to look for. Besides this, a medical insurance policy may also offer ambulance services, a certain payout per day, called hospital cash, to take care of extraneous expenses, convalescence benefits, etc.

'One may also go for a basic medical insurance which covers one up to a certain amount, and then also add a super top-up medical insurance to provide cover over the basic medical insurance. One needs the right mix of basic cover plus super top-up, so that one would have an adequate amount of medical insurance.

'Some people believe that if they are covered by their employer, they need not have a separate cover of their own. This may not work well always. Today, people are mobile and move from one job to another from time to time. While the pay may be better when one shifts, the insurance benefits can be lower.

'We have found that in some cases when one shifts from one employer to another, the insurance benefits come down. Also, some people take the entrepreneurial route at some point. In that case, the family will not have any insurance cover at all.

'Hence, it may be a good idea to have a separate personal medical insurance policy too, even if the employer-given policy is there.

'**Accident insurance policies:** Accident insurance policies are also something that one may need to consider. They cover death, partial and total disability situations as well as temporary total disablement (TTD).

'Total temporary disablement (TTD) is a condition where after an accident, it may so happen that one may be indisposed and would need to be on a long period of rest. During this period, one may not receive income, as paid leaves might have been exhausted and one would essentially be on unpaid leave.

'The TTD clause offers a certain payout during such situations and is a necessary clause to have in an accident policy. Such a payout will always be lower than one's income, as there needs to be an incentive for a person to start going back to work.

'Even this lower payout would come in very handy for the family when there are many expenses but the income has stopped.

'There are many small benefits from an accidental policy which could be useful. Accident policies cover hospital expenses up to a certain amount. These policies offer reimbursement of ambulance charges as per the policy conditions, arranging blood, modification of residence, if necessary, cost of prosthetics and a certain sum of money called hospital cash to take care of incidentals for every day of admittance in the hospital. Some policies also give a convalescence benefit.

'Home insurance policies can be taken to cover the structure and contents. The cover for the structure offers reimbursement or reinstatement if the structure gets destroyed or damaged due to fire, water, earthquake and the like (the perils covered may vary somewhat from policy to policy). The contents pertain to what is in the house.

'The contents coverage will include reimbursement or reinstatement of those household effects destroyed or damaged by fire, inundation or other perils like burglary. A home insurance policy comes at a low cost and is handy to have.

'When there were floods in Chennai several years ago, many people were caught unaware and did not have insurance to cover their homes. As a result, they had to foot the bill of renovating their homes and buying all the household goods afresh.

'Another insurance that has gained prominence these days is critical illness insurance. This is a good-to-have insurance unlike the must-have ones like life and medical insurance.

'Critical illness policies cover anywhere between eight to thirty (or even more) dreaded diseases. This is a benefit policy in that it offers a payout if the disease or condition is confirmed by a medical practitioner, without getting into whether one has spent that much money or not.

'Critical illness is costly to treat, and the costs go well over the medical insurance cover that one may have.

'The critical illness policies supplement medical expenses that invariably ensue on the onset of a critical illness. Even medical insurance policies cover any kind of medical treatment that involves hospitalisation, including critical illnesses.

'But a critical illness may not always involve hospitalisation and may still entail spending substantial sums of money on diagnostics, medicines, consultations, etc. Also, it may diminish one's ability to earn a living. This policy gives a helping hand in such a situation.

'For instance, if one is diagnosed with cancer and has a policy of ₹10 lakh, there will be a payout of ₹10 lakh on confirmation by a medical practitioner, irrespective of the expenses that have been incurred or may be incurred for treating cancer.

'There are other policies which may be useful that may have to be taken on a need and applicability basis.

'**Why insurance as an investment is not a great idea:** I had already mentioned that insurance products which have an investment component generally offer low yields. Insurance products are very long-term products, and the low yields over a long period of time result in poor accretion of wealth.

'Also, due to the long-term nature of the insurance product, the premium commitment is also for a long period of time, which in some cases may be inconvenient as one cannot skip premium payments. Skipping premium payments will result in the cessation of insurance coverage, which is one of the reasons why the insurance policy would have been taken in the first place.

'Investing substantially in insurance, especially traditional products like endowment, money-back, whole-life policies, will also result in locking up in one kind of asset class, with no possibility of changes (as the product is a long-term one).

'That is precisely why we always suggest a good term insurance policy to offer the required life cover and a bouquet of investments that together would meet the various goals. Such an investment bouquet can be rebalanced and money inflows over time can be properly channelised into appropriate assets. This kind of an approach results in investments being better aligned to personal situations, over time.

'**Insurance needs after retirement:** Many people ask whether life insurance is needed after retirement. Let us look at the fundamentals of why we take insurance in the first place.

'Insurance is a security net to protect the needs and goals of a family, which would depend upon the income generated by the income earner. Suppose the income earner were to suddenly pass away and the needs and goals of the family may not be met by the assets and investments created. There may also be liabilities.

'Life insurance is taken to ensure that the needs and goals of the family go on uninterrupted even on the unfortunate demise of the income earner. If a life insurance policy with a sufficient life cover is taken, then the family would receive the claim amount, which, along with other investments, would ensure that the family is comfortable financially.

'One would earn an income till a certain age. In many cases, it would be sixty. The insurance is to cover the financial loss incurred by the family in view of the income suddenly stopping. Viewed this way, there is no need to have life insurance beyond the retirement age.

'Many people want to have life cover till eighty years and sometimes even beyond. The mortality charges (based on which insurance premiums are calculated) are high in the later years. This unnecessarily pushes up the premium throughout the tenure.

'The insurance company charges the same premium throughout the tenure, which is called the level term premium. This would exert unwanted pressure earlier in life and would mean paying premiums after one has stopped earning, assuming that one may die in the premium paying period.

'Even this may not be true and one may survive the period and get nothing. In case of very long tenure payments, calculations show that even if policyholders do get the claim at the ripe old age of, say, eighty years, the premium they had paid and the returns from them would be more than that, if one adjusts for time value of money. For instance, a premium of ₹20,000 paid thirty-five years back would have multiplied ten times, assuming a 7 per cent return on investments to the insurance company.

'Hence, one should take life insurance and even accident insurance only to the extent of one's working life.

'Other insurance policies like health, critical illness, home insurance, etc., have no connection with whether one is earning an income or not. If it has been determined that it is needed for the family, these policies should be continued throughout life.

'**Calculating the insurance cover needed:** In the case of life insurance, there is a way of determining it. We need to find the value of all the important goals that would be there, even if the primary income earner is no more. Then the expenses of the surviving members throughout life needs to be derived. The present value of both these needs to be determined, and from that, any investments need to be subtracted. Loans, if any, have to be added. The resultant figure would be the life cover that needs to be taken.

'Life insurance needs to be primarily taken for the earning member in the family. Homemakers, though they do not earn an income, also contribute greatly to the family by the various services they render. In their absence, paid services may become necessary. One can estimate this and opt for this cover, if deemed necessary.

'In case of accident insurance, there is no such formula. We will need to estimate the amount based on the life cover taken, type of job, criticality of the goals, etc.

'In case of medical and critical illness insurance, the amount of insurance cover to be taken is a factor of the kind of medical healthcare that the family is expected to seek, their medical history and the probabilities of the medical cover taken covering most situations.

'Some people want very high covers in case of medical insurance, as they feel that there is a possibility of some serious illness at some point. While there is always a possibility, we need to look at the probability of such an event happening. If the probability of that happening is quite low, we need to take a cover which takes care of most situations and keep contingency funds handy for situations which go beyond that.

'We may have to keep contingency funds for our parents, as getting a medical insurance policy at an advanced age may not be feasible, if it is not already in place. There is just no other way to handle this, unless one's employer has an insurance policy that covers parents.

'Medical insurance covers should be taken without consideration for whether they are income earners or otherwise.

Any medical outgo would impact the family, and hence an appropriate medical insurance cover for all the members of the family is essential.

'One can take a cover for the family, where an umbrella cover is available to all family members. This would generally be somewhat cheaper than individual policies. However, one should take a sufficiently high medical cover here, as any family member can use it. A higher cover is needed because there can be a possibility where some or all the members need hospitalisation during the year.'

All this while, both Anshuman and Krupa were listening patiently. Anshuman's phone rang. As he stepped out to answer the call, I asked Krupa whether she wanted anything by way of refreshments. She answered in the negative. She just wanted to use the washroom.

Anshuman came in after completing his call. He told me that it was the new employer who was discussing a case he would be entrusted with. He was happy when he said this.

Anshuman started talking excitedly about the new project he was taking up. He explained to me about the research work he would be overseeing as well as futuristic developments in the field of automobiles. He was animatedly discussing electric cars, hydrogen-powered vehicles and solar-powered vehicles.

By this time, Krupa came back and our discussion tapered.

Krupa wanted to know a bit about how people set their goals, if there was a specific way to go about finding what goals one should have.

'There is no such thing as finding the goal. It is your own goal, which you need to come up with. If you think about it, it is not that complicated at all,' I said.

'Children's education, buying a home, vacations, buying a car, one's own retirement are some of the common goals. But there can be really unique goals. One of our clients had a goal of starting a school in his native village. Another wanted to start teaching children in his area, without monetary compensation. So, for different folks, it is different,' I concluded.

She was absorbing this.

'When we plan, will we be investing some money for each goal?' she wanted to know.

Goal-tagging approach versus pool-of-funds approach

'There are two philosophies here. In one philosophy, the investment for each goal is made separately. This is easy to relate to. Psychologically, one would not touch money assigned to important goals.

However, in this approach, there are a multitude of investment schemes, as an appropriate asset mix needs to be achieved for each goal. Rebalancing also needs to be done for the different portfolios, as necessary. The portfolio becomes bloated, and any portfolio review will need to look at multiple small portfolios, created for different goals. This is not a very efficient way of handling investments.

There is a different approach where the available funds are pooled and invested as per the asset allocation requirements of that person or family. In this approach, we divide the funds into those needed for the short term (up to three years), which are invested in safe and steady investments that will be least affected by market volatility.

The rest is invested as per the long-term asset allocation needs. The amounts needed as one moves on will keep getting moved to safer instruments. In this method, one will have money provided for goals coming up in the next three years.

In this approach, the portfolio so created will be compact, easy to manage and efficient. We follow this pool-of-funds approach,' I concluded.

She nodded but did not talk. I waited, for it was clear that something was turning in her head.

'What is your view regarding loans? I hear differing views on this. My parents are dead against any loans. But then, I have read many articles that say that loans are not bad if they are taken within limits for the right reasons,' she queried.

Loans and credit

'Loans are not toxic as such. In situations like buying a home, one cannot buy a home without a loan, considering prevailing home prices. This is an important goal for many. Housing is also a priority for the government, and hence the loan rates have been kept low, there are tax deductions available on the interest and principal paid on a home loan and long tenures to pay off the loan. This cannot be considered a bad loan.

'When we take a loan, we spend what we don't have. We are discounting our future earnings today on the assumption that those earnings would be possible. If there are any disruptions, it can pose a problem in loan servicing. There are many cases where we have seen that future income assumed is no longer there.

'Hence, credit should be availed only when the goal for which you take the loan is extremely important. Before taking the loan, one should understand the implications of one's decision, and be ready to make the repayment over the tenure of the loan. Even these important loans should be at an easily serviceable level. Else, there may not be much money left for other goals and expenses.

'Generally, after both monthly and annual expenses, one could go to the extent of 75 per cent of the surplus for loan servicing, for all loans together that one may have. The balance 25 per cent of this surplus should be used for investments towards other goals.

'Since these loan EMIs will be a static amount but income will go up over the years, the amount of money going to service the loans as a percentage of the surplus will keep coming down.

'Many who have availed home loans prepay some portion at regular intervals. This brings down the EMI amount for the rest of the tenure. However, if one would like to finish the loans faster, the EMI can be retained at the original level. In this way, more principal will go towards the repayment of the loan and the loan tenure will come down.

'Many home loan borrowers also use their bonus, incentives, ex-gratia amounts, etc., that they receive to partially retire their loan. This is a good strategy to bring the outstanding loan amount to comfortably manageable levels.'

I paused to take a swig of water. I looked at Krupa to see if she had any questions. She did not stir at all. Anshuman, sitting beside her, could have been a statue from the temple. He was sitting stoically and hearing all that was being said without comment.

'What about other loans which people take like loans for cars, vacations, white goods, etc.?' asked Krupa.

'Vacations and white goods are not very high value spends. Cars can cost anything at all today. Generally, we suggest that one should accumulate the amount necessary for these before spending. Where is the sense in spending ₹1.5 lakh on a vacation, if one does not even have that amount with them? These kinds of loans are generally costlier than home loans.

'You may hear of zero per cent interest loans. That's just optics. When one offers a no-interest or a low-interest loan, the price discount which would otherwise be available will not be there. A person willing to fund their purchase by themselves would get the benefit of a lower price.

'Even in the case of a car, taking a loan is not advised. Car is a depreciating asset and an item of consumption. A loan taken for the car adds to the price being paid. My general advice is that if one cannot afford a big portion or the full price of the car, one should wait for a later time to buy it.

'The other problem with credit is that people buy products on credit before properly evaluating whether they can repay the amount and then end up in a debt trap. Many who use credit cards go on a buying spree without realising that the money spent through the card is not free money and has to be repaid.

'Some of them are unable to pay the credit card bill at the end of the billing cycle. Hence, they pay the minimum balance allowed and revolve the credit at enormous interest rates. Interest rates can go as high as 48 per cent a year!

'Hence, it is imperative to settle at the end of the billing cycle. To ensure that the bill gets paid, one can link the credit card bill payment to one's bank account.

'So, if one can delay the gratification a bit, one can save for the object of desire or the goal and then spend without getting dragged into a debt trap.

'Credit cards can also be misused by fraudsters. It is always a good idea to have a card with a lower limit for online transactions, and setting daily transaction limits to lower chances of major misuse.

'To sum it up, I would say that one may access credit or loans only if they are truly necessary.'

'I suppose education loans also come under the category of extremely important loans. What is your view?' she asked.

Loan for education

'Education is an important goal. When one gets further educated, it always improves one's prospects. In that sense, it is good to spend money here. Hence, a loan taken for this can be justified.

'Even in the case of education, one should carefully consider the cost and benefits of a course. There are many expensive local and international courses now. One needs to examine if it makes any financial sense to take them up.

'Even after doing some of these courses, the incremental financial benefit is small. Hence, one will not even be able to recover the costs in some cases. This needs to be properly considered while pursuing further education and taking a loan towards that.

'But if there is a good course to be pursued, then an education loan may be taken. The Government of India has offered the entire interest on education loan as a tax deduction, after one rejoins the workforce once they complete their education.

'Is there anything else you want to know?' I asked. She signalled no.

I then went into a few more things regarding the information required from them, so we would be able to craft a plan. Anshuman had promised that he would send all the information by the weekend.

He was now in a frame of mind to accept and carry out any advice I offered. I wanted to use this position to sort out their financial situation.

After they were gone, I was still pondering over their situation. Anshuman's situation would clarify itself over the years, if he managed to keep the job. I did not have any doubt about his ability to keep his job, or his resolve to make his life and finances work.

Various other cases had also progressed well. Raj and Naina had gone on to implement our recommendations. Our operations staff had completed the implementation of the recommendations. Advisors from our office were in touch and were hand-holding them through this critical stage.

Preeti now seemed quite happy. She was devoting time to her children and taking care of them. This was her duty, her prayer. She had now settled into a routine and was enjoying it. Badri Vishal had brought further joy into their household. The two children were fawning over their infant brother, making for a very lively, loving household.

Then I eased myself into work which was vying for my attention and got immersed into it. When I looked up and saw the watch, it was well past my usual time.

At home, I showered and had my dinner. I was in the frame of mind to ruminate and take stock. I was thinking about the other cases, like Bala's. Bala had gone back to London, and so had Malvika. Things were going on fine there.

I picked up the paper and was flipping it, browsing the headlines. There was the usual news—robbery in a far-flung suburb, a traffic pile-up, a murder, a young girl who was lost was united with her family, etc.

Suddenly, I could hear water flowing with some force. I realised that I was near a river. I knew this river, this place. I walked towards the river. The thick forests were familiar environs to me. I sat on the banks, taking in the roar of the river. I must have sat there motionless for quite some time just looking at the swirling waters and listening to the song of the river.

It soothed and calmed me like only a mother could have. The river was sharing its love and munificence by feeding and nourishing the terrain that it was flowing through. I was one with nature and experienced the sublime oneness of creation.

There was someone on the opposite side of the bank waving to me. Who could that be? I thought.

It looked like Vishal. On closer scrutiny, I realised that it was not. It was the driver who had been with me in my previous outing in the forest. I waved back. How did he reach there? The other side of the river had no access at all. The only plausible explanation was that he must have swum across. Considering the strong water flow, that would have been near impossible. But yet, he was there.

I heard him. He was communicating telepathically. That surprised me even more.

He conveyed his greetings and told me that he was happy to see me again. He was happy that Badri Vishal was born and the infant was healthy. He expressed his contentment about the fact that Preeti had eased well into the job of taking care of her three children. I was very surprised he knew all of this. He was smiling.

He was now saying that I had handled my clients' cases well and had discharged my duty as a fiduciary in its true spirit. He congratulated me on the way I had handled Anshuman's case.

I wanted to protest that I did not do much to bring them together and was a mere player in the act. It had just happened. While I was thinking thus, I was struck by the fact that he knew all this.

He was saying that we are all a part of a play and that we are actors who come in at the appropriate time to play the part. This was all too familiar.

He said, 'We just have to play our parts well. We need not worry about the outcome. The outcome is the result of multitudinous factors. People get the outcome they are working towards. We sometimes call that destiny.

'Destiny is what happens when we have the vision and clarity of what we want to achieve, focus our efforts in a certain direction and take definitive actions to move towards a certain outcome. When we do this, we most probably will be crowned with success. The entire universe aligns and reconfigures so that we can reach our goal.

'Sometimes the desired outcome is not reached, and events overtake us, leaving us bewildered, disappointed and bitter. This is part of the overall coaching we get in life. This is part of the plan to make us strong internally. It is part of growing up and can even be seen as a rite of passage into life.

'If everything happens as we anticipate, we may become arrogant. Besides, there are just too many variables and interactions, which results in a particular outcome. Hence, there is a certain unpredictability to the result. That is why we say that one needs a bit of luck to achieve anything. What we mean is that many things have to align correctly to reach the desired outcome.

'People like you are part of the grand plan. Your job is to help your clients as best as you can. You are planning well for your clients and are putting in place a financial architecture so that the clients may reach their desired results. That is your karma, your puja in this life,' he said. He was laughing now.

I was confounded as to how he knew almost everything that I was doing. I was even a bit irritated by what I considered an impertinence on the part of the driver.

Divine music was now playing over the roar of the swirling waters.

While I was watching, the driver morphed into Lord Krishna. I was ashamed to think that I had not guessed this earlier, even after the Lord had indicated so last time, after I had shared what the driver had said.

He did not say exactly that He was the driver, but it was reasonably clear. He had appeared so many times and expounded on the philosophy of life itself and yet I was unable to grasp even this basic thing. I was cross with myself.

I felt a cool breeze caressing my body and a wave of bliss coursed and permeated my body. It was an indescribable, sublime feeling. It was somehow different every time I experienced it.

The compliment from the Lord about my client handling was the highest praise I could have hoped for. It was a huge morale boost for me. It was a thumbs up that I was doing the right thing, and doing it right!

He was now communicating with me again.

'Every client is my child. They are my manifestation. Serve the clients like you would serve me, if you knew who I was. That is in essence what a professional like you who has a fiduciary responsibility needs to do.

'Your clients are your world. That is your part in this life.' I thanked the Lord. While advisers like me serve clients to meet their financial goals, it was also important to engage with them about the larger meaning and purpose of life itself. If we are able to make that happen for our clients, then we would truly play a transformational role in their lives. I felt the responsibility towards my clients even more. And felt truly happy playing my part in making the clients' lives wholesome and well lived.

EPILOGUE

It has been seven years since Vishal passed away.

Preeti has settled down to a peaceful life and is very happy with her three children. The eldest, Shreyan, now in standard seven, is taller than his mother. Ashitaa looks just like her and has turned out to be a very responsible child; she even helps Preeti around the house.

Badri Vishal, the apple of everyone's eye, is a naughty little kid and very clearly a precocious child. He is adept at mathematics and helps Ashitaa and even Shreyan with their maths homework as well. He is going to abacus classes, and has breezed through the levels in under a year. He has also undergone training in Vedic mathematics.

His performance in school is phenomenal. He does not spend too much time studying but is able to grasp everything the teacher explains in the classroom. His teachers have told Preeti that he is a model student. When they teach, he listens with rapt attention. He is far ahead of everyone in his class and is already held in awe by fellow students and friends.

He has also become a wizard at chess and is a state-level player and should very soon be playing at the national level. When

Preeti talks of Badri Vishal, she is often in tears. His achievements are staggering and his talents multifarious, even at such a tender age. She always rues the fact that Vishal is not there to see the meteoric rise of the scion.

Financially, the family is on an even keel. For the most part, I take care of the finances but keep Preeti in the loop. Though she keeps a track of the broad contours of their finances.

Things are not so great with Naina and her family. Naina has left her job and is working as a freelancer. The family's finances are in precarious shape. They keep coming to me from time to time. But I have not been able to do much. Their spending has not reduced, which leaves little money to put aside for their future.

Ritika is now doing her bachelor's program in engineering. The college in which she has gotten admission is one of the more expensive ones. They are paying about ₹7 lakh per annum for it. They had not accepted my suggestion that Ritika take up an education loan and are now struggling to make ends meet. Their modest corpus is depleting fast. Naina is desperately trying to look for a stable job so that she can bring home a regular income when it is sorely needed.

Ajay and Arundhati are doing well—in fact very, very well. Ajay has gotten promoted and is in the top management of his company. He has been given ESOPs and is a valued member. He regularly features in the media these days. His income has also grown substantially. Arundhati, too, has progressed well and has ascended the corporate ladder with elan.

They still do not have children. When I spoke with them last, they both laughed and said they just don't have any time to bring up a child even if they wanted to. They seem to prefer it that way and are reconciled with it.

They were doubting Thomases when they came to me. But not anymore. Now, they have pretty much left everything to me. I have a quarterly meeting to give them a broad update as well as get feedback about the happenings in their life. They have transformed into one of the most trusting and ideal clients for us.

Bala is still in London. He has had a spectacular run there. In these seven years, he has done so much business there that he has risen to become the deputy CEO. His earnings now are stratospheric—a far cry from the days when he was staring at the possibility of job loss.

Malvika is still in London. She is working in a financial services firm. I have heard that she is doing well, though I have not seen her in a long time. She is now married to Ranga, who is someone she met in college. Coincidentally, Ranga was distantly related to her—which she did not know initially. He is a fund manager in one of the global firms in London. They are very much a power couple, who now call London their home.

Anshuman is a spectacular success. He has risen like a phoenix and has covered himself with laurels. He is the head of R&D at a multinational firm and a globe-trotter. He addresses conferences and publishes papers on the subject of transportation and mobility.

He talks to me once in a while. His wife, Krupa, is in touch with me regularly. She comes over to my office every quarter, though I keep telling her that we can have this discussion over Skype. She says this personal, face-to-face meeting helps. She often tells me that she likes the philosophical approach I take towards life and money and that she looks forward to our quarterly meetings.

Things have panned out quite well for many of them and I say this with enormous satisfaction.

I forgot to mention something about Badri Vishal. He has also taken a keen interest in quizzing. You may ask me what a seven-year-old can do in that area. That was precisely my thought too.

When I last met him a few days back and asked him a bit about world affairs, science, history, geography, etc., surprisingly Badri answered them all! And to each answer, he added a lot more context and further information about the subject matter, of which even I was not aware.

He also had knowledge of philosophy. He gave me a glimpse of his understanding of the *Vishitaadvaita* of Ramanujacharya, which is qualified monism. Even I do not claim to understand these precepts well. But here was a mere child, holding his own on one of the deepest philosophies in the Hindu pantheon.

This happened at Preeti's home. Preeti was there, and her eyes were filled with unshed tears. The sheer breadth of his knowledge at this tender age, his dazzling brilliance and his profundity were breathtaking!

Badri Vishal is the Lord's special gift to Vishal's family. It seemed imminent that Badri Vishal will blaze forth a trail so bright that the entire world will be spellbound with amazement.

The time ahead will be interesting—to witness the rise of the scion, the Lord's special child.

ACKNOWLEDGEMENTS

Writing a book is a daunting exercise. Sometimes one baulks at the enormity of the effort. That certainly happened to me.

But during the times when I felt low and the road ahead seemed to stretch beyond the horizon, there were those who acted as anchors and those who revived my dull spirit. I have felt at times that they had more faith in me than I had in myself.

My cousin, Sudarrsan, is one such soul. He has been encouraging me to write a book since 2007, after I had written my very first article. I put off writing the book by giving all kinds of excuses. The book is now in your hands because of Sudarrsan's dogged perseverance. Thanks, pal!

A friend of mine, a financial planner himself, has been coaxing and cajoling me to write for the past seven years. The last time we attended a conference at Udaipur, he even offered a pen to the Lord in one of the temples we visited. He must have concluded that only divine intervention could make this stubborn guy write. This good friend is Hemant Beniwal who I am very thankful to.

The other person who has been telling me to write for a long time is my friend and client, Kartik Sharma. He tried to kindle a fire which had not been there till very recently. Thanks again, Kartik, for your faith in me.

Gaurav Mashruwala, a friend and fellow financial planner, wanted me to share my wisdom with the society from which we have learnt so much. He also gave me a connection to the publishers. Thanks, Gaurav, for egging me on!

There are countless others who have shown their appreciation for my writing and have very kindly planted the thought in me that I can, indeed, write a book. Thank you all for being liberal with your praise and your faith in my abilities.

I am thankful for the wonderful work done by Avdyushka and Sonia Madan, which has made the book far more readable. Their painstaking editing has made the writing tighter and weeded out repetitive content which has made the narrative taut.

And, most of all, I would like to thank everyone in my immediate and extended family for patiently putting up with the long periods for which I would stay glued to the computer and skip fraternising.

Thank you, O Lord, for giving me the thought to share my learnings.